KU-164-076

# Contents

# Acknowledgements

There are many (too many to name individually) academics who have been influential in the writing of this book – but thank you all! However, I would like to thank students at South Bank University, Bedfordshire University, London Metropolitan University and the Ecole Superieure d'Hotellerie, Paris who were willing, but not always witting, guinea pigs exposed to some embryonic material used in the writing of this book.

At Goodfellows, I would like to thank, in particular, my editor Sally North who has been, once again, very supportive and helpful and Mac who took my not very well formatted text, and turned into this attractive book!

I would like to thank especially my wife Patsy who largely tolerated my long, and frequent absences at the computer, and even offered to help at critical times! Thanks also to my (grown-up-now) children, Jess and Will who, when they were around, looked on supportively.

As with all such creations however, any remaining blemishes are my responsibility.

*Peter Mason,*
Catfield, Norfolk, September, 2017

# Geography of Tourism

## Image, Impacts and Issues

**Peter Mason**

LIVERPOOL JMU LIBRARY

3  1111  01512  1864

ublishers Ltd

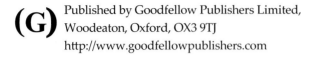

Published by Goodfellow Publishers Limited,
Woodeaton, Oxford, OX3 9TJ
http://www.goodfellowpublishers.com

British Library Cataloguing in Publication Data: a catalogue record for this
title is available from the British Library.

Library of Congress Catalog Card Number: on file.

ISBN: 978-1-911396-43-7

Copyright © Peter Mason, 2017

All rights reserved. The text of this publication, or any part thereof, may not
be reproduced or transmitted in any form or by any means, electronic or
mechanical, including photocopying, recording, storage in an information
retrieval system, or otherwise, without prior permission of the publisher or
under licence from the Copyright Licensing Agency Limited. Further details
of such licences (for reprographic reproduction) may be obtained from the
Copyright Licensing Agency Limited, of Saffron House, 6–10 Kirby Street,
London EC1N 8TS.

All trademarks used herein are the property of their repective owners, The
use of trademarks or brand names in this text does not imply any affiliation
with or endorsement of this book by such owners.

 Design and typesetting by P.K. McBride, www.macbride.org.uk

Cover design by Cylinder

Printed and bound in Great Britain by Marston Book Services Ltd, Oxfordshire

# Preface

This book is aimed primarily at undergraduate students and has been written in such a way that early chapters present largely factual material and later ones discuss and analyse theories, as well as considering critical concepts and issues. It uses a large number of case studies, at different scales, focusing on locations from many areas of the world, including the UK, Spain, France, Italy, the USA, Australia, New Zealand, Africa, Asia and Antarctica.

The book is divided into four sections.

- Introduction to the Geography of Tourism
- Impacts of Tourism
- Issues in Tourism
- Planning and Managing Tourism

The first section is concerned with the rationale for the geographical study of tourism, the key motivations for tourism and the resources for tourism. A whole chapter of this first section is devoted to an understanding of weather and climate. Weather and climate can be considered as 'resources' for tourism, but are more important than this, being the context in which so much tourism takes place. Without an understanding of the nature and causes of variations in climate globally, it will be very difficult to understand how and why climate is changing today, and the issue of climate change is discussed in detail in the third section of the book. However, the final chapter of the first section is concerned with the nature of tourism destinations, as it is here that impacts and issues are particularly significant and can be readily observed and researched. This chapter additionally focuses on the image of destinations, as this can be a major factor in the long term sustainability of tourism locations. The second section of the book considers tourism impacts and presents separate chapters focusing respectively on environmental, socio-cultural and economic impacts. It also shows how these impacts, in reality, are frequently multifaceted, and this section also sets tourism in a wider socio-economic context. The third section of the book discusses and critically evaluates major issues facing tourism, but where, in some cases, tourism is also a significant contributor to these issues. Global development, climate change and crises and disasters are the topics discussed at length, with each the focus of a separate chapter. The fourth chapter in this section investigates the relationship between the aims of conserving landscape, and yet also allowing recreation and tourism uses, through a discussion of protected areas. The need to manage tourism is the major concern of two of the chapters in the fourth section of the book, one of which considers the nature of tourism planning and management and the other is focused on an evaluation of concepts of sustainability and sustainable tourism. The final chapter of the book presents for critical analysis a number of possible scenarios for the future direction of tourism.

# Introduction

The first section of the book provides an introduction to the study of the geography of tourism. Chapter 1 discusses the nature of both geography and tourism and how the subjects are linked. The second chapter indicates the major motivations for tourism and then considers how these can contribute to demand for tourism experiences. Chapter 3 discusses tourism resources, including features of the natural environment, as well as human factors that can act as tourism attractions. The entire fourth chapter is devoted to an investigation of the importance of weather and climate, both as resources for tourism, but additionally as key factors influencing the nature and location of many tourism activities. Chapter 5 focuses on destinations, as it is here that tourism resources and attractions are geographically focused. The image of tourism destinations is also a major concern of this chapter. It is in the destination that many of the impacts of tourism are located, which means that this chapter acts as introduction to the second section of the book.

# 1 Geography and Tourism

## Introduction

This first chapter provides an introduction to the geography of tourism. It initially discusses the nature of geography, and indicates the major topics that the subject is concerned with, as well as presenting the types of questions that geographers ask. It then considers the activity of tourism, giving a brief overview of its importance and a discussion and consideration of definitions. The links between the two areas of study are presented, as well as a brief overview of different approaches to the relationship between geography and tourism.

## The nature of geography

In simple terms, geography is about people and places (Mason, 1992). The key word in connection with geography is location. So geography is about the location of places and also the location of people. It is about the relationship between different locations or places. This relationship is often described as a *spatial* relationship (Hall and Page, 2014). 'Spatial' is in effect another word for 'geographical'. However, geography is not defined in the same way by all authors interested in the subject, and the term 'spatial' is more specific and a more scientific concept as it refers to just space on the earth. The concept 'spatial' is not just two dimensions on the surface of the land, but also includes mountains, hills and river valleys as well as the depths of oceans and seas. So the concept of 'spatial relationship' does not necessarily have to refer to specific geographical features, be they physical or human geographical features. However, the concept of 'spatial relationship' is that it is concerned with the relationship between different geographical features.

Investigating spatial relationships can help in finding patterns (Hall and Page, 2014). Geographers are frequently involved in looking for patterns in the environment, as these can help understand, for example, features in a natural landscape. It also means that it may be possible to suggest that as a pattern has been discerned in relation to certain features in a specific location or area, if these features are found elsewhere, then this pattern may be evident again in this other location. It may therefore be possible, if certain patterns are found, to make predictions about future relationships. Being able to predict what may happen in the future, or suggesting similar patterns between what is currently known and a new context, can be very useful for those who are planning future human activity.

Conventionally geography is subdivided into physical and human elements (Robinson, 1976).

- The physical aspects of geography are, for example, landscape features such as mountains, rivers, seas, oceans, coastlines and glaciers. The word *environment* is often used as a shorthand way of indicating physical geography, although this can be misleading as the environment can also refer to the human landscape.

- Human geography is concerned with human activity in the environment and will involve study of for example settlements, farming, fishing and forestry.

Whether it is physical geography or human geography, the geographer is interested in a major question – '*where?*' The geographer wants to know where certain features are, be they rivers, lakes, cities or forests (Robinson,1976). Geographers also want to look at relationships between different physical features in the landscape, such as rivers and coastlines. Geographers will also be interested in the relationship between human aspects of the landscape/countryside such as farming areas and towns. Physical and human geography are linked when, for example, a geographer studies the type of landscape and soil in an area in relation to the use of the land for farming or forestry.

Geographers are not just concerned with the question '*where?*', but other very important related questions. The question '*what?*' will be concerned with precisely what is there in a landscape, or in a particular location. This can involve simply studying and describing for example, different types of rocks, or landscape features such as waterfalls, or river valleys. However, it is likely to also involve investigation of, for example, what types of buildings are in a village, or the types of farming activity in a region. In fact, geographers are very likely to be asking the questions *where* and *what* together. They will want to know *what* is there in the landscape and precisely *where* it is (Robinson, 1976).

The geographer is also concerned with the question '*when?*'. The landscape/environment has evolved over a long period of time and will continue to change in the future. When certain activities take place now and have taken place in the past is very significant. Geographers may therefore be interested in looking back one hundred years, or even a thousand years, to investigate how, for example, a town has grown. In the case of a mountain landscape, a physical geographer will want to investigate several thousand years of development to try to understand why it looks the way it does today. However, a geographer may also look at a much shorter time period, such as for over one year, particular in relation to for example seasonal changes in the weather or plant growth. So the question '*when?*' can be extended to '*for how long?*'

The sentence at the end of the previous paragraph has used the word *how* and this is another important question that geographers will ask. What geographers will be interested in is *how*, for example, a landscape has developed over time. This will require an understanding of the processes operating in that landscape. Some of this may be what we usually call 'natural' processes. These include the effects of climate such as rain, snow, wind and sunshine and, for example, the wearing away of the land through erosion by water or ice. Nevertheless, *how* the landscape or an environment in any one place has changed over time will frequently be a result of human activity, in terms of, for example, how we have farmed the land and built houses and roads.

However, probably the most important question a geographer will ask is *'why?'* A geographer may want to know why a particular city is located where it is. Trying to answer this question will focus on particular features of the landscape that have favoured the growth of the city, such as a river, or a natural harbour or the presence of raw materials for industry, such as coal or oil. A geographer will also want to answer the question: 'why is *this* city more important than a town that is nearby'. This will involve far more than a description of 'what is there and where it is'. It will require analysis of the processes in the physical environment and also activities by people and the reasons why particular decisions were taken. The relationship between these processes is often complex, meaning that answering the question *'why?'* is frequently difficult (see Mason, 2014). However, it is a very important question for all geographers, as answers to this question may provide information that can help change existing features and activities, may be useful to predict future processes and events and may provide opportunities for improvements to be made.

A further question that geographers are interested in is *'with what effects?'*. In relation to the question *'why?'* we have noted that attempting to get answers to the question will involve consideration of the reasons certain decisions were taken. 'With what effects?' is the question that considers, for example, what has happened following a decision taken by people in relation to a landscape/environment. 'With what effects?' may also involve the impacts that some features of the natural landscape have had on other parts, such as a glacier on a river valley. It can also involve consideration of what the natural landscape can do to a human landscape, such as a tsunami hitting settlements in a coastal area. 'With what effects?', however, is often a question concerned with what people do to a landscape such as drop litter, or trample vegetation, but can also involve consideration of how visitors to a heritage site can help contribute to its upkeep through the payment of an entrance fee.

Some of the questions in which geographers are interested enable *description* of, for example, a river valley or an urban landscape to be made. Answering the questions *'where?'* and *'what?'*, will enable this type of description to be achieved. However geographers usually want to do much more than just describe what they see in a landscape – they also want to carry out a process of *analysis*. This means attempts to explain and understand what is found in a landscape and not just describe what is there. This processes of analysis will usually require certain key activities. One of these is the process of *comparison* (see Mason, 2014). For example, geographers will compare one landscape with another, in an attempt to look for both similarities and differences. This comparison will involve attempts to *explain* any similarities and/or differences. The process of comparison is also likely to involve comparison of the current landscape, with that same area in the past, in an attempt to explain what happened previously that may have contributed to what is there now. Similarly geographers will study human processes and the results of human activities that have spatial dimensions and through analysis attempt to explain similarities and differences. The process of analysis is not just used to explain, but is frequently used to predict what may happen in the future, based on the explanation of what has happened before. When conducting this processes of analysis, geographers will be asking questions such as:

- Why is this geographical feature where it is?
- Why is this type of human activity taking place here?
- For how long has this activity taken place here and how has it changed?
- What effects is this activity having and why is it having these effects?
- What can be done to change (and improve?) the activities?

## The nature of tourism

Tourism is concerned with the movement of people between places. This movement clearly involves travel. Although travel has been a key aspect of human life for thousands of years, for much of recorded history, it was difficult. It was often uncomfortable and expensive and frequently dangerous (Williams, 1998), yet journeys were undertaken. In the distant past, these journeys may have been connected with the search for food or water, or the need to escape from other groups during war or conflict. Many of these journeys were concerned with survival. Hence, until relatively recently, very few people travelled for leisure purposes. However, in the last 150 years, as travel has become more affordable and less difficult, some of those who travelled were prepared to openly admit that pleasure was one of the motivations for their journeys. Travel for leisure pursuits is the key origin of tourism.

By the 21st century, tourism has become a global industry involving hundreds of millions of people in international, as well as domestic travel, each year. The World Tourism Organization (WTO, 2014) indicated that there was, for the first time more than one billion international travellers in 2012. By 2015 almost 15% of the world's population had been involved in international travel (WTO, 2014). However, some of this activity may comprise the same travellers involved in more than one journey per year and hence the precise scale of tourism as an industry is in some doubt (Leiper, 1999). Globally, millions of people work directly in the industry, in for example, hotels, tour operators and travel agencies and many more are employed indirectly in the industry, for example in bars and retail outlets. Hundreds of millions of people are on the receiving end of tourism activity as they live in what are termed destination areas, in supposed 'host' populations.

As recently as the 1960s, tourism was an activity in which relatively few participated, and was mainly confined to Europe, North America and a small number of other locations. International travel, prior to the 1960s, involved a wealthy minority who had the time as well as the money to be able to be involved in long distance sea or air travel. Major changes in the second half of the 20th century led to the rapid and massive growth of the phenomenon known as modern tourism.

With approximately 51% of international arrivals in 2015, Europe remained, in the early part of 21st century, the single most important region for international travel arrivals (WTO, 2016) although this percentage has fallen from 55% in 2006 (WTO, 2007). In fact in 2015, Europe had five countries in the top ten tourism destinations globally – France, Spain, Italy, the United Kingdom and Germany, with France (first in the top ten) and Spain (third in the top ten) having combined totals accounting for 13% of total international arrivals (WTO, 2014).

This brief overview of the importance of tourism, however fails to indicate that there is no full agreement on the meaning of the term *tourism*, nor is there complete agreement on what a tourist is and because of this, the section below contains a brief discussion of these concepts.

In the early 1980s, two of the earliest researchers on the impacts of tourism, Matthieson and Wall (1982: 1) indicated that tourism comprised:

> *The temporary movement of people to destinations outside their normal places of work and residence, the activities undertaken during the stay in those destinations, and the facilities created to cater for their needs.*

More recently, in 1991, the World Tourism Organization (WTO) created a definition which was largely designed to help those whose responsibility it was to collect and publish tourism statistics. This definition is as follows:

> *The activities of a person travelling outside his or her usual environment for less than a specified period of time whose main purpose of travel is other than for exercise of an activity remunerated from the place visited.*

This may appear a rather technical definition, but it clearly makes reference to travel, time away from home and that the purpose of tourism is not concerned with work.

The impacts of tourism are an important aspect of Jafari's (1981: 3) definition. As he stated:

> *Tourism is a study of man (sic) away from his usual habitat, of the industry which responds to his needs and the impacts that both he and the industry have for the host socio-cultural, economic and physical environments.*

This definition fails to make reference to women, but Jafari probably intended the term 'man' to summarise all humans. However Jafari does stress that tourism is an industry and that as such an activity has impacts on society, the physical environment and economies.

Most definitions of the term *tourist* are based on the concept of tourism. Usually, such definitions make reference to the need for the tourist to spend at least one night in a destination to which he or she has travelled. Tourists can be distinguished from a day tripper or excursionist in such definitions, as a day tripper is someone who visits and leaves without staying a night in a destination (Prosser, 1998). The reason for different terms is that those who stay overnight clearly require some form of accommodation and hence the impacts they have are likely to be different from those who just visit for a day and do not stay, particularly in relation to economic impacts.

However, as Prosser suggested, it is not that uncommon for the two terms to be combined. In fact, it is often the case that the term *visitor* is used in preference to either *tourist* or *excursionist*. Theobold (1994), for example, used the concept of 'visitor ' to combine the elements of a tourist and an excursionist.

When discussing some types of impact of tourism, a classification involving terms such as day tripper, excursionist or tourist is not particularly helpful. For example, in relation to the impacts of the feet of a group of walkers on a mountain slope, it matters little whether the group involved is classified as tourists or excursionists, as the feet are very likely to have the same effect!

As the actions of day trippers/excursionists and those of longer stayers may be almost indistinguishable, the view that a definition of tourism does not necessarily need reference to an overnight stay has been become far more acceptable in the last 20 years or so (Williams, 1998).

In addition to the importance in definitions of for how long a tourist stays or visits an area, the distance travelled has also been seen as significant in relation to definitions of both tourism and tourists. However, there is no commonly accepted international distance used in connection with definitions. There has been a good deal of debate and unresolved confusion about distance travelled and tourism definitions. For example, the US, Canada and Australia in the first decade of the 21st century each used a different distance travelled to define tourism – in the US it was 100 miles, in Canada 50 miles and in Australia 25 miles!

Nevertheless, if there is no complete agreement on the definition of tourism, it is still important to understand the key aspects of the processes of tourism and the reality of being a tourist. Prosser (1998: 374) presented a succinct and useful statement when he indicated that the central components of any definition of either tourists or tourism are as follows:

> *movement, non-permanent stay, activities and experiences during the travel and stay, resources and facilities required and impacts resulting from the travel and stay.*

# Geography and tourism

The focus of the geographical dimensions of tourism is largely on two separate and yet related locations. First, the location of places that attract tourists, usually known as destinations; and second, the places where tourists come from – the generating locations/regions. Tourism is very much concerned with the movement of people from the generating location to the destination. Leiper (1990) attempted to show this relationship as a system and Figure 1.1 indicates the generating region and the tourism destination, with the link between them (Leiper's 'Transit Route'). Figure 1.1 shows, as well as the movement from Generating Region to the Destination, that there is also a return of tourists moving in the opposite direction. Leiper set his two locations and the movement between them in a wider context of environmental, economic, socio-cultural, political, technological and legal factors.

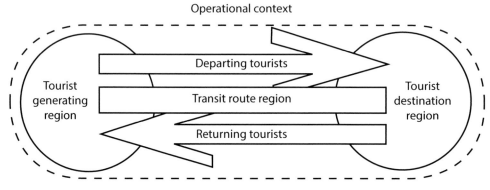

Operational context includes economic, socio-cultural,
political, technological, legal and environmental variables

**Figure 1.1:** Leiper's (1990) Tourism System

Leiper's tourist generating areas are the origin areas of the tourists, and these are usually the home area, although they could be a stopping-off point if a tourist is in transit for a long period and stops off on route to a destination. As Boniface and Cooper (2001) state, a key dimension which is very important to any discussion of the geography of tourism is the demographic structure of the generating area, as this has a significant impact on the demand for tourism (Boniface and Cooper, 2001). The socio-economic make-up of the origin area is also very important in relation to demand. All other things being equal, it is possible to argue, that the greater the wealth/disposable income of those in the origin area and the amount of leisure time, the greater the demand for tourism will be. The nature of tourism demand is discussed in greater detail in Chapter 2.

Tourism destinations are places where tourists visit and stay temporarily (Boniface and Cooper, 2001). In the destination are the facilities for tourists such as accommodation, restaurants, bars, retail outlets and attractions, including entertainment facilities. Together these facilities can be considered as the tourism industry in the destination. It is partly for the reason that several major sectors of the tourism industry are located here, and that as a result many tourism impacts occur here, that the destination can be considered the most important part of the tourism system (Boniface and Cooper, 2001). The destination is clearly a major example of the tourism/geography nexus and is therefore a significant focus of this book.

The third part of Leiper's system comprises the transit routes. In a domestic context these are likely to mean road and rail links, whilst in relation to international travel may involve both these forms of transport, but will also very likely include air and ship-based travel.

One of the first in-depth textbooks of geography and tourism was published over 40 years ago. In his book, *A Geography of Tourism,* Robinson (1976) indicated six factors which he considered were the key parts of a rationale for geography as a subject area to be concerned with tourism. These six factors are presented, in italics, below, and further comments in relation to each have been added:

1 *Geography is particularly concerned with the environment, the location of phenomena, their spatial distribution and relationships.* Tourism is concerned with spatial conditions, the location of tourist areas or destinations and the relationships between places generating tourists and the destinations and the movement of people between them.

2 *The phenomenon of tourism is closely related to the structure, form, nature, use and conservation of the environment.* Tourism has, in summary, two types of impact on the landscape – it changes the landscape through the impact on it via, for example, the building of hotels and second, it helps to conserve the landscape as a result of the creation of, for example, national parks, sites of scientific interests and nature reserves. These two impacts can be viewed as most probably conflicting land use effects. Geography has a role in reconciling tourist activity with other demands on environments.

3 *Tourism is often very significant in remote or peripheral areas.* So, for example, areas such as the Swiss Alps would have relatively few residents, were it not for tourism creating jobs and providing conditions that enable areas that would be subject to major depopulation to maintain a population. Geographers have long been interested in this relationship between economic conditions and demographic change.

4 *Tourism is an important commercial activity in many parts of the world.* It is therefore worthy of study by economic geographers. Tourism is a major part of the economy in many European countries, such as France, Spain, Greece and Italy, as well as in Australia, New Zealand and North America, and increasingly in parts of Asia and South America. It employs large numbers of people and makes significant contributions to gross domestic product in many countries, as well as providing tax revenue. Tourism has also been used to assist economic development on a regional basis in many countries. This is important in promoting economic growth, which is a topic frequently studied by geographers.

5 *Tourism features as a part of international trade and is one of the biggest items in this trade.* Hence, tourism can play a major role in a country's balance of payments. For some countries, such as Spain, France and Ireland, tourism is a vital component in helping to balance trade between imports and exports (appearing as an export in calculations). The amount spent by some tourists, historically Americans (but more recently Japanese and Chinese), greatly benefits the economy of countries such as Mexico, the Bahamas and the UK.

6 *Tourism has far-reaching social and cultural effects.* It helps create jobs, promotes the development of underdeveloped areas and the money gained may be used to improve a country's infrastructure. In the widest sense, tourism can bring about development, which in extreme cases can mean a radical change in, for example, an undeveloped country's 'traditional' culture.

Although Robinson's ideas were written more than 40 years ago, it would appear, in the second decade of the 21st century, that they are still very much relevant. However, there has been a change of focus since the time that Robinson was writing. There is now an even greater concern with the environment than in the 1970s, particularly in relation to major issues including climate change. Also, certain socio-economic factors have become even more important, in particular the benefits and costs to local, or host, communities of tourism and new forms of tourism, such as ecotourism, have been developed. In the past 40 years, as well as positive impacts of tourism, an increasing number of negative effects have been recorded, and this is partly the explanation for a greater emphasis on planning and management of tourism to offset, or overcome, these detrimental effects. Hence, planning and managing tourism has become a major area of focus in the relationship between geography and tourism, and the concern of much of this planning recently, has been on attempts to bring about sustainable forms of tourism.

Hall and Page (2014) produced a useful overview of the development of the geography of tourism, including recent approaches in the relationship between the two areas, and this is summarised in Table 1.1.

Table 1.1 indicates a range of possible approaches to the relationship between geography and tourism. The work of researchers and authors may fit within any one of these approaches or indeed more than one. The different approaches indicate the dynamic nature of the relationship, and suggest that it is likely there will be new approaches developed and employed in the future.

**Table 1.1:** Approaches to geography and the relationship to the study of tourism. (adapted from Hall and Page, 2014).

| Approach | Key concepts |
|---|---|
| Spatial analysis | Locational analysis, maps, systems, networks, positivism |
| Behavioural geography | Behaviourism, environmental perception, mental maps, decision making, spatial preferences |
| Humanistic geography | Human agency, subjectivity of analysis, place, landscape, phenomenology, ethnography |
| Applied geography | Planning, governance, remote sensing, Geographical Information Systems, public policy, regional development, carrying capacity |
| Emerging approach: sustainability | Integrated resource management, sustainable development, sustainable tourism |
| Emerging approach: environmental change | Global environmental change, ecological footprint |
| Radical approaches | Neo-Marxist analysis, role of state, gender, globalisation, localisation, post-colonialism, post-modernism, post-structuralism, role of space |
| Emerging approach: 'cultural turn' | Cultural identity, gender, post-colonialism, the body, sexuality, visual methods. |

## Summary

Geography is a subject, frequently referred to as a discipline. It is a way of organising our thoughts about the world and helps structure and focuses these on specific topics, themes and issues. Its particular approach is to study spatial relationships on the earth's surface. It focuses on both the physical world and the human world and is concerned very much with the relationship between these two. One major concern of geography is to consider the nature of the impacts of human activity on the earth's surface. Additionally it considers major global issues that have important spatial dimensions. Tourism is a human activity, which has social and economic dimensions. It uses significant resources from both the physical and human worlds and has important impacts on the earth and people. It has major geographical dimensions, because of the spatial links between the origin regions of tourists and the locations, or destinations, that tourists visit. It both contributes to, and is affected by, some of the current major global issues that have significant geographical dimensions. Tourism's use of resources and that the activity has significant impacts has meant an increased need for planning and management.

## Student activities

1  What type of questions are geographers interested in finding answers to and why are they particularly interested in these questions?

2  Why are geographers interested in studying tourism?

3  Why is it difficult to define what a tourist is?

4  Figure 1.1 shows the tourism system. Using this explain what the 'tourism system' is.

5  In 1976, Robinson presented six factors (as indicated above) which he considered were the key parts of a rationale for geography to be concerned with tourism. In small groups (3/4), discuss these factors and put them in descending order of importance. Consider any other factors that should be added to this list today.

# References

Boniface, B. and Cooper, C. (2001) *Worldwide Destinations*, Oxford: Butterworth Heinemann

Hall, C.M. and Page, S. (2014) *The Geography of Tourism and Recreation* (4th ed), London: Routledge

Jafari, J. (1981) Editor's Page, *Annals of Tourism Research* **8**, 7

Leiper, N .(1990 *The Tourism System*, Palmerston North, New Zealand, Massey University, Dept of Management Systems

Leiper, N .(1999) Ten Myths about Tourism, Conference Proceedings 1999, CAUTHE National Conference, Adelaide, pp 1-11

Mason, P. (2014) *Researching Tourism, Leisure and Hospitality for your Dissertation*, Oxford: Goodfellows

Matthieson, A and Wall, G (1980) *Tourism: Economic, Social and Environmental Impacts*, London: Longman

Prosser, R. (1998) Tourism in : *Encyclopaedia of Ethics* Vol 4, Chicago IL.: Houghton Mifflin, pp 371-401

Robinson, H. (1976) *A Geography of Tourism*, London, Macdonald and Evans

Theobold, A (1984) *Global Tourism*, Wallingford, UK: CABI Pub lications

Williams S (1998) *Tourism Geography*, London: Routledge

WTO (1991) *Yearbook of Statistics*, Madrid: World Tourism Organization

WTO (2007) UNWTO World Tourism Barometer, Vol 5, No 2, World Tourism Organization

WTO (2014) UNWTO Tourism Highlights, 2014, Madrid: World Tourism Organization

WTO (2016) *Tourism Highlights 2016*, Madrid, World Tourism Organisation

# 2 Tourism Motivation

## Introduction

Tourists are motivated to be involved in tourism for a variety of reasons. An obvious motivation is to have an enjoyable experience, but there are many different ways to achieve this. Some people will be happy to lay in the sun on a beach and do very little, however, others may want to be very active and spend time climbing a mountain. Getting away from the 'normal' environment of home or work, in other words, following the dictum, 'a change is as good as a rest' can be another reason for being involved in tourism. In reality, it is often a combination of factors that leads people to travel, although some of these may be more important than others. In the first part of this chapter, tourism motivation is discussed; the second section is concerned with how motivation can be converted into demand.

## Key perspectives

In any tourism journey, there is likely to be at least one factor, and quite possibly a number of reasons which, when combined, can be considered as the motivational factors for the trip. These can be characterized as *push* and *pull* factors. The *push* factors are a number of perceived negative factors about the location in which the potential tourist currently finds himself or herself and which will contribute to a desire to leave this place. The *pull* factors are perceived positive factors of a potential or real destination. The nature, extent and significance of particular push and pull factors will vary according to the particular tourism context.

The use of the terms *push* and *pull* is linked closely with the psychological model of tourism motivation developed by Iso-Aloha (1980), who was one of the first researchers to investigate tourism motivation in depth and detail. The two dimensions in the model can be summarized as *seeking* motives and *escaping* motives (Pearce, 1993). In Iso-Aloha's model, individuals seek personal and interpersonal rewards, which they hope to find in the place that is exerting the pull, and at the same time wish to escape personal and interpersonal environments, or what can be considered as the push aspect of the current location of the potential tourist.

The main criticism of Iso-Aloha's model is that with only two dimensions, it is somewhat limited. Having only the concepts of push and pull may oversimplify a complex process. However, investigating motivations in an attempt to understand the behaviour of tourists has always been important in tourism research (Ryan, 1997). Understanding what motivates tourists can help with their categorisation, as well as provide a better understanding of their impacts. Knowing the motivations can also help link the desires of tourists with where they wish to travel to and the activities in which they want to engage, which is important for tourists themselves and the tourism industry.

Tourist behaviour can be influenced by a number of demographic factors, including gender, age and ethnicity, but also cultural conditioning, social influences, perception and education can be very significant (Mason, 2016). However, as Crompton and McKay (1997) indicated motives generally precede the decision-making process that leads to particular types of behaviour.

# Psychological and sociological theories

The related fields of psychology and sociology have provided the foundations for many researchers to develop significant theories on motivation. For example, in the field of cognitive psychology, motives are viewed as largely a function of what will happen when humans behave in a particular way, or putting this more formally, the expected consequences of future human behaviour (Dunn-Ross and Iso-Aloha, 1991). In this sense, motives can be considered as internal factors that have initially aroused a person, and following on from this internal reaction, these factors then direct the individual's behaviour (Iso-Aloha, 1980). In summary, it is possible to suggest that the key components of a general psychological model of motivation are:

  i) *needs* and *motives*,
  ii) *behaviour* or *activity*,
  iii) *goals* or *satisfactions* and
  iv) *feedback* (Harrill and Potts, 2002).

The link between these concepts are as follows: *motives* (or needs) drive behaviour, this behaviour has certain *goals*, the overarching one of which is to achieve *satisfaction*.

The concept of feedback relates to whether satisfaction has been achieved, or not, in the particular context. Mannell and Kleber (1997: 190) indicated the conceptual relationships very well, when they stated:

> *People who have a strong need or desire to be with others* (motive) *may attempt to engage in leisure activities, such as going to bars and drinking, that allow them to increase their interactions with other people* (behaviour) *in hopes of developing more friendships* (goal and satisfaction).

The feedback element of the conceptual relationship is concerned with whether or not the initial needs and motivations have been achieved (Harrill and Potts, 2002). Hence, during an activity, an individual interacts with the environment in which the activity takes place and possibly with others involved in the activity and this may then result in new, or perhaps, different motivations.

Sociological theories have also been developed to try to explain tourist motivation. One of the earliest was that of Cohen (1972) who sub-divided tourists into four types, based on motivation. He argued that the two main factors forming the basis of his theory are *strangeness* versus *familiarity*. Cohen developed a continuum based on this two-fold classification, and indicated that at one end was the 'organized mass tourist', who wanted some degree of familiarity in holiday surroundings, while at the other end, the 'drifter', (the term he created), is willing to accept far more strangeness and actually wants to become absorbed by the local culture and possibly settle in the new location. Between these two are two groups – one group who wish to have some freedom, but a degree of organisation for their tourist experience and Cohen referred to these as 'independent mass tourists', and a second group who want, to some extent, the unfamiliar/strange in terms of where they go to, but still desire a number of the comforts of the mass tourist, and Cohen termed such tourists as 'explorers'.

Cohen developed his theory to investigate how various types of tourist might interact with host communities. This approach also influenced Plog (1973) who devised a continuum, using two concepts that he created. He indicated at one end of the continuum were *allo-centrics* and at the other *psycho-centrics*. Plog suggested that psycho-centric individuals are inhibited and relatively non-adventurous and are concerned primarily with the self. In terms of tourist behaviour, psycho-centrics want the familiar in relation to people and places, and are unlikely to travel great distances to their chosen tourism destinations. At the other end of the spectrum, Plog asserted allo-centrics seek out the unfamiliar when travelling and are confident and naturally inquisitive. Such tourists will be prepared to travel significant distances, wish to meet new people and desire unusual experiences.

Despite the fact that Plog's theory is largely psychological and Cohen's sociological, there are similarities in terms of the concepts of familiarity and strangeness that each author uses in their respective theories. Also the resultant classification of different types of tourist share some features, in that Cohen's 'organised mass tourists' would probably fit into Plog's psycho-centric conceptualisation, whilst Cohen's explorers would most likely fit within Plog's allo-centric classification. Both Cohen's (1972) and Plog's (1973) theories have been tested, but with varied success and have not met with universal acceptance. Nevertheless, they remain as key theories in relation to tourism motivation, although both are largely descriptive rather than explanatory (Harrill and Potts, 2002).

# Motivation categories

It may appear in relation to sociological and psychological theories, that motivation tends to be a fairly static concept. However, Pearce (1988), using the concept of a *travel ladder*, suggested that motivations are multivariate and dynamic. He suggests that demographic factors are important and motivation will change particularly as a result of ageing and life-cycle stage. He also suggested that fashion can affect motivation and individuals can be affected by other people's ideas and activities. Pearce acknowledged that he was influenced by the work of the psychologist Maslow (1954), who created a hierarchical range of needs from low level, primarily physical needs, to high level intellectual needs. Maslow termed these needs, in ascending sequence, as physiological, safety, social, self-esteem and self-development. Pearce, using Maslow's (1954) ideas, proposed the following tourism motivation categories:

- Relaxation,
- Excitement and thrills,
- Social interaction,
- Self-esteem and development,
- Fulfilment.

In attempting to summarize the major motivations of tourists, Ryan (1991) drew on the work of Cohen (1972), Crompton (1979) and Matthieson and Wall (1982) and presented eleven major reasons for tourist travel. These are as follows:

1 Escape
2 Relaxation
3 Play
4 Strengthening family bonds
5 Prestige
6 Social interaction
7 Sexual opportunity
8 Educational opportunity
9 Self-fulfilment
10 Wish fulfilment
11 Shopping.

This list of eleven motivations for tourist journeys can also be seen to be linked to the concepts of push and pull factors with, for example, *escape* certainly a push factor and *prestige* clearly a pull factor. These eleven factors are very varied and several appear quite different from others, for example *social interaction* and *play* will involve tourists being fully engaged and active, whilst others such as *relaxation* are more contemplative and less likely to involve active participation. However, some of the eleven factors may be linked, such as *strengthening family bonds* and *social interaction*. Nevertheless, this list indicates that there are potentially many different motivating factors that could influence tourism activity.

Ryan (1991) indicated, that often, holiday choices are based on a combination of motivations. At the time the choices are made, they represent a set of priorities by the potential tourist. However, it is possible, and even probable, that these priorities will change over time. Some tourists may even deliberately delay achieving certain needs and this may be based on the cost of, access to, or availability of, the means to achieve these needs (Ryan, 1991; 1997).

Chadwick (1987) provided a more simplified categorisation of the reasons for tourist-related journeys than that provided by Ryan, when he summarized the motivations for, and purpose of travel, under three main headings. These are as follows:

1 *Pleasure*: leisure, culture, active sports, visiting friends and relatives (usually abbreviated to VFR).
2 *Professional*: meetings, missions, business, etc.
3 *Other purposes*: study, health, transit.

At the end of the 20th century, the Annual International Passenger Survey carried out by the British Tourist Authority distinguished five types of tourism-related visit (cited in Prosser, 1998). These reasons for visiting, shown immediately below, are closely linked to the idea of motivation, with the first two referring specifically to a holiday, whilst the third category is clearly different in terms of motivation, with its reference to business. The fourth category, Visiting Friends and Relatives, stresses the importance of friends and family as a motivating factor in tourism visits.

1 Holiday independent
2 Holiday inclusive
3 Business
4 Visiting friends and relatives (VFR)
5 Miscellaneous

The VFR segment is important in the United Kingdom and Europe (Prosser, 1998; Seaton, 2005) and particularly significant within Australia, New Zealand and Canada, with as many as 20 per cent of visitors to Australia being regularly in the VFR category (Mason, 2016). Partly in relation to this high figure, Prosser (1998) suggested a 3-fold categorisation of visitor motivation, as follows:

(i) pleasure,
(ii) business and
(iii) VFR.

Despite a number of the theoretical perspectives being originally produced over 25 years ago, with the emergence of new forms of tourism in this period, for example ecotourism, volunteer tourism and pro-poor tourism, the theoretical perspectives on motivations discussed in this section could appear to be outdated. However, using volunteer tourism as the particular example of a new form of tourism – one which may at first glance appear to have very different motivational factors than more traditional forms of tourism – it is still possible for this type of tourism to fit with earlier classifications. Therefore, using Ryan's (1991) categories, *self–fulfilment* and *education* appear to be at least two of the major motivational factors for volunteer tourism and also this activity would most probably involve *social interaction* and possibly *prestige* as key motivations.

The following case study, set within the context of a historical cross-country trail, El Camino de Santiago in Spain, provides an example of the range of possible motivations relating to a tourism experience and indicates that some factors have changed over time and that those once important have declined and additionally new motivational factors have emerged.

## Case Study : El Camino de Santiago

The Camino de Santiago can be regarded as the very first tourism route and a particularly early example of mass tourism. El Camino de Santiago means the 'Way of Saint James' and is also known as the 'Pilgrims Way'. Santiago de Compostella is a town in North Western Spain and the destination of those who walk the Camino. Santiago is reputedly the location of the body of Saint James ('Santiago' is the Spanish for 'Saint James'). Saint James was the cousin of Jesus. How the bones of Saint James reached this corner of Spain, following his execution in Jerusalem, has been debated for centuries, which has helped maintain interest and acted as a form of marketing. Whatever the reality, a large number of Catholic Christians believe, or want to believe, that the body of the Saint is in the cathedral in Santiago.

For the first pilgrims the main motive for their walk related to their religious faith. The pilgrims believed that St James had miraculous power and that their pilgrimage to his remains in Santiago would guarantee them a reduction of half the time that their soul would spend in Purgatory after they died - Purgatory is the place that Christians believe that the human soul goes to after death and before the soul goes to either Heaven or Hell. In Holy Years (every six years, when Saint James's feast day is a Sunday) pilgrims who walked to Santiago could achieve even greater benefits – they could bypass Purgatory completely.

A sign on part of the Camino de Santiago near Santiago de Compostella in Spain

**2**

The reason for the significance of Santiago as a place of pilgrimage for Spanish and other European Catholics relates to the religious and political history of Spain. Although Saint James' body disappeared, after his death in Jerusalem, for over 750 years, it reputedly reappeared in Santiago. The bones were found in AD 813 by a hermit, who was drawn to a location on a hillside by visions of stars. The Latin for the location was known as *campus stella* (field of stars) and soon after became known as Compostella. Hence, Santiago de Compostella.

The 'discovery' of the bones coincided with a very important time in Spanish history. For the century leading up to 800, the Moors (originally from North Africa) had been progressing through Spain, but had not yet reached the far northern coast – the regions of Asturias and Galicia which is the location of Santiago. The Moors, who were Muslims and had been inspired by the prophet Muhammed, who had died in AD 632, had embarked on a *jihad* or holy war and were attempting to make the whole of Spain Islamic. Spanish Christian Catholics used Saint James as their symbolic champion, or talisman, to fight back against the Moors. During the next five hundred years the Moors were slowly driven out of Spain. In the battles that took place between Catholics and Moors, the Catholics frequently called upon Saint James to help them defeat the Moors, and if they won, Saint James became even more important to them.

Traditionally the pilgrimage should start in the pilgrim's home location, which means there are many potentially different paths to Santiago, but for the majority in the past, and even today, the town of Roncesvalles in the Basque region of the Spanish Pyrenees is the starting point. This still means a lengthy 750 km. trip in each direction to and from Santiago, along what is known as the Camino Frances, and this is likely to take several weeks. However, for pilgrims to earn their certificate of pilgrimage (known as the *compostella*) today, they need only walk the final 100 km of the Camino, or it is possible today, instead of walking, to cycle the last 200km.

As the number of pilgrims grew during medieval times, monasteries and charitable organisations provided cheap accommodation and food along the route-way. New villages appeared and older ones developed places to stay and places to eat and drink. An order of knights was created to protect the pilgrims, and what is probably the first tourist guide was written by a French monk who discussed the landscape and cultural habits of the people who lived along the route.

By the early 21st century approximately 70,000 pilgrims make the journey along the Camino de Santiago each year, but the numbers have risen from less than 20,000 annually, 50 years ago. In the 'Holy Years' the number of pilgrims doubles to more than 150,000. This increase in the number of pilgrims suggests that it has become a fashionable thing to walk the Camino.

Although the original reasons for almost all pilgrims to make the journey was linked to their Catholic faith, and there are still those who undertake the walk for religious reasons, in the 21st century, there exists many more motivations. For some, it is a personal challenge – they want to demonstrate to themselves and, probably friends, that they have walked on an old, famous European route-way.

One of the first references to a pilgrimage to Santiago in English literature in fact was by Chaucer in his Canterbury Tales, in which he referred to his character, the Wife of Bath and that she had made a pilgrimage to Santiago for personal reasons.

For many pilgrims in the past (and also for some in the present), journeying by foot or by cycle has been a social event with groups of three and upwards travelling the route together, joined by friends and possibly family members for part of the route. Others travelling alone, hope to meet like-minded pilgrims. Yet others may hope to meet a future partner – so there is also a romantic dimension to the reasons for travelling the Camino.

Some tourists will be travelling the Camino, motivated by the desire for adventure, and an increasing number of these are young pilgrims. A criminal element was also attracted by the pilgrims in the past, as they could be easy targets for robbery or mugging, if walking alone. Criminal activity still occurs today, with the occasional theft and the more serious occurrence of rape or mugging. Some of those on the Camino will be motivated by the desire to see examples of Spanish history, heritage and culture. Whatever the motivations, and some travellers will have a combination of reasons for walking or cycling the Camino, many return year-after-year to attempt a different section of this famous route-way.

*Source*: adapted from: Baskett, S., Brown, J., Dubin, M., Ellington, M., Fisher, J., Garvey, G. and Stewart, I., *The Rough Guide to Spain*, Twelfth Edition 2007.

The importance of motivation for tourists' activities and experiences, in terms of the geography of tourism, is that if we consider that the concepts of push and pull are in their theoretical constructs by definition linked, then we are discussing two different locations. In other words, the location of the push factors will be different from the location of the pull factors. These locations therefore exist in different geographical places and what links them is travel between the two, and as we have seen previously travel is a key component of tourism. So, for example, we could be discussing a large industrial town from where a potential tourist wants to escape (a push factor) to travel to a coastal resort to relax or play (pull factors). Or, to take another example, a potential tourist from a relatively isolated rural community could wish to escape (push factor) to meet friends and shop at major department stores (pull factors). Although in each example, the push and pull locations are very different types of place, the similarity is that each has a push location and a pull location. Geographically linking the two locations is a route and some form of transport. The relationship between the origin location of the potential tourist and the destination location is shown in Figure 1.1.

# Demand

This chapter so far has discussed the motivation for tourism activities and experiences, but there is a very important related concept to motivation – this is demand. According to Pearce (1995), tourism demand is the relationship between a tourist's motivation to travel and their ability to do so. In other words, this is when the desire to travel as a tourist is translated into actual travel and related tourism activities.

Demand is most often considered to be an economic term and a very important one, particularly in relation to the concept of supply. It is commonly accepted within most western capitalist societies that there is a close relationship between demand and supply, particularly in terms of the effect that this relationship has on the price of goods and services. Hence, if there is a high demand for a product or service and there is only a small supply, then the price is likely to be high. A very good example of this is the precious metal gold, of which there is only a limited supply, which means, as the demand is high, that its price is usually very high. Conversely water which is generally in very large supply in most, although not all, parts of the world, has a low demand and consequently a low price.

In economics, demand has a specific meaning which according to Cooper *et al.* (2005: 38) is as follows:

> *The schedule of the amount of any good or service which people are willing and able to buy at each specific price in a set of possible prices during a specific period of time.*

The economist is concerned, when considering the concept of demand, with the relationship between the ability to buy and how much a potential consumer is willing to pay for a good or service. The geographer's concept of demand in relation to tourism is somewhat different and according to Mathieson and Wall (1982: 71) can be considered to be 'the total number of people who travel, or wish to travel to use tourist facilities away from their place of work and residence'. Psychologists have yet another angle on the concept of demand and are interested in the relationship between motivation of tourists and their behaviour.

It is nevertheless important to ensure a full understanding of the economic perspective on tourism demand, particularly in terms of the links between demand and supply and there are in fact three different and yet related concepts of the term (Cooper *et al.*, 2005):

- *Effective demand* or *actual demand*, which is the number of tourist who are travelling at a given time or in a given time period. Most tourism statistics and measures concerned with demand as a concept are referring to effective or actual demand.

- *Suppressed demand*. This refers to those who do not travel, for whatever reason, at a particular point in time. The reason may be a lack of financial resources or a lack of time. Although increasing numbers of people are travelling, many at the global scale still do not. This is particularly the case in relation to international travel, where it is a minority who do actually travel between countries. According to Cooper *et al.* (2005), suppressed demand has two components, *potential demand* and *deferred demand*. Potential demand relates to the ability of some people to be able to travel in the future, as they will have, for example, more money and/or time to do this. Deferred demand refers to the inability of some people to travel at a given moment, because of the lack of availability of a specific destination to travel to, due, for example, to non-availability of accommodation, or the lack of a means of transport to get there.

■ *No demand.* This refers to the fact that there are always likely to be, in a given context, some people who are unwilling to travel to be tourists.

The concepts of *actual demand, suppressed demand* and *no demand* are applicable to most economic activities and sectors and not just tourism. However, demand in tourism can also be viewed in other specific ways. The demand for tourism can change, if the chosen destinations is not available and the tourist selects a different destination. This is called *redirection of demand* (Cooper *et al.*, 2005). It may also be the case that a tourist changes his or her mind on the type of accommodation that they wish to use, from, for example a hotel room to self-catering accommodation. This is an example of *substitution of demand* (Cooper *et al.*, 2005). Yet another situation can occur when there is the creation of a new destination or a new activity. This leads to a change in supply of tourism resources or activities. (Note that tourism resources are discussed in detail in Chapter 3 and 4). However this change in supply is likely to cause:

■ Redirection of demand

■ Substitution of demand

■ New demand.

Leiper's model of the Tourism System (Figure 1.1) indicates that there are flows between the generating region and the destination region. In effect these flows are the product of tourism demand from the consumers in the origin region to the supply of a range of tourism products in the destination. Therefore, being able to measure and understand these flows of tourists is an important component of measuring and understanding tourism demand.

Tourism demand is influenced by a large number of factors. These factors can be summarised under three headings and Figure 2.1 indicates in summary that these are economic factors, socio-psychological factors and external (or exogenous) factors. Some of the important economic factors, as Figure 2.1 shows, are the amount of disposable income available to a tourist, the price of goods and services and relative pricing of one destination in comparison with another. Socio-psychological factors include the image of a destination, attitudes towards a destination and travel time available, whilst important exogenous factors include the availability of the supply of resources in a destination, accessibility of a destination and the existence (or absence) of natural disasters, war or terrorism.

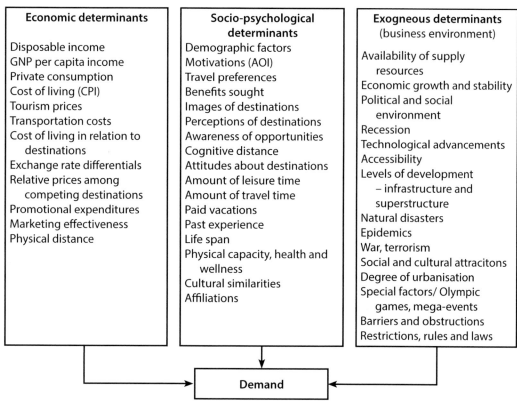

| Economic determinants | Socio-psychological determinants | Exogeneous determinants (business environment) |
|---|---|---|
| Disposable income<br>GNP per capita income<br>Private consumption<br>Cost of living (CPI)<br>Tourism prices<br>Transportation costs<br>Cost of living in relation to destinations<br>Exchange rate differentials<br>Relative prices among competing destinations<br>Promotional expenditures<br>Marketing effectiveness<br>Physical distance | Demographic factors<br>Motivations (AOI)<br>Travel preferences<br>Benefits sought<br>Images of destinations<br>Perceptions of destinations<br>Awareness of opportunities<br>Cognitive distance<br>Attitudes about destinations<br>Amount of leisure time<br>Amount of travel time<br>Paid vacations<br>Past experience<br>Life span<br>Physical capacity, health and wellness<br>Cultural similarities<br>Affiliations | Availability of supply resources<br>Economic growth and stability<br>Political and social environment<br>Recession<br>Technological advancements<br>Accessibility<br>Levels of development<br> – infrastructure and superstructure<br>Natural disasters<br>Epidemics<br>War, terrorism<br>Social and cultural attracitons<br>Degree of urbanisation<br>Special factors/ Olympic games, mega-events<br>Barriers and obstructions<br>Restrictions, rules and laws |

Demand

**Figure 2.1:** Factors influencing tourism demand (source: Uysal, 1998)

It is possible to consider tourism demand both at the individual level and at the national level. At the individual level it is possible to consider demand in relation to two major sets of factors (Cooper *et al.*, 2005). The first set of factors can be summarised as *life-cycle*, meaning, for example that age and domestic circumstances (e.g. whether married or single, with or without children) are important, whilst the second set can be summarised as *lifestyle* and these include education level, income level, nature of employment, amount of holiday time provided and mobility (Cooper *et al.*, 2005). Taken together, these two sets of factors will affect the nature and amount of tourism demand.

In relation to life cycle factors, for a child under the age of, for example, ten years, the amount of control over demand for tourism experiences is relatively low. A child's parents will select a holiday destination, although a child may have been asked their preferences (or may have expressed these anyway, whether requested or not!). Adolescent children have more control than younger ones, but will still often need parents' permission and will usually require funding from adults, so their power in relation to demand is still limited. Young adults will be in a far stronger position in relation to demand, but may lack the necessary finances. Parents with young children will often have different factors influencing demand than those without children, and providing holiday experiences for their children may be the major motivational factor for such people, which will affect the nature of their demand. Senior citizens who no longer need to support their children will have yet different factors affecting their demand, which are likely to include the amount of time that they have available to be involved in tourism, while their age my preclude their participation in some forms of activity, but lead to an interest in others, that were not important when they were younger.

In the discussion of life-cycle factors, some life-style factors have been hinted at. In particular income, or more specifically disposable income, which is the income that is left over after all bills and other necessary payments have been made, is very important. The more disposable income an individual has, then the greater demand for tourism experiences would appear to be a logical con-nection. However, the relationship is more complex as the demand depends on an individual's attitude to a holiday – if it is regarded as luxury, then even an individual with a high income may not engage in tourism, conversely a low income individual may view a holiday as essential and spend less on other items to be able to take the holiday. Also of great importance in relation to life-style factors is time, as it is difficult to be a tourist if an individual does not have time to be involved. Of particular importance in relation to growing demand for tourism over the past one hundred years has been paid holidays. Most jobs in European countries have an entitlement to paid holidays – in other words the worker has an entitlement to time away from work, but still receives pay while away from work. In many countries, there are significant numbers of people who have time to be involved in tourism, but they lack employment, so do not have the ability to take holidays. Such people are often referred to as being 'time rich, but money poor'. There are also a number of people in many countries who have money but their work limits their capacity to take holidays and they are frequently referred to as 'money rich, but time poor'. Both sets of such people are significant in relation to tourism demand.

There are a number of other life-style factors that affect demand for tourism. Education levels can be important, with those who have higher levels of edu-cational attainment likely to have a higher demand for tourism (Mason, 2016). Personal mobility is also important, with those owning cars more likely to travel to engage in tourism than those without vehicles, and ownership of a car actually stimulates a desire to travel for tourism purposes (Cooper *et al.*, 2005). Race and gender are also important influences on tourism demand. Traditionally it has been argued that white males are more likely to have a higher demand for tour-ism than others (Cooper *et al.*, 2005). However, it is a far more complex situation, varying from place to place, country to country and one that is changing anyway.

Although life-cycle factors and life-style factors have been separated in the discussion above, in reality they are entwined as, for example, a high status job, will usually attract a high income, will probably be carried out by a well-educated person and is likely to occur when an individual has reached at least middle-age. It is also important to be aware that these two sets of factors are *influences* on tourism demand and not *determinants*, and also to acknowledge that conditions influencing demand are in a continual state of flux.

# Summary

There is a range of reasons why people are motivated to be involved as tourists. Some of these are to do with some negative aspects of the place where the potential tourist is located, so this can lead to a decision to 'escape' – from work, or home, or just the normal routine of life. But there is usually something that attracts people about a place that they want to visit which is away from their place of residence. These two sets of factors can be considered as push and pull' factors. Frequently the push and pull factors act together and are the combined motivations for a tourist. However, before the tourist actually travels there has to be demand. This is the relationship between the tourist's desire to travel and their actual ability to do so. The nature of demand has been discussed in this chapter as well as the factors, particular life-cycle and life-style that can affect demand.

## Student activities

1   Ryan provided eleven motivations for tourism. Working in pairs consider this list and discuss what you believe are the **five** most important motivations. When you have agreed your list of five, compare your list with another pair of students and discuss reasons why you selected your five motivations.

2   Consider a recent tourism experience you have been involved in. List the motivations for this tourism activity and then put the motivations into order of importance.

3   In relation to the case study of the Camino de Santiago, working in pairs, discuss which historical motivations are still important today and which new motivations can be found in the case study.

4   What is tourism demand?

5   The section on Demand has stated that demand is affected by life-cycle factors and life-style factors. What do you understand by life-cycle factors and life-style factors?

# References

Baskett, S., Brown, J., Dubin, M., Ellington M., Fisher, J., Garvey G. and Stewart I., (2007) *The Rough Guide to Spain*, 12th Ed. London. Rough Guides

Chadwick, R. (1987). Concepts, definitions, and measures used in travel and tourism research. In *Travel, Tourism and Hospitality Research: A Handbook for Managers and Researchers* (J. R. Brent Richie and C. Goeldner, eds). New York: Wiley.

Cohen, I. (1972). Towards a sociology of international tourism. *Social Research*, **39**, 164–82.

Cooper, C., Fletcher, J., Fyall, A., Gilbert, D., and Wanhill, S. (2005) *Tourism: Principles and Practice*, 3rd ed. London: Prentice Hall.

Crompton, J. (1979). Motivations for pleasure vacations. *Annals of Tourism Research*, **6**, 408–24.

Crompton, J. and McKay, J. (1997). Motives of visitors attending festival events. *Annals of Tourism Research*, **24**, 425–39.

Dunn-Ross, E. and Iso-Aloha, S. (1991) Sight-seeing tourists' motivation and satisfaction, *Annals of Tourism Research*, **12**, 256-62.

Harrill, R. and Potts, T. (2002). Social psychological theories of tourist motivation: exploration, debate and transition. *Tourism Analysis*, **7**, 105–14.

Iso-Aloha, S. (1980). *The Social-Psychology of Leisure and Recreation*. Iowa: Brown

Mannell, R. and Kleber, D. (1997). *A Social Psychology of Leisure*. Pennsylvania: State College Venture Publishing.

Maslow, A. (1954). *Motivation and Personality*. New York: Harper.

Mason, P (2016) *Tourism Impacts, Planning and Management,* 3rd ed., London, Routledge.

Pearce, P. (1988). *The Ulysses Factor: Evaluating Visitors in Tourist Settings*. New York: Springer Verlag.

Pearce, P. (1993). Fundamentals of tourist motivations. In D. Pearce and R. Butler, (eds.) *Tourism Research: Critiques and Challenges*, pp. 113–34. London: Routledge.

Pearce, D. (1995) *Tourism Today: a geographical analysis* (2nd ed.) Harlow, Longman

Plog, S. (1973). Why destination areas rise and fall in popularity. *Cornell Hotel and Restaurant Administration Quarterly*, **12**, 13–16.

Prosser, R (1998) Tourism in : *Encyclopaedia of Ethics* Vol 4, Chicago IL.: Houghton Mifflin, pp 371-401

Ryan, C. (1991). *Recreational Tourism*. London: Routledge.

Ryan, C. (1997). *The Tourist Experience*. London: Cassell.

Seaton, A. (2005). *Handbook on Tourism Market Segmentation,* Brussels: European Travel Commission.

Uysal, M. (1998) The determinants of tourism demand: a theoretical perspective, in Ionnides, D. and Debbage, K. (Eds.) *The Economic Geography of the Tourist Industry*, London: Routledge, pp 79-98.

# 3 Geographical Resources for Tourism

## Introduction

Chapters 1 and 2 made brief reference to a number of potential geographical resources for tourism. Some of these resources are located within the physical environment, such as landscapes, and include coastal area, moorlands and mountains. Others are part of the human environment, including towns and cities and historic monuments – in summary this is usually known as the built environment. These physical resources and human resources are not necessarily located separately but are often found together. For example, a coastal tourism destination has a physical environment which may be made up of a beach, a shoreline, the sea and it could be backed by cliffs. This will be coupled with a human environment of, for example, hotels, restaurants and bars and possibly, a harbour or marina. This chapter considers the physical and human resources for tourism.

## Key perspectives

Approximately 50 years ago, Peters (1969) provided an attempt to classify tourist attractions. His classification, which was made in relation to international tourism, had five categories, which are as follows:

- **Cultural:** (e.g. sites of archaeological interest, historical buildings and museums, political institutions)
- **Traditions:** (e.g. festivals, music, folklore, arts and handicrafts)
- **Scenic:** (e.g. National Parks, wildlife, flora and fauna, beach resorts, mountain resorts)
- **Entertainment:** (e.g. zoos and aquaria night life, cinema, theatre, theme parks)
- **Other attractions:** (e.g. climate, health resorts, spas, unique attractions not available elsewhere)

(source: Peters,1989)

Not long after Peters put forward his fivefold classification, Robinson (1976) argued that very many tourism attractions are, in fact, geographical and suggested that there are seven geographical aspects of tourism. These seven aspects are shown in Table 3.1.

**Table 3.1:** Geographical components of tourism (after Robinson, 1976)

| |
|---|
| Accessibility and location |
| Space |
| Scenery – landforms (e.g. mountains), water (e.g. rivers) vegetation (e.g. forests) |
| Climate – sunshine, cloud, temperature conditions, rain, snow |
| Animal life – wildlife (e.g. birds) hunting and fishing |
| Settlement features – towns and cities, historical remains, monuments , archaeological sites |
| Culture – ways of life, traditions, folklore and arts and crafts |

There is some similarity between the aspects indicated by Robinson (1976) and those suggested by Peters (1969). However, there is more detail on physical geographical elements such as landforms and landscape features, including plants and animals, in Robinson's categorisation. Study of both Peters (1969) classification and that by Robinson in Table 3.1 may appear to suggest that almost all of the physical and human landscape can act as tourism attractions. However, it is important to be aware that not all resources of the physical environment and not all parts of the human environment are actual tourist attractions. Nevertheless, there is a very large range of attractions and many resources that are currently tourist attractions and yet others that have been attractions in the past.

Although not all geographical features are necessarily tourist attractions, Robinson (1976) suggested there are certain geographical factors that encourage tourism, or as he put it:

> There are … principal elements or ingredients which predispose towards tourism development (Robinson, 1976:42)

Robinson argued that there are six such elements, and these are outlined below:

- Good weather
- Scenery
- Amenities
- Historical and cultural features
- Accessibility
- Accommodation

Boniface and Cooper (2001) used a somewhat similar approach to both Peters (1969) and Robinson (1976) and subdivided geographical resources for tourism under two broad headings: physical resources and cultural resources. Although, in many ways their headings mirror the classification points made by both Peters (1969) and Robinson (1976), Boniface and Cooper (2001:25) stated that there are three main characteristics of the resources for tourism, and suggested that:

- The concept of tourism resources is usually taken to mean tangible objects which are considered to be of economic value within tourism

- The resources are not just used by tourists, but tourism resources are shared with a number of other uses, such as agriculture, forestry, water management and services used by local people

- The resources are perishable. This means that in the case of some resources, such as landscape, they can be damaged by tourists. Another meaning of perishable here is that some tourists' resources, such as accommodation (for example hotel beds) cannot be stockpiled and also unused tourism resources cannot be stored and will perish.

**3**

## Good weather

Robinson (1976) suggested that 'good weather' is important for tourism. However, he failed to define precisely what 'good weather' actually means, but he gives a number of examples. Robinson argued that fine weather is very important for beach based tourism and as he says it 'can make or mar a holiday' (Robinson 1976:43). Robinson (1976) went as far as actually claiming that weather is the most important resource for tourism, whilst Boniface and Cooper (2001) went even further and claimed that it can be considered as more than a resource, as it has a major influence on all outdoor tourism activities and 'bad weather' can restrict tourist behaviour. For this reason, a complete chapter (the one following this) is devoted to discussing weather in this book, and this is done in relation to climate.

## Scenery

Both Peters (1969) and Robinson (1976) make specific reference to scenery as a geographical resource for tourism. It is also usually the case that when scenery is referred to, it means that natural or semi-natural landscapes are being discussed. It is important to note in relation to our understanding of scenery, that until only two hundred years ago, much of what is considered to be attractive scenery today, such as rugged mountain ranges, or high moorlands, was avoided by most travellers, if it was possible to do so. So, for example, the European Alps were not considered to be attractive to tourists up to the mid-1700s, but instead as a barrier to the movement of goods and people between northern and southern Europe.

In the UK it was the Romantic Movement poets, such as William Wordsworth, who started an interest in 'raw nature' and 'wild places' by writing about the English Lake District, which is a region of relatively low, but by UK standards, remote hills and mountains. Wordsworth also visited the French and Swiss Alps in the 1740s and wrote about his experiences there, which acted as a form of marketing for others of his generation to visit, and also to inspire many more in the last 250 years.

Nevertheless, the word *scenery* can be considered a rather vague term. For a passenger sitting on a bus or train, what is outside and apparently passing the window is the scenery. This implies the concept of scenery is everything that can be seen by an observer. This is not what is usually understood by the concept, however. The term scenery is usually linked to concepts of attractiveness and beauty. So there is usually an aesthetic dimension to scenery in relation to tourism. Hence, a tourist may use a phrase such as: 'This is a beautiful valley' or 'What a wonderful view of the land from this hilltop'. An important issue in relation to this aesthetic dimension, is that beauty is often very subjective – in other words what one individual may find very attractive, another may not react to positively at all. So, for example, there are anecdotal stories of travellers from the Netherlands, which is largely a flat country, who have not previously left their homeland, travelling south and when they reach the Swiss Alps, becoming so disturbed by the sight of high mountains, that they have immediately turned round and driven home! How much truth there is in this is not clear, it nevertheless raises the issue of the likelihood of some types of tourists, based on their cultural experiences, reacting differently to other types, in relation to scenery. This means that what a tourist from the UK, for example may find attractive in a destination, may not be what an Indian, Chinese or Japanese visitor finds attractive in the same location.

However, although scenery is comprised of different elements, landforms are a key aspect of scenery (Robinson, 1976). In relation to physical resources for tourism, Boniface and Cooper (2001) suggest that there are a number of different landforms that can act as resources. These include major features such as mountain ranges, but also specific types of mountains, such as volcanoes. Some mountain ranges are particularly important for tourism as they have relatively few permanent inhabitants and have landscapes that are highly valued. Such areas have been designated as national parks or protected areas in many countries and tourism is an important activity within them, and Chapter 13 discusses such protected areas in more detail. However lowland areas, where agriculture is important can also be significant for tourism, and water on land can be a tourism resource, particularly in the form of rivers and lakes (Boniface and Cooper, 2001).

Over 70% of the earth's surface is water, mostly in the form of oceans and seas, and water in this form can also act as tourism resources. However, it is particularly where land and sea meet in coastal areas that there are important locations of tourism resources. Hence, many islands act as tourism resources. Coastal cliffs are relatively small scale landforms that also attract tourists.

Forests are also significant tourism resources that can make up what we refer to as scenery and they range from tropical rain forests to temperate region, coniferous and deciduous forests. As with many of the other tourism resources, forests have multiple uses and this indicates that planning and management in relation to these resources is vital. The theme of resource management is discussed in the final section of this book, in Chapters 14 and 15.

# ■ Wildlife

Any discussion of scenery as a tourism attraction would not be complete without reference to the creatures that are found in the landscape and help to make up the scenery. For example, those involved in taking a safari holiday in Kenya are interested largely in the wild animals they observe in a landscape, rather than the landscape itself. The plains, or to give the correct geographical term, the savannah regions of East Africa, are where it is possible to observe the big cats (e.g. lions, tigers and cheetahs) as well as elephants and rhinoceros and other species such as deer and wildebeest 'in the wild'. Without these animals as the key resource, tourism would be very different and probably much smaller scale.

Wildlife, including particularly birds, are a very important attraction for certain types of tourist. These animals may only be found in a particular country or region. In the UK county of Norfolk, for example, there is a particular type of butterfly known as the swallowtail, which is only found in small wetland parts of the county. Tourists will visit the area to see this butterfly, although it may not always be possible to do so as it is very rare. The notion of rarity is a factor in the motivation of many tourists who are birdwatchers. The rarer a bird that tourists of this type have seen, the more satisfied they will be. Such tourists may spend hours, days or even weeks seeking out the rare species in a specific area. They may never observe what they came to see, but they almost certainly will have contributed to the economy of the area they have visited.

Some animals are emblematic of a country or region. For example, many international visitors to Australia have the sighting of a kangaroo, or a koala bear, high on their list of 'must sees'. Visitors to New Zealand may try to hunt out the kiwi, but they will usually be unlucky, as the flightless birds are nocturnal and difficult to spot. The most likely place to observe a kiwi is in a zoo. Zoos are themselves another type of wildlife tourist attraction, although the wildlife is in captivity which for many potential visitors is controversial (see Mason, 2000). Nevertheless, zoos are important urban tourist resources and may encourage visits to the actual area where zoo animals can be seen in the wild, as well as make tourists aware of important animal resource conservation messages (Mason, 2008).

In the not too distant past, much wildlife was a resource that could be hunted and killed by tourists, and in some parts of the world this is still the case. Such animals include the big cats, but also deer and rabbits. In the past 30 years or so, there has been a growing realisation that many animals are endangered, some as a result of direct human activity, others as a result of loss of habitat, or eco-system change. With growing concern about declining wildlife numbers, new forms of tourism have emerged, particularly eco-tourism. These types of tourism are designed to help conserve particular species and the ecosystem in which they are found, but they are still relatively small scale and specialised compared with more conventional mass tourism. However some popular forms of recreation, for example fishing, are becoming less consumptive of the resources that make the activity possible. Hence, in angling, some fish caught in freshwater or salt water environments are now likely to be returned to the water, rather than taken to be eaten or stuffed and mounted to advertise the prowess of the person who caught the fish.

It is not just rare or unusual animals that are tourism resources, but farm animals are also important attractions. Agro-tourism, or farm tourism, in many parts of the world makes use of domesticated animals such as cows, pigs, sheep and goats, chickens and ducks, as well as the working animals, including horses and donkeys, to draw in tourists, particularly families with young children.

## ■ Cultural activities, festivals and events

Peters (1969) and Robinson (1976) make specific reference to culture as a geographical resource for tourism, and Boniface and Cooper (2001) also discuss cultural factors which they consider important for tourism, and regard the following to be cultural components that act as attractions for tourists: language, art, music, festivals, folklore, handicrafts, food and what they term 'way of life' (Boniface and Cooper, 2001:29).

Robinson (1976) considers cultural features to exert a powerful attraction for many tourists. He makes reference to specific locations associated with important cultural factors, such as William Shakespeare and Stratford-on-Avon in the UK, the Egyptian pyramids and the Parthenon in Athens. It is not just that a majority of international tourists' arrival point in the UK is London, that leads them to stay in the city, it is largely a result of the cultural and historical attractions there, that it is a 'must-see' for such tourists (Robinson, 1976). The same point could be made in relation to the international visitor to France, who goes to Paris, and the tourist to Italy, who visits Rome.

It is possible to recognise a number of broad cultural regions at a global scale. These regions do not always fit well within continental boundaries, but one good example is European or 'Western' culture (Boniface and Cooper 2001). European culture can be seen to date from the Renaissance period in Europe, but in the last seven hundred years or so, has spread to many other parts of the world via colonialism, trade, emigration and technology. However, in parts of Asia and Africa, Western culture is relatively marginal or superficial. This is particularly the case in countries in South East Asia, which are predominantly Buddhist and in the Middle East and North Africa where Islam is dominant. These cultures are different from Western culture and the manifestations of differences (in terms of for example architecture, art, music, dance, festivals and food) are what attracts many 'Western' international tourists. Cultural differences are a motivating factor for significant numbers of tourists from Asia, particularly Japan and Korea, but increasingly China and India to visit Europe and North America.

Religion is an important dimension of culture and a shared religion can be a major motivating factor for international travel. For millions of Muslims around the world, at least one visit to the holy shrine in Mecca, in Saudi Arabia is considered essential. For Christians, there are several places that they can visit, including

Jerusalem and as indicated in Chapter 2, Santiago de Compostella, in Spain, has become a major place of pilgrimage for Christians.

In the sixteenth and seventeenth centuries, the sons of wealthy Europeans travelled around Europe, particularly in Italy and Greece, but they also travelled to North Africa and Turkey to visit places of classical civilisation, to see art treasures, visit museums, historic sites and ancient monuments. These travellers were involved in what is termed the Grand Tour and this was considered an important part of the education of this elite group of tourists.

What attracted the travellers involved in the Grand Tour several centuries ago, is still a major dimension of tourism. This is termed *heritage tourism* and it is concerned with places, monuments, other human manifestations and natural features that are considered to be worthy of preservation. Many heritage locations are regarded as being of such importance (and therefore resources for tourism) that they have been given special designation by the United Nations Education, Scientific and Cultural Organization (UNESCO) as World Heritage Sites (WHS). Achieving WHS status from UNESCO will not only help with preservation, but also act as marketing that will encourage more tourists. As discussed in Chapters 14 and 15, this brings with it potential issues and management problems.

As noted above, many cultural resources for tourism are historical in nature, but some cultural features are particularly modern, yet act as a major resource for tourism. One such factor is sporting events. Some sporting events are local in nature and not aimed specifically at tourists, but there are significant numbers of international sporting events, such as the Olympics, the Soccer World Cup and the 'Euros' (the European Nations Soccer Championship), as well as other major events such as international tennis championships and international golf championships that are aimed largely at tourists and have become important resources for tourism in particular locations..

These events can also be seen to fit within Peters (1969) tourism category of 'Entertainment'. There are clearly many other types of entertainment including cinema, theatre and musical events. Some of these events are festivals which may be held annually, or biennially or on some other regular basis. Often such events attempt to capture an audience which is not just made up of locals, but brings in domestic visitors from other parts of a region or country, but additionally some international visitors. If the events make use of some historical themes then it can be seen that they will fit within Peters (1969) category of 'Traditions'. However, as noted by Boniface and Cooper (2001) it is important to remember, that many events, be they modern or historical in their focus, are not just aimed at tourists, but are also resources for local communities.

## ■ Accommodation

It has been indicated above that some resources for tourism are also used by locals. However, there are specific types of accommodation that are aimed almost exclusively at tourists, and are therefore very important resources. As by definition tourism involves travel away from home, tourists require accommodation. The most obvious form of tourist accommodation is the hotel. However, there is a very large number of types of hotels, ranging from five (or more) star luxury hotels, to those that have no star category at all, large scale, international chain hotels and smaller, independent boutique hotels. Some hotels offer full-board accommodation, meaning in addition to a bed for the night, the staying guests receive three meals a day. It is also possible to have only two meals a day (half-board) or just bed-and-breakfast, and some accommodation providers specialise in just serving breakfast in addition to providing accommodation. Some hotels also provide entertainment, usually in the form of music and/or dancing. Yet other hotels cater for specialist groups such as those involved in wedding celebrations.

Accommodation can also be in the form of self-catering in apartments or houses, where guests provide their own meals. For example, in France there has been for many decades, a particular type of self-catering accommodation which is usually a whole house or cottage in a rural tourist area, which is rented by visitors for a week or longer, and is known as a *gite*. A relatively new form of accommodation is Airbnb, where private individuals rent out their property, or a part of their house/apartment to individual tourists for a period of time which could be just a few days or several weeks. Such accommodation is frequently in urban areas, is often much cheaper than hotel accommodation, may be better located, can provide more space and is more like a home-from-home than a hotel room.

Another form of accommodation is in the form of campsites that cater for motorhomes, caravans and those staying in tents. Although the visitors provide their own accommodation (e.g. tents and caravans) the different types of accommodation have to be located on a specific site where there are also the types of facilities that would be found in other forms of accommodation, such as a restaurant, bar, toilets, showers and bathrooms.

Although accommodation is being discussed here as a geographical resource for tourism, it is often the case that a particular form of accommodation is actually a significant attraction for tourists. Hence, some tourists return regularly to a particular hotel because of, for example, the quality of its food and drink, or the attention and service of its staff, or the general ambience of the hotel. It may also be that the guests meet up regularly with other visitors in the hotel who are staying there at the same time as them, so in this way the hotel is not just an accommodation provider, but an attraction for tourists.

## ■  Amenities

It is possible to regard accommodation as an amenity specifically provided for tourists. However, as we have noted earlier, some types of accommodation are also tourist attractions. There are also a number of other amenities for tourists. Robinson (1976) indicated these amenities are usually of two types: i) natural facilities, such as beaches for sunbathing, the sea for swimming, locations for fishing and locations to obtain panoramic views, and ii): built amenities, such as entertainment facilities including theatres and cinemas, but also swimming pools and Thalassa therapy centres. Clearly there is an overlap between some amenities (e.g. theatres and cinemas) and cultural resources that have been referred to above. Also some of these amenities will include those that are for use by both locals and tourists, such as swimming pools.

One particular type of built amenity, that has become a very significant tourism resource in the 50 years or so, is the theme park or amusement park. Earliest forms of theme parks can be found in coastal locations, such as Blackpool in the UK. Blackpool combines the 'natural' amenity of a long, wide, sandy beach with a forerunner of the modern theme park. Dating from the late 19th century and greatly assisted by the railways, Blackpool developed a significant array of built attractions to complement its beach. So it had by 1900, and still has, the Tower, (built in 1894, but still operating today with a viewing area, known today as the Blackpool Eye, dance ballroom, circus, dungeon and children's adventure playground), the Pleasure Beach, where there are fairground rides, similar to more modern theme parks, and its 'Golden Mile', a road running along the sea front with amusements arcades, cafes, bars and food stalls. All of these are amenities targeted primarily at tourists.

Modern theme parks were developed from the original activities found in Blackpool in the UK and Coney Island, New York in the last decade of the 19th century. World famous theme parks include those established by the Disney Corporation, such as the major European park 'Disneyland Paris'. Other similar types of park to those of Disney include Alton Towers in the UK, which also has a variety of fairground type rides. Different types of theme park have also been developed, such as Puy du Fou in South West France, which provides experiences based on the history and heritage of France from medieval times.

## ■ Settlements

There is a (misguided) conception that tourism takes place away from towns and cities, as it is largely located at the beach, in the mountains, in forests or on farmland. This idea may come from perceptions that urban dwellers need to escape from the city for several weeks in the summer to recreate themselves in the countryside or at the coast. In France, for example, it is a commonly held view that the capital Paris 'closes down' in August as Parisians head 'en masse' to the south or west in the direction of the sea. With this perception in mind, it is easy to forget that Paris is one of the leading tourist destinations in the world, and the single most important tourism location in France.

A very large number of the world's capital cities, such as London, Rome, Berlin, Madrid, Mexico City, Beijing, Kuala Lumpur and Delhi are major tourism destinations. Other large cities such as New York, Rio de Janeiro, Shanghai, Hong Kong also act as tourist magnets. The main reasons are linked to topics already discussed in this chapter – cultural attractions such as museums, art galleries monuments and festivals and events are located here. Some world cities such as

Barcelona, Sydney and Auckland are also on the coast, so it is possible to have a combined urban- and beach-based tourism experience.

Urban areas also have large numbers and different types of one of the major types of tourist attractions – shops or retail outlets. Shopping is something conducted by locals and many shops are aimed primarily at local residents. But many major cities have retail areas that are targeted specifically at tourists. For example, Oxford Street and Kensington High Street, in London have a range of department stores, clothing, food and souvenir shops that are aimed primarily at tourists. In terms of total number of visitors to an attraction, in the early years of the millennium, Oxford Street, London had over 200 million visitors a year, the great majority of whom were tourists including both domestic and international visitors (Moore, 2001). In an attempt to attract large numbers of tourists, the Middle Eastern country of Dubai, which has a desert climate, has built a number of very large indoor, air-conditioned, shopping malls. These contain Western supermarkets and boutiques and shops, as well as local Arab and Indian retail outlets.

Large cities are also important tourism resources as they are frequently the arrival point by air for international tourists. They may start and complete their journeys in their chosen destination country or region from these cities. International migration has contributed to large numbers of immigrants in world cities. Tourists from the migrant origin countries are drawn to these cities, not just by the cultural attractions and shopping facilities, but often to visit friends and relatives there as well.

## Accessibility and location

Although not strictly speaking resources for tourism, both accessibility and location greatly affect the use of geographical resources for tourism, and are considered important factors by both Peters (1969) and Robinson (1976). Physical isolation of a location is likely to inhibit its development for tourism, although this is not inevitable, as can be seen in the fact that the most remote continent, Antarctica has a growing tourism industry and has had tourist visits for at least half a century. However, it is also generally the case that locations, with the potential to be developed for tourism, which are close to major urban areas are more likely to become tourism destinations than those at a significant distance from the urban areas. Hence, the proximity of the British seaside resort, Brighton to London, has helped it grow as a tourism destination over the past 250 years.

However, it is not just the actual location of potential places for tourism, but also how accessible they are. As noted earlier in this chapter, the Swiss Alps were regarded as a barrier to the movement of people and goods for many centuries until about two hundred years ago. The Alps are relatively well located in relation to the whole of Europe in terms of centrality, but the height, steepness and ruggedness of the mountains made transport and communications difficult, until transport and technological changes, such as the railways, enabled greater access.

Aircraft radically changed tourism, beginning in the 1960s with the use of the jet engine allowing much longer flights. Then from the 1970s, the development of wide-bodied jet aircraft, such as the Boeing 747 (the Jumbo Jet), provided the possibility of loads of up to 300 passengers per flight (Mason, 2016). A key result of this was much cheaper air travel, enabling what had once been an elite luxury form of transport, to be available to millions of people who had not had the opportunity to fly before. Specifically in relation to this discussion, once very distant places from Europe, such as Australia and New Zealand, could be reached within a matter of hours rather than the weeks that travel by ship had taken.

The case study below, focusing on Disneyland Paris, provides evidence of the importance of location and accessibility and it discusses one particular type of geographical resource for tourism, referred to previously in this chapter, the theme park. It also introduces the topic of destination image, and the importance of image will be discussed in more detail later in this book.

# Case study: Disneyland, Paris

The Walt Disney Corporation (WDC) was founded in 1923 by Walt Disney and since then has developed into one of the biggest entertainment companies in the world. It has five key areas of work: The Walt Disney Studios, Disney Consumer Products, Media Networks, Disney Interactive and Disney Parks and Resorts. Walt Disney as the founder had considerable impact on the vision of his corporation and he wanted the company to project certain values and a wholesome image. The values underpinning Disney, as set out by the WDC, to create the desired image are:

- ☐ **Innovation**: WDC is committed to creativity and innovation
- ☐ **Quality**: WDC strives to set a high standard of excellence
- ☐ **Community**: WDC attempts to create positive and inclusive ideas about families and provide entertainment for all age groups
- ☐ **Storytelling**: WDC uses timeless and engaging stories to delight and inspire
- ☐ **Optimism**: At WDC entertainment is about hope, aspiration and positive outcome
- ☐ **Decency**: WDC honours and respects the trust people place in it.

These values have created a distinctive image for Disney and affected all five sectors of its entertainment business. It has been particularly obvious in Disney films, but has also become evident in its other activities, including its theme parks.

The first of the WDC theme parks was established in California in 1955. This was successful and as the Corporation developed and became more profitable it wished to expand beyond the USA and become a well-known global brand. Following the success of Walt Disney World in Florida, plans to build a similar theme park in Europe emerged in 1972 and other parts of the world. Tokyo Disneyland opened in 1983 with a good deal of success, forming a catalyst for further international expansion. In late 1984, a list of approximately

1,200 possible European locations for a European park had been identified. By March 1985, this had been reduced to four – two in France and two in Spain.

Both Spanish sites were located near the Mediterranean Sea and offered a subtropical climate similar to Disney's parks in California and Florida. Disney had also shown interest in a site near Toulon in southern France. The landscape of that region, as well as its climate, made the location a major competitor for what would be called 'Euro Disneyland'. However, the underlying geology would have made construction here very difficult. Finally, a site in the rural town of Marne-la-Vallée, north of Paris, was selected with following rationale given:

☐ its proximity to Paris

☐ its central location in Western Europe

☐ it was no more than a four-hour drive for 68 million people

☐ it was no more than a two-hour flight for a further 300 million people.

Initially, it was decided that 5,200 Disney-owned hotel rooms would be built using an exclusively American theme in which each hotel would depict a region of the United States. For a projected daily attendance of 55,000 customers, Euro Disney planned to serve an estimated 14,000 people per hour and in order to accomplish this, 29 restaurants were built inside the park. Menus were dominated by American flavours and Disney's precedent of not serving alcoholic beverages was continued in the park.

The prospect of a Disney park in France was controversial. Critics denounced what they considered to be the cultural imperialism of Euro Disney encouraging an unhealthy American type of consumerism in France. For others, Euro Disney became a symbol of 'America within France'. In June 1992, French farmers blockaded Euro Disney in protest at farm policies supported at that time by the United States and a Parisian celebrity, named the Euro Disney a "cultural Chernobyl", a reference to the Russian nuclear power station accident that had occurred in 1989.

Other controversies included Disney's American managers requiring English to be spoken at all meetings and Disney's appearance code for members of staff, which listed regulations and limitations for the use of makeup, facial hair, tattoos and jewellery. French trade unions mounted protests against the appearance code, which they saw as "an attack on individual liberty", whilst others criticised Disney as being insensitive to French culture, individualism, and privacy. Disney countered by saying that a ruling that barred them from imposing such an employment standard could threaten their image. As a Disney manager responded "Without the code, we couldn't be presenting the Disney product that people would be expecting."

Euro Disney Resort and its theme park, Euro Disneyland, officially opened in April 1992, but the first few years were difficult financially. In 1994, there were rumours that Euro Disney was getting close to bankruptcy. However in May 1995, a new attraction opened at the theme park, "Space Mountain de La Terre", and in July 1995, it reported its first ever quarterly profit .

In 2002, Euro Disneyland underwent a name change to Disneyland Resort Paris. The reason given by Disney's Chief Executive Officer was:

> As Americans, the word 'Euro' is believed to mean glamorous or exciting. For Europeans it turned out to be a term they associated with business, currency, and commerce. Renaming the park 'Disneyland Paris' was a way of identifying it with one of the most romantic and exciting cities in the world.

In 2004, having been open fewer than fifteen years, Disneyland Paris had become the number one tourist destination for Europe. In August 2008, the Resort's 200 millionth visitor was welcomed, at this point it was the third consecutive year of growth in revenues, and it also achieved a record of 15.3 million visitors.

A study reviewing Disneyland Resort Paris' contribution to the French economy was released in time for the Resort's 20th anniversary in March 2012. It found that the Resort's had generated "37 billion euros in tourism-related revenues over 20 years," and provided on average 55,000 jobs in France annually.

(adapted from: Tribe, J. *Strategy for Tourism* 2nd Edition, 2016 and Euro Disney, 2010)

## Summary

There is large range of both physical and human resources for tourism. The landscape and particular features within in it comprise important tourism resources. Mountain ranges and places close, or actually adjacent, to water frequently act as tourist attractions. Human resources include settlements, with urban areas important, although at first glance this may not seem that obvious. Rural landscapes, with farming and forests are also important attractions. Flora and fauna in a landscape can also be important attractions. As indicated in the case study of Disneyland Paris, dedicated tourism attractions such as theme parks have also become major attractions in the past 75 years or so.

## Student activities

1   What is the main link between motivations for tourism and tourism resources?

2   The Mediterranean region of Europe is a major holiday area. What are the key resources for tourism in the region?

3   Why are mountain areas important tourism resources?

4   In what ways do hotels act as tourism resources?

5   Why are urban areas not always perceived as resources for tourism?

6   Why are European capital cities, such as Amsterdam, Madrid and Berlin, major tourism resources?

7   With reference to the case study of Disneyland Paris, why did the Disney Corporation decide to locate their first European theme park near Paris?

8   With reference to the case study of Disneyland Paris, what types of tourist will be attracted to the theme park?

9   Consider a tourism area/destination close to where you currently live. List the major resources found in your area. Which are the main resources for tourism in your area?

10  In groups of 3 or 4 discuss why resources for tourism have changed over time.

11  In small groups discuss the following question: What do you believe will be the major resources for tourism in 2050?

# References

Boniface, B. and Cooper, C. (2001) *Worldwide Destinations*, Oxford: Butterworth Heinemann

Euro Disney (2010) Reports Fiscal Year, Results *Disneyland Paris: Corporate*. Euro Disney S.C.A. Retrieved 19/03/2017.

Mason, P. (2000) Zoo tourism: the need for more research, *Journal of Sustainable Tourism*, **6**(4) 333-339.

Mason, P. (2008) *Tourism Impacts, Planning and Management*, 2nd ed., London: Routledge

Mason, P. (2016) *Tourism Impacts, Planning and Management*, 3rd ed., Oxford: Elsevier

Moore, T. (2001) *Do Not Pass Go: from the Old Kent Road to Mayfair*, London: Vintage

Peters, M. (1969) *International Tourism*, London: Hutchinson

Robinson, H. (1976) *A Geography of Tourism*, London: Macdonald and Evans

Tribe, J. (2016) *Strategy for Tourism*, 2nd Ed., Oxford: Goodfellow Publishers

# 4 Weather and Climate

## Introduction

Weather can be regarded as a vital resource for tourism, and Robinson (1976) suggested weather was a major element which contributes to tourism development. Although it is seen as less important in Peters' (1969) grouping (see Chapter 3), Boniface and Cooper (2001) devote a separate chapter to climate, suggesting its importance for tourism, and this book follows suit with an entire chapter containing a discussion of weather and climate. However, it is climate ('average weather conditions over a period of time') that is particularly significant and Holden (2016) considers it to be the most important factor affecting tourism.

This chapter discusses weather as a resource for tourism, and stresses that weather (and the related concept of climate) provides a very significant context for many tourism activities. The discussion below indicates that variations in climate occur in regular annual cycles and we refer to these as seasonal changes. The seasons, the cause of which is explained below, are a very significant aspect of tourism and the seasonality of tourism is largely the result of climate.

## Key perspectives

Boniface and Cooper (2001) indicate that climate can be viewed as a significant resource for tourism, but they emphasise its importance, when they also state that it imposes constraints on tourism in terms of limiting the appeal of a destination. However, climate can be viewed as a particularly important resource for tourism for the following reasons:

- Climate includes a number of aspects (e.g. temperature, snow, wind speed and direction) that are major influencing factors on certain types of tourism. So, for example, beach-based tourism is linked strongly to high levels of sunshine, whilst ski tourism requires snow, and sailing and kite surfing need wind of a certain strength to make the activities possible.

- It is often a *combination* of climate factors acting together, such as sunshine hours and high temperatures for sunbathing, or snow and low temperatures for skiing, that enable certain types of tourism activity to occur in particular locations.

■ Much tourism takes place out-of-doors, so even with modern technology, it is not possible to avoid weather and climate in relation to these types of tourism activity.

■ There are climate zones around the world with differing climate conditions, some of which encourage tourism, others which do not.

■ Climate has been very important historically in assisting in the creation of certain types of tourism destinations, such as coastal resorts and mountain ski resorts.

■ Climate continues to be important, both in relation to domestic tourism and international tourism, leading to regular movement of people at certain times of the year from tourist origin areas to tourism destinations. This is what is termed 'seasonality' in tourism and is linked closely, although not exclusively, to climatic seasons.

■ Climate change is one of the most significant factors affecting all life on earth in recent history and has important impacts on tourism (this issue is discussed in detail in Chapter 11).

As indicated in Chapter 3, Robinson (1976) indicated that 'good weather' is important for tourism, but he does not give a clear definition of 'good weather'. Robinson indicated when fine weather is important and how 'bad weather' can seriously affect tourism activities. Indeed, when discussing tourism in Britain, he stated that British weather is notoriously fickle and there is a general lack of sunshine, despite mild conditions, even in much of southern Britain. This, he argued, is why the Spanish Costas, as well as the French Mediterranean coast and large parts of the Italian and Greek coasts have become desirable destinations for British tourists who are seeking 'guaranteed sunshine'.

However, it is also the case that 'good weather' includes snow for winter sports and related activities. Mountain areas such as the Alps have become popular for winter tourism activities because of the almost guaranteed snow cover which allows skiing for several months of the year. Nevertheless, as discussed later in Chapter 11, global warming is affecting the nature and length of the ski season, as well as the actual location of ski tourism.

What is considered 'good weather' for certain types of tourism is perceived in relation to 'bad weather' elsewhere, by potential tourists. This contributes to the travel behaviour of these tourists that takes place at particular times of the year. Hence, from November to the end of February, northern Europe usually has generally cool, often cold weather, accompanied by cloud and frequent rain and also the strong possibility of snow in the period. This perceived 'poor weather' in the northern part of Europe has led to the development of 'winter sun' locations. These locations are almost always south of the northern European countries, such as the UK, Germany, the Netherlands, Belgium, Sweden, Norway and Denmark.

The winter sun locations are however relatively close to these countries, in terms of being two to three hours' flight time away from the northern European generating areas, or at most, two to three day's drive time. These European 'winter sun' destinations are located particularly in Spain and Portugal, but also on the French Mediterranean coast and the southern Italian coastal areas. In the last 20 years or so, countries in North Africa such as Tunisia and Morocco, have also become popular winter sun destinations for northern Europeans.

In the USA and Canada, the US southern state of Florida, as well as islands in the Caribbean have become 'winter sun' destinations for North Americans. These locations all have much higher temperatures and longer sunshine hours than northern locations in the USA and Canada. For Australians and New Zealanders, the islands of Fiji and the Indonesian island of Bali have become, in the last 30 years, important 'winter sun' destinations. The reasons for this are the same as for the winter sun attractions of the Caribbean for North Americans – the contrast between winter weather at home and the probably better weather in the destination.

A key difference between the Northern hemisphere countries, such as the UK, France and the USA and those countries, such as Australia and New Zealand, in the southern hemisphere, is that winter and, hence, 'winter sun' holidays occur at different times of the year. A 'winter sun' holiday for an American will be in the period from November to February, but for an Australian, a winter holiday will take place between May and August. But why is this? And why is that southern European countries have different weather conditions at different times of the year to northern European countries, or that the northern parts of North America have different weather to the Caribbean? The answer to these related questions requires an understanding of, first, the power of the sun to heat the earth, and second, the way the earth moves in space.

# The relationship between the sun and the earth and effects on weather and climate

It is a result of the earth revolving around the sun (taking 365 and a quarter days) and that the axis of the earth (an imaginary line that passes through the centre of the earth from the North to the South Pole) is not vertical, that gives the earth different weather conditions at different times of the year and this is explained below.

The earth is a planet of the sun. This means, along with other planets such as Mars, Venus and Jupiter, that the earth revolves around the sun. This is a regular movement, and as indicated above, this takes a set length of time – what we call one earth year. This revolution has been going on for millions of years. Another regular movement of the earth is that it rotates about its own axis. This takes a period of 24 hours. It is a combination of the revolution of the earth about the sun and the rotation of the earth about its axis that contributes to different weather conditions. As these conditions are similar on a year-by-year basis at different times of the year – for example, each spring in the UK (or Australia, or the USA for that matter) is similar to the spring of the previous year, in that particular place (and over many springs, conditions in each place are known to be similar) that we average weather conditions in each period of time, and call this concept 'climate'.

The earth is heated by the power of the sun – this is solar radiation. The sun is felt to be hottest when it has a high angle in the sky in relation to the earth's surface. If the sun is at its maximum angle of 90 degrees (vertical to the earth's surface), it will provide concentrated heat on the surface. If the sun is at an angle of only 30 degrees to the vertical, then the heat is spread over a far bigger area and will be far less powerful. The analogy of a torch may help here. Imagine holding a torch one metre above the ground and shining the torch vertically straight down, at 90 degrees to the ground. The beam of light will be concentrated. But if the torch, still held one metre above the ground, was at an angle (not vertical), but still pointed at the ground, then the area of the beam will be far larger, as the light is far less concentrated. If the torch beam analogy is replaced by the concept of solar radiation, then it should be clear why it is hotter (think of the vertical torch beam) than when the sun (think again of non-vertical torch beam) is at an angle much less than 90 degrees.

Figure 4.1 is an attempt to show the effect of the angle that the sun's rays hitting the earth's surface has on heating. It uses the analogy of the torch beam to show this. The torch on the right is vertical and the distance across its beam is shown as 'A'. The area on the ground of this torch beam is the same width as the beam's width, shown as 'A'. The torch on the left is at an angle to the vertical (it is not at 90 degrees, but less). Although the width of the beam in the left side torch is 'A' (the same as the right side torch), when the beam reaches the ground it spreads out over a larger area – shown as 'B'.

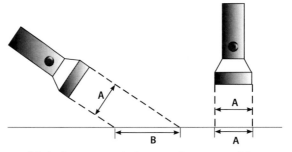

**Figure 4.1:** When a beam of light is at anangle it spreads over a wider area.

Figure 4.2 shows the effect of the curve of the earth's surface on the sun's heating capability. In Figure 4.2 the sun's rays are shown approaching and striking the earth – in this example from the left side. The rays are the same distance apart in space before they reach the earth. When the rays strike the earth at the Equator the length of 'A' on the earth's surface is the same as the width of the rays in space. However, on Figure 4.2, the rays striking nearer the North Pole are further apart at this location than at the equator. Here the heat is less concentrated, so this area on the earth's surface will have lower temperatures.

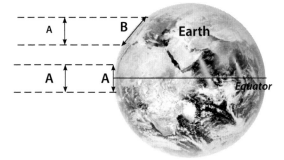

## 4

**Figure 4.2:** The effects that the curving of the earth's surface has on heating from the sun's rays.

If we consider the earth in relation to the sun, then the curve of the earth's surface means that the highest temperature of the sun will be near the middle of the earth's surface (the Equator in Figure 4.2) and low angles of the sun will be found near the North Pole and the South Pole. Although it is not the full explanation, this should help with the understanding of why some parts of the earth (e.g. the Caribbean) are usually hot while other parts (e.g. northern Sweden) are cold.

It is not quite as simple as this however, as we know that it is usually much colder high up a mountain than standing by the sea. So, although the temperature may be 30°C on a beach at the Equator in the East African country of Kenya in July, it can be 0°C near the top of Mount Kilimanjaro, also in Kenya, and very close to the Equator. How is this possible? The answer is also to do with heat from the sun. Solar radiation is of a particularly type (it is known as short wave radiation) and it is unable to directly heat gases, but can only heat up liquids and solids. The earth's atmosphere is a mixture of gases and the sun's radiation generally passes straight through. It then reaches the surface of the earth and heats the solid ground and any water surfaces (such as oceans, seas and rivers). Heat is then passed upwards, as long wave radiation, moving from the earth's solid and liquid surfaces, which have been heated up. So this should help to explain why land adjacent to the sea (we call this 'sea level') on the earth's surface is usually much warmer than on the top of a 6000 metre mountain.

Complicating matters somewhat further, but essential to an understanding of the nature and location of tourism and the importance of geography affecting tourist activity, is what we refer to as the seasons. Figure 4.3 is a diagram representing the position of the earth in relation to the sun at four times in a year to help to explain the cause of the seasons.

Earlier in this chapter, the axis of the earth has been referred to – the earth turns one complete rotation about its axis in 24 hours. However, the angle of the axis is tilted (in other words it is not vertical) in relation to the sun. The angle of tilt is approximately 23.5° to the vertical. It is the combination of the tilt of the axis, and the fact that the earth revolves around the sun, that causes the seasons.

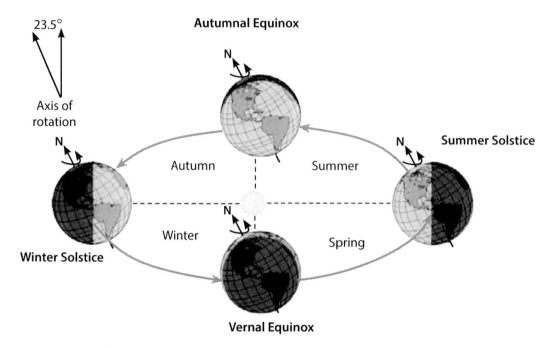

**Figure 4.3:** The seasons on Earth

Figure 4.3 shows what happens at different times of the year in relation to the seasons. The sun is shown at the centre and the earth in four positions which corresponds to four specific dates in the year. The tilt of the earth's axis can be seen (where 'N' is written at the top of each). This tilt is approximately 23.5° to the vertical. The curved arrow under each of the earth diagrams indicates the direction of rotation (from west to east). The rotation means that places in the east see the sun rise first, before places further to the west. The diagrams also show that a section of the earth is in daylight for part of the rotation and in darkness for the other part – this gives us day and night during the rotation period of 24 hours.

The tilt of the axis results in the seasons. In Figure 4.3 on the right hand side, the earth is shown at what is known as the 'Summer Solstice' – this date is usually June 21st. However, it will be one day different in some years because of the calendar, and therefore could be the 20th or 22nd, but for simplicity we will use the 21st. On this day, the northern hemisphere is tilted towards the sun, due to the tilting of the axis. The sun strikes the earth at 90° on June 21st at a point 23.5° north of the Equator. As the earth is also rotating about its own axis all the time, the sun hits at 90° to the earth's surface along a line. This is a line of latitude, known as the Tropic of Cancer. and is at 23.5° north of the Equator.

Looking again at Figure 4.3 there is a position on the opposite side of the sun to the Summer Solstice. This is known as the Winter Solstice, and here the northern hemisphere is tilted away from the sun. The sun is directly overheard (90°), south of the Equator on this day, which is usually December 21st (as with the Summer Solstice, this could also be the 20th or 22nd because of differences in the calendar) and strikes at 90°along a line of latitude 23.5° south of the Equator. This line is known as the Tropic of Capricorn. Figure 4.4 shows the two positions of the earth in relation to the sun at the June 21st Solstice and the December 21st solstice.

**June Solstice**                                                    **December Solstice**

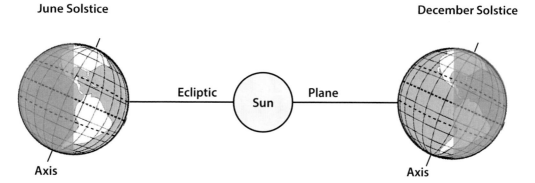

**Figure 4.4:** The earth at the June 21st Solstice and the December 21st Solstice

Figure 4.3 also shows two other positions of the earth. One is March 21st and the other September 21st. Neither the northern hemisphere nor the southern hemisphere is pointed towards the sun on these two days. The sun actually strikes the earth at 90° (on both days) at the line of latitude knowns as the Equator (it divides the earth into two equal halves, hence its name). Figure 4.5 shows the earth at the September 21st Equinox and the March 21st Equinox.

**September Equinox**                                                  **March Equinox**

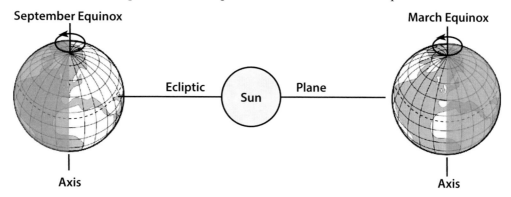

**Figure 4.5:** The position of the earth at the September 21st Equinox and the March 21st Equinox.

What does the tilt of the earth's axis and revolution of the earth around the sun mean for weather and climate, during the year? When the sun strikes at 90° along the Tropic of Cancer, at the *summer* solstice, there will be most heat available in the northern hemisphere, and temperatures will, on average be higher than at other times of the year. At the *winter* solstice, when the sun strikes the earth to the south along the Tropic of Capricorn, the angle of the sun in the northern hemisphere will be at its lowest and temperatures at this time will be at their lowest.

When the sun is overhead at the Equator (March 21st and September 21st) the temperatures on average, in the northern hemisphere are not as high as on June 21st, but not as low as December 21st. The two dates in March and September coincide with the seasons of *spring* (March 21st) and *autumn* (September 21st). These two dates are known as equinoxes. The term equinox is explained below, but first we need to consider what is happening to weather and climate in Australia, New Zealand and South Africa at different times of the year.

So far this discussion has had a 'northern hemisphere bias', so those of you in the southern hemisphere may be still trying to understand the relationship between the tilt of the earth's axis and the seasons. To explain what is happening on the four dates (the two solstices and the two equinoxes), in the southern hemisphere, it will help to look again at Figure 4.3.

When it is the summer solstice in the northern hemisphere, the sun strikes the earth at 90° along the Tropic of Cancer. This is the time in the southern hemisphere when the angle of the sun is at its lowest, so this is southern hemisphere winter – June 21st is the winter solstice. On December 21st, the sun strikes at 90° along the Tropic of Capricorn. This is the highest angle of the sun for the southern hemisphere, so here on this day (December 21st) it is the summer solstice. Conditions are similar on March 21st and September 21st to those found in the northern hemisphere, as on each date the sun is overhead at 90° at the Equator. However, as December 21st is the summer solstice in the southern hemisphere, March 21st is the autumn equinox and September 21st is between winter and summer, and so is the spring equinox. In brief, the seasons are at opposite times of the year in each of the hemispheres. So, summer time in the northern hemisphere is winter time in the southern hemisphere (and vice versa), spring in the southern hemisphere is autumn in the northern hemisphere (and vice versa).

To return to the term *equinox*. The tilt of the earth's axis not only gives us the seasons, but it affects the length of day and night, which varies throughout the year. In the northern hemisphere summer, we have long days and short nights and in northern hemisphere winters, we have long nights and short days. The cause is precisely the same as the reason for the four seasons. On June 21st, with the northern hemisphere pointed towards the sun, the days are at their longest. On this day, as the earth rotates about its axis, the sun never sets at the North Pole and it is in continual daylight for 24 hours. Further south, but still in the northern hemisphere, days are much longer than nights and for everywhere in the northern hemisphere this day is referred to as the 'longest day of the year'.

On December 21st, day and night conditions are very different. The northern hemisphere is tilted away from the sun and the North Pole will have no daylight – it will be continual night. For everywhere else in the northern hemisphere, night will be longer than day. So, this day is the 'shortest day of the year'.

The conditions in the southern hemisphere are once again 'opposite' to those in the northern hemisphere. So on June 21st the southern hemisphere is tilted away from the sun, meaning the South Pole is in continual darkness, the rest of the southern hemisphere has longer nights than days and it is the shortest day of the year in the southern hemisphere. On December 21st the southern hemisphere is tilted towards the sun, the South Pole has continual daylight, everywhere in the southern hemisphere has days longer than nights and this is the longest day of the year.

From the discussion of the seasons we have found that on March 21st and September 21st the earth is not tilted towards the sun, but the sun is overhead at 90°at the Equator. This means that on both days in both the northern and southern hemisphere, there is an equal length of day and night (12 hours). The name for March 21st and September 21st is *equinox*, which is from Latin and translates as 'equal night'. One of these days is called the spring, (or vernal) equinox, the other the autumn equinox. Whether March 21st is the spring equinox or the autumn equinox will depend on whether it is the northern or southern hemisphere.

So, combining what happens in relation to the tilt of the earth and its effects in creating the seasons and variations in the length of day and night, we find that on June 21st in the northern hemisphere the sun is at its highest angle and days are at their longest, and the result is, on average, high temperature conditions. On December 21st in the northern hemisphere, the sun is at a low angle and the days are at their shortest, so temperatures are usually low. In the southern hemisphere on June 21st, the sun is at its lowest angle and days are short so temperatures on average are low and on December 21st the sun is at its highest angle and days are long, so temperatures are generally high. On March 21st and September 21st with the sun overhead at the Equator, day and night are of equal length and temperatures, on average are higher than in winter but lower than in summer.

## Other factors affecting weather and climate conditions

The discussion of the seasons and length of day and night at different times has used, on a number of occasions, the term 'on average' in relation to temperature. This is because temperature is affected by several other factors than the position of the earth and the sun, and there is much more to weather than just temperature.

Rain, snow, sleet, hail, fog, wind direction and wind strength are just some of the terms we use in relation to weather and climate, and all of these factors may affect tourism. We have seen earlier in this chapter that temperatures are usually higher at sea level than at high altitude on a mountain top. Hence, the specific location (at sea level or on a 6000 metre mountain) is quite likely to be as important, if not more important, on a particular day, in giving weather conditions, than the specific season.

Although short wave solar radiation does not heat the air above the earth, as discussed previously, it can only warm solids and liquids, the rate at which it heats up liquids is different to the rate of heating solids. Hence, this solar radiation warms liquids at a slower rate than solid surfaces. However, solid surfaces are not only heated up more quickly than liquids but also cool down more quickly. As 70% of the earth's surface is water, (mainly in the oceans and seas), then this variation in heating between land and water, is very important in affecting weather conditions, particularly in coastal areas, (which are often important for tourism).

Strong winds and rain can also affect temperature. These conditions are usually associated with different atmospheric conditions. The atmosphere, (what we usually refer to as 'the air') is made up of different gases (including oxygen, nitrogen and carbon dioxide) as well as water, some of which is in the form of clouds. The atmosphere rotates with the earth's daily movement about its axis. This rotation helps to produce wind and mixes the gases and the water within the atmosphere and this is likely to affect temperatures.

Therefore, the fact that the earth's surface is a combination of solids and liquids and has high points, such as mountains and low areas including beaches, and that the atmosphere above the earth's surface is almost constantly in motion and changing, means that relying solely on an understanding of the seasons to predict temperatures is not necessarily a sensible idea. Temperatures on earth are affected by a range of factors, of which only one is seasonal fluctuations.

## ■ Climate zones

A major result of the combination of climatic factors discussed so far, including the angle of the overhead sun, heating differences at the earth's surface, particularly whether it is made up of water or land, and the effect of altitude, is that the earth has a series of climate zones. In basic terms, the zones with high temperature are close to the Equator and those with low temperatures are near the two Poles. However, it is more complex than this, partly because of the effects of altitude, particularly where there are mountain ranges, and also in relation to locations close to, or distant from, oceans/the sea. As indicated above, water takes longer to heat up and longer to cool down than the land surface. This means that locations close to the sea have a smaller range of temperature than those at a distance from the sea where, on average, it is both colder in winter and hotter in summer, than at the coast.

Figure 4.6 shows these climate zones. These zones have been created using five factors, three of which have already been discussed in this chapter. Of particular importance is latitude or the position of a zone in relation to the Equator. Second, and previously referred to, is altitude or height above sea level, and we have discussed before that temperatures generally fall as altitude increases. Third, is distance from the sea and we have noted the moderating effect of the sea on temperature. The two new factors are wind direction – winds from warm places raise temperatures, whilst winds from cool places decrease temperatures and the fifth factor is aspect. Aspect refers to the direction a slope faces in, with those facing the sun having higher temperatures, than those facing away from the sun. When climate conditions are discussed in each zone the key dimensions that are measured are the temperature and precipitation (e.g. rain, sleet snow).

Figure 4.6 indicates the importance of latitude, as to a certain extent the climate zones are parallel to the Equator, and this is particularly the case in Europe, Asia, Africa and Australasia. However, this is not the case in South America and North America. This is because of the Andes Mountains in South America that run from north to south along almost the entire length of the continent and in North America, the Rocky Mountains which also run from north to south.

● Equitorial
○ Arid
◔ Mediterranean
● Mountain
◕ Polar
● Temperate

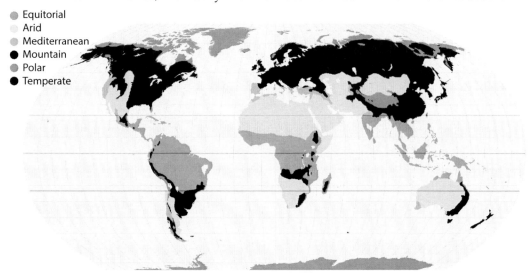

**Figure 4.6:** Climate Zones of the Earth (adapted from the UK Meteorological Office, 2017)

In summary as indicated in Figure 4.6, the Tropical Zones have high temperatures and a large amount of precipitation, although there may be a dry season and a wet season, Arid Zones have high temperatures but little rainfall, the Temperate Zones have neither particularly high or low temperatures, so can be referred to as having a mild climate, but also have rainfall throughout the year, whilst the Polar Regions have very low temperatures, but are relatively dry, as the precipitation is mainly in the form of snow. The two other zones are the Mediterranean Zone, which has mild winters, and hot, dry summers and the Mountain Zone which does not conform to the zones that are largely parallel with the Equator, but has generally lower temperatures and more precipitation than the corresponding zones that this cuts across.

Some of these zones are particularly suitable for tourism where climate is an important factor, others less so. For example, the advantage of the Mediterranean Zone in Europe is that during the period from May to September (the summer season) there is usually guaranteed sunshine and a lack of rain, and this is combined with long hours of daylight, as the summer solstice occurs during this time. The Mediterranean also has considerably milder winter conditions than northern Europe because it is further south, and the area is adjacent to the sea. Also, although the sun's angle is not particularly high from November to March, it is considerably higher than in, for example, the UK, the Netherlands and much of Germany.

The case study below uses data obtained at campsites in Southern Spain and Portugal, giving an indication of the nationality of caravan and motor home owners and considers factors that affect the selecting of destinations by this particular group of tourists.

# Case study: Nationality of vehicles using Spanish and Portuguese campsites

During northern hemisphere winter a large number of those who live in Northern Europe travel south to the Mediterranean coasts of Spain and Portugal. Many rent accommodation, some of them for several weeks, in the towns and resorts in these areas, some stay in hotels and an increasing number stay in motorhomes or caravans.

A motorhome is a large vehicle which is usually based on a commercial truck body, but in addition to the driver and passenger seat, it usually has an area with a table (a dining space), chairs, a bedroom area, a cassette toilet and shower and storage space for clothes and food. In other words, this is a home on wheels. In parts of continental Europe, these vehicles are known as camping cars and in North America, recreational vehicles, or RVs for short. A caravan is similar to a motorhome in that it is a form of mobile home, but it lacks an engine and has to be towed behind a car.

Motorhomes and caravans are relatively expensive to buy, but have been popular in continental Europe for over 40 years. In the UK they have grown in popularity particularly over the past 25 years. They appear to have become even more popular in the past five years or so. For example, in the UK in 2012, just over 10,000 new motorhomes were purchased, whilst in 2014 this figure was almost 12,000 (Camping and Caravan Club, 2017). Motorhomes can also be rented for a daily or weekly period or for even longer than this.

Motorhomes and caravans have certain advantages when compared with traditional hotels or rented houses or apartments. Owning a motorhome or caravan means that it is possible to travel at times that suit the tourist and not just in the tourist season as dictated by travel agents, tour operators and accommodation providers. During the tourist season, accommodation in hotels is in great demand and often in short supply, meaning that it is expensive. Motorhomes and caravans can travel when it is likely to be cheaper. Travelling at non-peak times of the year can also mean roads are less crowded with other tourists. It is also possible in a motorhome or caravan to move on from somewhere which has, for example, poor weather, or is crowded, or has other negative factors. It is then possible to go to a potentially better location without incurring significant costs.

Although a motorhome or a caravan being towed by a car uses more fuel than most cars, there is a much lower cost for the accommodation compared to a hotel room or rented apartment. A motorhome staying at a campsite on the Mediterranean coast of Spain in the month of February is unlikely to cost more than 20 Euros per night for two adults, and it can often be considerably cheaper. Costs can also be kept low, if the campsite user is a member of a club, such as the Dutch organisation ACSI. This organisation produces an annual guide with over 3000 European campsites, all of which offer significantly reduced charges out of season. In a motorhome or caravan, it is possible to travel at the pace favoured by the tourist and not have to follow bus and train timetables, or to travel rapidly to a destination to avoid 'en route' costs.

The table below shows the percentage of motorhomes and caravans, by country of origin, on four campsite (two sites on the Spanish Mediterranean coast, one near Almeria and the other Malaga, one on the Spanish Atlantic coast near Cadiz and the fourth on the Portuguese coast, near Faro) on four consecutive days in mid-February 2017. The total number of motorhomes/caravan over the four sites at the time of the survey was 261. The campsites were on average between one half and two thirds full at the time of the survey, and each one is at approximately Latitude 37° North of the Equator. The Spanish ones are all within three kilometres of the coast and the Portuguese one is actually on a beach on the south facing Atlantic coast of Portugal. All sites could be described as having a Mediterranean climate.

**Table 4.1:** Motorhomes and caravans on four camp sites on the Iberian Coast, February 2017, by nationality of the vehicle registration plate.

| Nationality of vehicle | Percentage (of all four campsites) |
|---|---|
| United Kingdom | 33% |
| Germany | 26% |
| Netherlands | 12% |
| France | 10% |
| Spain | 5% |
| Portugal | 5% |
| Sweden | 3.5% |
| Belgium | 2% |
| Austria | 0.75% |
| Switzerland | 0.75% |
| Others (Ireland, Norway, Bulgaria, Poland) | 2% |

Source: Mason, 2017

The case study of the nationality of motorhomes and caravans indicates how climate can affect holiday decision making and also the location of activities at certain times of the year. However, although we have noted that sunshine and high temperatures are key components of tourism, so that climate is influential in relation to tourism, it does not necessarily determine the nature and location of tourism. So, to put sunshine and temperature, as two very significant climate factors, into context, the hottest places on earth are in desert regions and traditionally deserts have not attracted many tourists. Other factors than hot sun must also be playing a part in tourism here.

# Summary

This chapter has discussed the importance of weather and climate as resources for tourism. The process and impacts of the movement of the earth around the sun has been considered and in particular how this causes the seasons. The rotation of the earth about its axis and the effect this has on length of day and night at has been discussed. Other factors affecting climate have also been considered. The resulting climate zones have been shown and their importance for tourism discussed. The impact of different weather and climate conditions at the same time of the year but in different locations in terms of a specific group of tourists has been investigated in the case study of campsites in Southern Europe.

## Student activities

1  Why are weather and climate important as resources for tourism?

2  Explain in relation to seasonal factors and length of day and night, why the Mediterranean region of Europe is a major area for 'sun, sea and sand' holidays?

3  Why do so many people from northern Europe travel south in winter to Spain and Portugal?

4  Why is Bali a winter sun destination for Australians and New Zealanders?

5  In small groups (3/4 students) discuss what would happen to climate on earth if the earth's axis was not tilted at 23.5 degrees to the vertical.

6  In relation to the case study of nationalities of motorhomes and caravans:

   a)  Why are there such high percentages from the UK, Germany and the Netherlands?

   b)  Why are there also some vehicles from Spain and Portugal?

   c)  What reason would you give for there being some vehicles from France, but not as high a percentage as from the UK and Germany?

   d)  If the survey was conducted in July, would you expect to find similar percentages from each of the country's indicated, or very different results? Explain your answer.

   e)  In small groups (3/4 students) discuss what other factors than climate are important as reasons for the large number of northern Europeans in Spain and Portugal during the time of the survey.

# References

Boniface, B. and Cooper, C. (2001) *Worldwide Destinations*, Oxford: Butterworth Heinemann

Holden, A. (2016) *Environment and Tourism*, 3rd ed. London: Routledge

Mason, P. (2017) *Nationality of Motorhome and Caravan Drivers at Spanish and Portuguese Campsites*, February, Unpublished Report

Peters, M. (1969) *International Tourism*, London: Hutchinson

Robinson, H. (1976) *A Geography of Tourism*, London: Macdonald and Evans

# 5 Tourism Destinations and Destination Images

## Introduction

The previous three chapters have discussed respectively, reasons behind tourists' motivation to travel, and the nature of resources that tourists will make use of, when they are involved in tourism. However, the discussion so far has not focused on precisely where tourists will travel to, why they have selected particular locations and/or activities, when they do this and the possible effects of this activity. This chapter considers to where tourists travel, and why they travel to these places. In this way it links the earlier chapters' concerns with motivations and resources.

## Destinations

'Tourism destination' is an important concept, because not only is this the location where amenities, services and facilities, such as hotels restaurants, bars and entertainment centres are located (in other words the resources for tourism), but it is where the tourists are found, and they may be present in large numbers. The destination is also the location where visitors will interact with the host (or local) population as well as be in contact with the local environment. Tourists are also likely to interact with other tourists in the destination area.

As a result of the concentration of tourism facilities and the interaction of tourists with other tourists, with local people and the local environment, it is here that many if the impacts, which will be discussed in the second section of this book, usually occur. If tourism impacts are viewed as being concentrated spatially, then the planning and management of the response to these impacts will also be focused here in tourism destinations. This concern with planning and management is discussed in the final section of the book.

It has been traditionally the case that tourism destinations are regarded as geographical areas. Such areas are usually considered to have well defined boundaries (Hall, 2000). It is relatively easy to envisage this concept of a destination when applied to a geographical feature such as an island. However, it is also the case that the notion of a destination can apply to entire countries and here it is primarily a political definition that is being used. Destinations can also comprise towns and cities – these are both geographical and political concepts. In relation to cities and towns, the tourism element of the settlement may be of significance, but is likely to be found alongside other important functions, related to, for example, manufacturing industry, banking, trade or transport. In other words, tourism destinations often have other functions than those just linked to tourism. Nevertheless, some geographical locations owe their existence almost exclusively to tourism. Such locations would include coastal towns in Britain such as Blackpool, Scarborough and Brighton.

However, a problem with the use of the concept of a tourism destination, which may be apparent from the discussion above, is that it can be used at a range of different scales. So a part of a city can be a destination, a small coastal town can be a destination, but an entire country or even a continent (Antarctica would fit into this category) can be considered as a destination. What is actually considered to be a destination seems to depend largely on the researcher's focus of enquiry (Augustyn, 1998).

Applying the concept of scale to tourism destinations, Ritchie and Crouch (2003) provide a six-fold classification. This classification, (which has an underlying formal, political, and jurisdiction aspect), is as follows, starting with the largest geographical area at the top:

- A macro-region consisting of several countries (e.g. Europe) or a region that crosses several borders e.g. the Alps
- A nation or state
- A province or state within a country e.g. Ontario in Canada
- A localised region within a country e.g. South West England
- A city or town
- A unique locale, such as a national park, heritage site, memorial or monument that is significant enough to attract visitors.

A particularly useful definition of the destination which draws on the important geographical aspect is that of Murphy *et al.* (2000) who indicated that it is an amalgam of tourism products, available in certain geographic locations within a country, drawing tourists from beyond its boundaries.

However, there is an overlap between the concept of a tourism destination with other geographically based notions of the location or area where tourism is focused. So for example, there is a link between the concept of a destination and that of a resort. A resort can be narrowly defined as a localised self-contained tourism complex providing a variety of recreational activities in one location (Gunn, 1994). So, using this definition it is possible to put theme parks, some hotels that also provide significant entertainment activities, and even cruise ships into the category of resorts (see Laws 1993; Buhalis, 2000).

It has been argued that a key element of a tourism destination is that it has a *range* of different tourism facilities (Smith, 1994; Kozak and Rimington, 2000). Indeed, some authors differentiate a destination from a resort when they indicate that a destination has a variety and range of different tourism facilities and activities, whilst a resort tends to be focused on one single tourism attraction, such as a resort hotel (Ekinci *et al.*, 1998). However, the terms resort and destination are often used as if synonymous, and it should be clear how this is possible when a resort has been regarded by some researchers as a town or settlement, with a significant range of tourist activities and facilities or a region or even country in which several holiday centres are located (see Medlik, 1995; Laws, 1993).

It is also the case that the terms 'tourism destination' and 'tourism attraction' are frequently used as if they are synonymous. However, an attraction is usually considered to be just one object or aspect of tourism that draws in tourists (Swarbrooke, 1999). Swarbrooke provides a fourfold classification of visitor attractions (Figure 5.1). As Figure 5.1 shows, visitor attractions range from built heritage features, including historic monuments, such as Stonehenge, other historical built features, which may have had a previous purpose, such as country houses and castles, through natural/semi-natural attractions, for example National Parks to entirely manufactured attractions, including theme parks, art galleries and museums. In some cases a visitor attraction becomes a destination and this is particularly the case with theme parks such as Disneyland Paris or Alton Towers in the UK (Holloway, 2009). In both cases, the location of the theme park was not important as a tourism destination until the theme park itself was built.

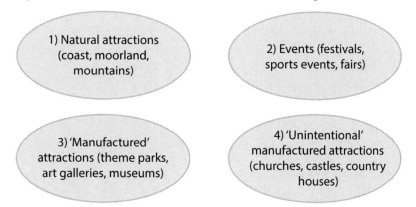

**Figure 5.1:** Swarbrooke's classification of visitor attractions (based on Swarbrooke, 1999).

## Destination image

A key question in relation to visitor attractions is: What attracts tourists to these different types of destinations? If a person has visited before, then to a great extent, they know what to expect, but if someone has not visited the destination before, then it must be information that the potential tourist has obtained in advance and this will be linked to the image of the destination. As Ooi, (2010: 252) stated:

> *People form their own images of a place based on their experiences, and what they have learned from different sources, such as news programmes, travel programmes, films, geography lessons, and travel tales from friends and relatives.*

From the quotation above, the notion of image may appear to be relatively simple, and the way in which a destination image is formed seems relatively straightforward. However, a large number of authors have suggested that image is actually complex, but nevertheless it is a critical factor in a destination selection process (see in particular Crompton, 1979; Dann, 1996; Echtner and Ritchie, 1993; Gartner, 1989, 1993). Perhaps, because of its relative complexity, there has also been general agreement that few researchers have been successful in accurately conceptualising image (Fakeye and Crompton, 1991; White, 2005).

Echtner and Ritchie (1993) were among the first researchers who attempted to rectify the perceived weaknesses in conceptual and measurement issues relating to image. They were concerned that early definitions of destination image were vague in terms of the nature of the image, as it was frequently referred to simply as a combination of 'impressions', 'beliefs, 'knowledge', 'prejudices', 'expecta-tions' and 'feelings' towards an individual, group, object or place.

Echtner and Ritchie (1991) proposed that destination image should be seen in both 'attributes' and 'holistic' terms. In other words, image is made up of separate components (or attributes) but also can be viewed holistically. They also argued that destination images can range from those based on 'common' functional traits and psychological traits, to those based on more 'unique' functional and psychological traits. By functional attributes, Echtner and Ritchie meant, for example, what could be termed as the tangible destination elements or attributes, so this would include climate and scenery. The psychological traits of image are largely related to the responses of the tourists to the destination, so would include whether tourists regard the local inhabitants of a destination as friendly and hospitable and also whether tourists feel the destination is safe. Echtner and Ritchie (1991, 1993) also stated that most destinations have elements that are commonly found in other destinations, but some unique elements are found there as well. They proposed a framework for analysing image, which was based on their classification of the following: attributes/holistic, functional/psychological, and common/unique image dimensions.

Researchers of destination image components have also indicated that there are different components in terms of the reaction of the tourists to an image (see for example Baloglu and Brinberg, 1997; Dobni and Zinknan, 1990; Gartner, 1993). These components are usually classified under the headings of cognitive and affective. 'Cognitive' aspects of image refer to *knowledge and understanding* of, and beliefs about, the destination, whilst the 'affective' dimensions refer to *feelings or emotions* about a place (see e.g. Baloglu and Brinberg, 1997; Gartner, 1993; Zimmer and Golden, 1988).

It appears logical to assume that knowledge of a destination (the cognitive elements of image) is a particularly significant aspect, as a tourist equipped with accurate reports and data can make an informed choice about a possible holiday destination. However, it is also the case that much of the image of a destination is not about the tangible elements, but feelings regarding the location. The emotional response may be based on previous visits, and repeat visitation is common in different forms of tourism, including visits to the same hotel over several years, or to a particular festival or a theme park.

Feelings generated by previous visits may be such that they override the rational response to a current problem in the destination, so that despite the problem there, the tourist still visits. In this way the tourist is trusting their own experience, and their feelings in relation to this experience, that has led to the image that they hold. Paradoxically, it may also be the case that a tourist who has not visited a destination before, relies heavily on the received image from the media rather than other sources of information, which could include their experience of a similar destination, in making a decision about whether or not to visit. So, for example, Weiping (2010) found that British tourists who had never visited the island of Bali, were less likely to go there in the future, than those who had previously visited. The main reason behind the different choices between these two groups was that those who had previously visited were using their own experiences and memories and emotional reaction to help make a decision, and this would have required the ignoring of several negative media stories about Bali and terrorism that were prevalent when Weiping conducted her research. However, those who had not visited Bali before were relying on media material in assisting them in making decisions. Hence, lacking their own personal experience of Bali, these tourist were persuaded much more by the media, than those tourists who had actually visited the island. Weiping's (2010) findings concerning differences of views of those who have visited a destination and those who have not, are supported by other studies, particularly, MacKay and Fesenmaier's (1997), and this particular piece of research is discussed in more detail later in this chapter.

Gunn (1988) recognised that image creation is not a simple linear process and argued that image develops from two different sources of information. The first he termed the 'organic' image, which is formed from non-commercial sources of information, including friends and relatives, but also through education and generally from a variety of media sources, including newspapers, TV, film and radio. The respondents in Weiping's (2010) research, discussed above, who had not visited Bali, were clearly influenced by these organic images, which were mostly received from news media sources. Gunn indicated that the second source of information contributed to what he referred to as the 'induced' image, and indicated that this is formed from commercial sources, via advertising and promotion. Today we can add the world wide web to Gunn's (1988) sources of information for both organic and induced images.

Cooper *et al.*, (2005:63) indicated that Gunn's organic and induced images will be combined in what they suggest is the process of the development of a holiday destination image. They state that there are four stages in the development of what they term a holiday image:

1  The first stage is a rather vague, almost fantasy-like image that will have been created by a combination of advertising, education and word-of-mouth. This process will be before a tourist has thought seriously about taking a holiday in a particular destination.

2  The next stage occurs when a tourist makes a decision to take a holiday and needs to consider timing, type of holiday and the actual destination. At this point the image becomes modified, extended and clarified and an anticipatory image is created.

3  This stage is the actual holiday experience itself which leads to a change in the image. This process will involve removal of elements of the image that have proved to be invalid. It also reinforces the parts of the image that have proved to be correct.

4  This is the 'after-image', the memory or recollection of the holiday. The emotional reaction will possibly involve feelings of nostalgia, or regret or even fantasy. This stage will help create an individual's holiday concepts that will contribute to a new sequence of holiday images that will influence future holiday decisions.

Page (2003) has similar views on the process of image creation to those of Cooper *et al.* (2005) and stated that tourists use a process of elimination when selecting a destination to visit, and a key element in this selection process is the destination image. Page also follows Gunn's views when indicating that destination image is a combination of the actual knowledge that tourists have of a location, its media image and the opinions of individuals and group members that inform the decision-making process.

Where destinations have particularly memorable elements, these then form an important dimension of the image and this can greatly influence decision-making. Hence, the Eiffel Tower is regarded as a very important part of the image of Paris, and this can lead tourists to regard such an image as a very positive factor, resulting in them deciding to visit (Page, 2003). It can also mean at times when a destination is not regarded as safe (such as locations that have had a terrorist incident), a previous positive image can still lead to decisions to visit (see Mason, 2016).

The reference to terrorism incidents indicates that conditions in a destination can change over time and this can have an effect on its image. Studies of image change over time are relatively unusual, as most studies are one-off (Weiping, 2010). However, when there are situational problems such as political, economic or health-related issues at the destination, a number of studies have been conducted to measure the impact of the problem by comparing the results conducted before and after the negative event (see, for example, Gartner and Shen, 1992; Weiping, 2010). In relation to image change studies, Gallarza *et al.* (2002) categorized three types of studies: first, those which study the influence of the length of stay in a destination on the destination image, (e.g. Fakeye and Crompton, 1991); second, studies that were repeated after a period of time on the same destination (e.g. Gartner and Hunt, 1987); and third, those that investigated the effect of previous visitation on image structure (e.g. Ahmed, 1991; Dann, 1996).

In relation to previous visitation to a destination, MacKay and Fesenmaier's study (1997) suggested that there are differences in the images held by those who have visited before and those who have not. Hence Mackay and Fesenmaier concluded that individuals 'familiar' with a destination hold images closer to the 'holistic, psychological and unique' ends of the image dimension continuum, whilst, individuals 'not familiar' with a destination were more likely to have images closer to the 'attribute, functional and common' ends of the image continuum. In their study, familiarity was defined as 'previous experience with a destination' and originated in respondents own indication of how familiar they thought themselves to be with a place (Mackay and Fesenemaier, 1997).

## The power of image

Although a destination image may change over time, perhaps as a result of a political or economic crisis, the image may not necessarily change and Holloway (2009) indicated why this can be the case. As Holloway (2009) states, destinations depend on their image to be successful in attracting tourists, but the image may no longer be that up to date, or an accurate representative of the destination. So the image of London for many foreign visitors, is Big Ben, the Houses of Parliament, Buckingham Palace and horse riding guardsmen wearing red coats and busby hats. This image is very dated and includes little indication of the modern London, one of the most multi-cultural cities in the world and gives no indication at all of the terrorism events that took place in 2005 and again in 2017. However as Holloway (2009:185) argues:

> *The power of the image is the branding iron that drives tourism and to jettison it in favour of a modern, but less graphic image, is a far more difficult - and risky - task for marketing than keeping the original.*

So in summary, as long as images are positive, promotional organisations will want to keep them (Holloway, 2009), even though they may bear little resemblance to the actual destination that the images are attempting to promote.

The importance of a historically-based image can be seen in the case study of Scotland, in its use of tartan to market itself as a tourism destination, which is presented below. This case study also reveals how an image can change over time and that it can be a romanticised image that is used, rather than one closely linked to historical fact.

## Case Study: Tartan - Marketing a piece of Scotland's history to tourists

Along with haggis, the thistle, malt whisky, shortbread (and more recently, perhaps the deep fried Mars bar), a key part of Scotland's tourism image is tartan. Tartan, which is patterned material with different coloured vertical and horizontal lines (see Figure 5.2), is used to package many goods sold in Scotland including whisky and shortbread, and when the Scottish Football supporters travel to other countries they are referred to as the 'Tartan Army'. However a huge degree of myth surrounds tartan, and it is romantic fiction and commercial interests that have made tartan very big business for the tourism industry.

Dating back over 300 years, originally tartan was a type of patterned cloth known as *helande*, which was woven in Scottish Highland towns and villages. It was a very fine cloth that was both hardwearing and (almost) rainproof. It was woven into a single piece of cloth, about four metres long, originally known as a *plaid* and then, to wear it, a person wrapped the whole plaid around themselves with a belt around the middle and the upper part of the cloth thrown over the shoulder. The colours of the cloth were relatively soft and muted (nothing like the bright patterns of today) blending in with the Highland landscape. It provided very good camouflage and was worn as an everyday garment.

Up until the early 1700s, tartan was only worn in the Highlands, but from then on it gradually became acceptable for people of the Lowlands area of Scotland to wear it. What really started the myth-making around tartan was the Battle of Culloden and its aftermath. In 1745, Bonnie Prince Charlie (Prince Charles Edward Stuart) attempted to become the king of a united England and Scotland. Charles Stuart's father was the son of James VII, so Charles had a potential claim to the throne. However, he had not visited Scotland before he arrived from Paris in early 1745. He gained the support of Highland clansmen – the groups of influential families who lived in the Highland areas. The supporters of Charles were known as Jacobites and Charles led an army of Highland clansmen south into England, initially winning battles against the English. However, he was soon driven back and in 1746 his army was defeated at the Battle of Culloden near Inverness, although he himself escaped and was taken, in disguise, by a young Scottish islander, Flora MacDonald to the Isle of Skye, from where he eventually escaped back to France.

Following the defeat at the Battle of Culloden, the Highlanders who had supported Bonnie Prince Charlie were treated brutally, the stated reason being to deter others from rising against the English crown, and they were banned from wearing tartan for 25 years. Very soon, tartan had become a symbol for those who were Jacobites, or supporters of the Jacobites, as the ban had the effect of making tartan, for many, a symbol of repression and an expression by the Highlanders and other Scots of their resistance to English rule. In 1782, when the ban was lifted, tartan became a national symbol for Scotland. Following this, the different Highland clans, such as the Mackays, Campbells and the Macleods, began to develop their own specific tartan patterns, when previously the pattern depended largely on the individual maker. These patterns bore little resemblance to the original plaid, but were possible to produce as a result of the Industrial Revolution, and they used brightly coloured dyes and new weaving techniques, to make very distinctive material (see an example in Figure 5.2).

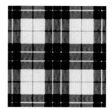

**Figure 5.2:** The Macleod clan tartan

Tartan also became an emblem for the many Highlanders who left, or were forced to leave, Scotland in the late 18th and early 19th century. By the early 19th century, with Scotland and England united, tartan was also being incorporated into the British Army where Scottish regiments wore tartan kilts.

By 1800, a romantic myth about Bonnie Prince Charlie had been created. This was expanded and spread by sentimental Victorians throughout Britain from the 1830s onwards. Accompanying the myth was the idea of the Prince and his supporting Highlanders wearing tartan patterned kilts. The kilt is a type of plaid – in other words a single piece of cloth belted at the waist and with a part thrown over the shoulder. The Scottish writer, Sir Walter Scott in the 1840s, further developed the myth of tartan as he also romanticised Scottish history, glamorised the Highland clans and put many of his Highland characters (and even the English King George IV) into tartan kilts. Queen Victoria had a strong attachment to Scotland, particularly the Highlands, and spent long periods each year at her castle, Balmoral, in the Highlands, north of Dundee. During this time the tartan kilt became an item of formal dress for Scottish (and other) men. It was worn at weddings, christenings, funerals and other formal occasions. Tartan kilt wearing continues to this day and for some Scottish people is a way to indicate their nationality.

Today, the Sottish tourists industry uses brightly coloured tartan to help sell kilts, or to hire them out, as they are usually very expensive to buy. There are also a large range of women's clothes, including skirts and trousers, which have a tartan pattern. As indicated above, in addition to clothes, tourist products such as shortbread and whisky are sold in tartan packaging, as are many other Scottish products for visitors including chocolate, toffee, jam, honey and beer.

(Adapted from: *The Rough Guide to the Scottish Highlands and Islands*, 2011, with additions).

As the case study of tartan indicates, Scotland has used its heritage – both historically accurate and a romanticised version – to create a particular image to promote its tourism industry. However, Scotland has also used its landscape to create a very different image. 'North Coast 500' is a route-way that runs around the northern coast of Scotland. The route begins and returns to the Highland town of Inverness and was opened in 2014. It heads westwards from Inverness to the Kyle of Lochalsh, travels up the remote and sparsely populated north-west coast, along the north coast to John O'Groats, the most northerly part of mainland Britain, before heading south along the east coast to return to Inverness. North Coast 500 is so called because it is approximately 500 miles long (516 miles precisely). The route passes some of the most impressive coastal scenery in Scotland, if not in the world. It is aimed very much at road trip enthusiasts, and is targeted in particular, at owners of vintage cars, sports cars, motorbikes and motorhomes. The scenery combined with the comparative difficulty of driving on narrow roads is what attracts drivers. However, from a Scottish Tourist Board marketing perspective it wants tourists to visit the most remote parts of mainland Scotland where relatively few tourists venture, except on their way to John O'Groats. The intention is to get tourists to stay, and specific groups of drivers, for example motorhome owners and campers are targeted, with suggestions on how far to travel each day, campsites/caravan sites to stay overnight and pubs, cafes and restaurants and tourist attractions to visit on route. The marketing is via detailed printed publications, dedicated North Coast 500 maps and a comprehensive, regularly updated website. It is also possible to join, for a small fee, the 'North Coast 500 Club'. As Woods (2016) claims, North Coast 500 is Scotland's answer to America's Route 66. The American route which runs from east to west across central USA has been made famous in books, songs and films. Indeed part of the marketing for North Coast uses precisely the same logo image as that for Route 66, as is shown in Figure 5.3. Although in existence for only three years at the time of writing, it appears that a significant number of users are returning regularly, often driving the route in the opposite direction to their previous visit.

**Figure 5.3:** 'North Coast 500' and 'Route 66' logo images

The section above has indicated how the image of destinations can change over time. However, some locations have changed to such an extent that they have actually become tourism destinations when previously they were not regarded as such. Birmingham in the English Midlands is a good example of this change. With over one million residents in 2015, Birmingham was for more than two hundred years considered to be England's second city, but its origins are strongly linked to the UK Industrial Revolution and it was known by the early 20th century for making a range of iron and steel items including weapons and motor vehicles. However, by the 1960s, as its main industries fell in to decline, it tended to be regarded as an unfashionable and unloved city, located in a provincial backwater (Heely, 2011).

In the 1970s, attempts were made to improve Birmingham's image and put it on the visitor map. In 1976 the National Exhibition Centre (NEC) was opened on the outskirts of the city, although there was still a feeling that Birmingham was not the appropriate location for a national centre. However these concerns proved unfounded as the NEC has hosted many major national/international events since, including the International Motor Show, the Confederation of British Industry National Conference, Crufts Dog Show and the Horse of the Year Show.

In the 1990s, the largely unattractive city centre underwent major redevelopment, which involved the building of the International Convention Centre, the National Indoor Arena and the Birmingham Symphony Hall. By the mid-1990s, Birmingham had over 40% of the entire UK conference and exhibition trade. Most of this development had involved public money, but there was also the creation, largely via private investment, of over 3000 hotel rooms and 250 licensed premises, located in what became known as the 'convention quarter' – this title being a part of re-defining of the image of the city (Heely, 2011).

**5**

By the mid-1990s Birmingham was addressing its old 'declining industry/boring city' image issues with new marketing, advertising itself as: 'Birmingham: Europe's Meeting Place'. Some evidence to support this claim can be seen in the Lions Club International decision to hold in the city what was reputed at the time to be the biggest global meeting ever, and following this the Eurovision Song Contest was held there and, in 1997, a G8 Summit (Mason, 2016).

In 2017, Birmingham could offer visitors not only a range of high quality traditional activities such as sporting venues, including several premiership/championship football grounds and an international test cricket ground at Edgbaston, but also one-off events at the NEC and National Indoor Arena. In the city centre, visitors could go to major art galleries, the Birmingham Symphony Hall and new tourist centres at the Rotunda and Birmingham New Street. The city was also realising its potential as a multi-cultural tourism attraction, with the creation of the 'Balti Triangle'. This was in recognition of the post-war migrants from Bangladesh who made Balti, a special type of curry dish, sold originally to Birmingham residents in restaurants and takeaways. By 2017, these food sellers were known not just locally, but nationally and even internationally, adding to the increasing number of attractions in what once had the image of an unappealing industrial city apparently lacking the type of resources to bring in tourists.

The discussion of Birmingham indicates how an old, industrial city with a poor image can be re-invented to become a tourist destination. The key factors in this process were planning decisions that were designed to turn Birmingham into a major event and exhibition centre; and what contributed to the success of this planning was a partnership between public and private sectors. The result of this was a significant change in Birmingham's image. The nature of destination planning and management is investigated in greater detail in Chapter 14.

Another European city, once important for industry and not until recently perceived of as a tourist destination, is Barcelona. There are other similarities between Birmingham's and Barcelona's development as tourism destinations, not the least being the importance of the hosting of international events, which has contributed to a change in image.

Barcelona is the second city of Spain after the capital Madrid. With a population in 2016 in excess of 1.5 million, Barcelona became important in the 19th century as Spain's leading manufacturing centre, focusing on the production of textile machinery and related products. However, Barcelona's potential for tourism was not recognised until the mid-1980s. This was very much the result of Spain's 20th century political history. During the Spanish Civil War in the 1930s, as a largely left-wing city, Barcelona supported the Republican cause and following Franco's victory, its economic development was held back. This was compounded by the strong desire of the Spanish region, Catalonia, of which Barcelona is the capital, to be independent of the rest of Spain, which put it in continual conflict with Franco's dictatorship based in Madrid.

After 1975, with the gradual transition to democracy in Spain, Barcelona began to develop its economy, including tourism, more rapidly. However, the real spur to Barcelona's tourism rise was its designation in 1986 as host for the 1992 Olympic Games. After 1986, Barcelona went through a period of re-assessing its role as a tourism destination and leading up to the Games there was a strong public/private sector partnership involved in the building of the facilities required for the Games. This partnership managed to secure much more sponsorship than any previous Games. The expenditure was primarily on venues and transport, but also used to improve run-down parts of the city, such as the harbour-side Port Vell area and the decaying industrial area, Poble Nou, and this helped counter the city's poor image (Mason, 2016).

The spirit of the Olympics was harnessed and used in an attempt to create a new image for Barcelona, with an identity based on urbanism, culture and style. There was also real endeavour to showcase the heritage, independence and regional identity of Catalonia. The Mediterranean climate and the distinctive cultural and architectural achievements of Picasso, Gaudi and Miro were emphasised as part of this new image-creating process. The effectiveness of the process has been such that successful urban regeneration linked to major events has become known as the *Barcelona model* (Heely, 2011).

Following the Games, the tourism strategy became less generic 'destination' marketing and much more tactical marketing, focusing on a range of different market segments, namely: meetings, culture, shopping, cruises, sport, gastronomy, gay and health. However, hosting major events is still very important for Barcelona's tourism economy, with for example, regular festivals and conferences, but also one-off events such as Gaudi Year (2002), Picasso Barcelona (2006) and World Architectural Year (2009). The city also has a number of other pre- and post-Olympic attractions, including the Sagrada Familia (Gaudi's unfinished church), Gaudi's Parc Guel, the Opera House, the Picasso Museum, the Miro Foundation, the Museum of Catalan Art and FC Barcelona's Football Museum. There are also new conference centres, including the Barcelona International Convention Centre opened in 2004 and the city has continued to host major events, such as the World Conference of the Association of Corporate Travel Executives and the World Mobile Phone Convention (Heely, 2011).

Despite a reputation for petty crime, which has had a negative impact on the city's image, Barcelona no longer fits George Orwell's Spanish Civil War description of a partially destroyed city with a 'gaunt, untidy look', but has become much more a global trademark of refined urban life, advanced design and Mediterranean hedonism, and in 2014 was Spain's single most important tourism destination (Mason, 2016).

The following case study discusses recent attempts to change an old UK city's image. It focuses on Norwich, which has a strong historical image, with a number of significant buildings and monuments, including its Norman castle and cathedral, several museums and art galleries, and it is recognised as a UNESCO City of Literature (UNESCO, 2014). All of these largely historical factors have helped develop tourism in Norwich. However, the city does not just want to appeal to those interested in what could be termed heritage-based tourism, and wants to offer a more modern perspective. It was once at the centre of a major agricultural area, particularly the production of wool in the Middle Ages, and in the last two hundred years was at the forefront of arable farming, with the grain crops of wheat and barley of great importance locally and nationally. Very recently, it has tried to use its reputation for the production of one arable crop, barley, but to create a new tourism image, as the case study indicates.

## Case study: Norwich City of Ale

Norwich is the location of a recent initiative which combines traditional image with a modern concern. Norwich owes much of its origins and wealth as a city to its role centred as a market place to the county of Norfolk and the agricultural produce of the area of East Anglia in the UK. In the period from 1100 to 1700 Norfolk was important for the production of cloth and textiles, using wool from the sheep that were kept on large numbers of farms and also in religious establishments. By 1700 Norwich was the second largest city . after London in England.

However, by the 1800s clothing and textiles were being produced increasingly in the north of England counties of Yorkshire and Lancashire. Norfolk, including Norwich, was largely bypassed by the industrial revolution as the areas lacked key resources, such as coal and iron ore. Norwich's importance as the second city began to decline, but it still maintained its close agricultural links, and arable crops that had been grown increasingly from about 1700 began to be the most important products. One such arable crop was barley, which was used partly to feed animals but also to produce beer. Norfolk barley was seen by many brewers as the best in the UK, so more of it was grown and large numbers of breweries grew up in Norfolk and the wider region of East Anglia in the 1800s. The importance of brewing and the provision of public house (pubs) can be seen in relation to the claim that by 1900, 'Norwich had a church for every week of the year and a pub for every day' – this was in a city with a population of less than 100,000.

Until 1970, Norwich maintained its tradition of breweries, with these generally serving local pubs. However, the local breweries were taken over or forced out of business by national breweries in the 1970s. The national breweries stopped brewing the local beers, usually referred to as 'living' beers (or real ale), as they contained yeast, which had unique flavours, but at times were sometimes unpredictable and therefore inconsistent. The national breweries replaced them with pasteurised, homogenised, standardised bitter and mild beers (the two most common British beers up to the 1970s) and increasingly standardised continental lager-style beers. Norwich went from being a city with a proud tradition of brewing real ale, to a virtual real ale desert. This lasted for approximately 30 years, but from about 2005 there was a growing interest in what today is called just 'ale', but is what those who were around in the 1970s would call 'real ale'. This interest was from a new younger generation of beer drinkers. It led to a boom in micro-breweries, (pubs that brewed their own beers and sold it on the premises, or other types of small-scale brewers), new styles of beer and the re-introduction of once defunct beers that were re-invented using the old recipes. This was also happening in other countries, including the USA, parts of continental Europe, and in other parts of the UK, but Norwich and Norfolk were at the forefront of this movement.

To capitalise on this renewed interest in ale from the older generation, and an awakening of interest from the younger generation, in 2011 Norwich established its first 'City of Ale' Festival. Directing the Festival was Norwich City of Ale Limited, a not for profit organisation with the mission to promote Norwich nationally and internationally as the UK 'City of Ale'. The objectives of the Festival, according to City of Ale website, were originally:

☐ To facilitate collaboration between local breweries and city real ale pubs;

☐ To organise an annual festival as a celebration of real ale from local breweries to be held throughout the city in real ale pubs and other venues selling real ale;

☐ To produce and distribute a programme of events, ales, pubs and breweries;

☐ To disseminate Norwich City of Ale to a national and international audience;

☐ To partner with organisations that share the ethos and support the objectives of the Festival;

☐ To engage in activities that support the achievement of these objectives.

By 2016, the Festival ran for 10 days, taking place in pubs all over Norwich. As many as 45 pubs took part and around 40 local breweries offered over 200 different ales. There were hundreds of events in the pubs and other venues. (cityofale, 2017). One of the major activities is a series of 'Ale Trails' in which drinkers visit a selection of pubs involved in the Festival and gain a stamp in a booklet (after consuming Festival beer) which then allows them to receive a commemorative badge and gives them the opportunity of being entered into a competition with the possibility of winning free beer.

The City of Ale Company uses various means to gain publicity for the event. Each year, the Festival supports a local charity by offering a special 'charity ale'. In 2016, the selected charity was the East Anglia's Children's Hospices. In relation to the specially brewed Festival beer, the brewery donated 20p for every pint sold.     Part of the publicity involves a competition to name the specially brewed beer, which is publicised by the local newspaper, the Eastern Daily Press (EDP). The winner receives publicity in the EDP, is given tickets to attend the opening of the Festival and also some free beer. As the 2016 pre-publicity 'City of Ale Festival' website indicated:

> 'The brand new beer will be available in many City of Ale pubs during the Festival and it needs a name! So a naming competition is announced, and the winner will receive two VIP tickets to the City of Ale Launch Party … on Thursday 26th May, where they will be presented with a demi-pin of the ale. As the Co-Chair City of Ale stated "This new, golden, fruity ale sounds delicious, and it's in support of a very special cause, so it deserves a very special name. We look forward to seeing the entries and selecting the winner. And tasting the ale, of course!"

Traditionally real ale has been associated with older male drinkers. However, the City of Ale Festival has tried to get away from this image. For example, as part of the 2016 Festival there were special sessions devoted to modern female brewers, of which there are a significant number in the region, with historical perspectives on female brewers from the past, as well as tastings of beers that have been especially brewed with women as the target consumers (City of Ale, 2016). The local newspaper, the EDP, also tried to attract more female drinkers to real ale as part of its publicity for the 2017 City of Ale Festival, and once again ran a competition to name the specially brewed beer for the 2017 Festival, which results in a prize similar to that of the 2016 for the winner and also 20p of every pint sold will go to charity. The continuing link between charity and the Festival can be seen in te fact that the winning beer name for 2017 was 'Hope in the Hop'.

(Source: City of Ale - cityofale.org.uk, accessed January 12, 2017, and the Eastern Daily Press, January 13th 2017 and May 23rd 2017)

# Summary

This chapter has focused on tourism destinations. It is here that the motivation and demand for tourism meet the actual resources for tourism. There is a great variety of tourism destination, ranging from coastal towns to old industrial cities, as well as including manufactured, dedicated attractions, such as theme parks. The image of destinations is a vital component of what makes them attractive to visitors. The chapter has indicated that there are different aspects of image, including the cognitive and affective dimensions, notions of destinations comprising different components, as well as also holistic perspectives of destinations. There has been discussion of how image is formed and how it can change as a result of problems in a destination, but also reasons why the image of, and actual events in, a destination, may not match. The way in which an image can be developed based on both accurate and romanticised historical information has been presented via a case study of Scotland. It has also been argued that changing the successful image of a destination, by bringing it up to date may be a damaging activity in relation to the reputation and brand of the destination.

## Student activities

1   Why are tourism destinations particularly important in the study of the geography of tourism?

2   What is the difference between a tourist attraction and a tourism destination?

3   With reference to Birmingham and Barcelona as discussed above, what are the main factors that have contributed to a change of image in each location?

4   There is thematic discussion of Scotland's image above. What are the main components of your own image of Scotland, and why do you believe you have this particular image?

5   a) Why has the city of Norwich, in England, decided to change its image?

    b) What factors are important in Norwich's attempts to change its image?

    c) How will Norwich know if its attempts to change its image have been successful?

6   Consider a tourism destination close to where you live.

    a) What do you regard as the key elements of the destination image?

    b) How has the image changed over time?

    c) How might the image change in the future?

# References

Ahmed, Z.U. (1991). The influence of the components of a state's tourist image on product positioning strategy. *Tourism Management.* **12** (4), 331-340.

Augustyn, M. (1998) The road to quality enhancement in tourism, *International Journal of Contemporary Hospitality Management,* **10**(4), 145-158.

Baloglu, S. and Brinberg, D. (1997), Affective images of tourism destination. *Journal of Travel Research,* **30**, 11–15.

Buhalis, D. (2000) Marketing the competitive destination of the future, *Tourism Management,* **21**(1), 97-116.

City of Ale (2017) https//www.cityofale.org.uk, accessed January 12, 2017

Cooper, C., Fletcher, J., Fyall, A., Gilbert, D., and Wanhill, S. (2005) *Tourism: Principles and Practice,* 3rd ed. London: Prentice Hall.

Crompton, J. (1979)  Motivations for pleasure vacations. *Annals of Tourism Research,* **6**, 408–24.

Dann, G. (1996). Tourists images of a destination: An alternative analysis, *Journal of Travel and Tourism Marketing,* **5** (1/2), 41–55.

Dobni, D. and G. Zinkhan (1990). In search of brand image: a foundation analysis. *Advances in Consumer Research,* **17**, 110-119.

Echtner, C. and Ritchie, J.  (1991). The Meaning and Measurement of Destination Image. *Journal of Tourism Studies,* 2(2): 2 — 12.

Echtner, C. and Ritchie, J. (1993). The Measurement of Destination Image: An Empirical Assessment. *Journal of Travel Research,* **31**, 3 -13.

EDP (2017a) Norwich City of Ale seeks charity partner for 2017 festival brew, *Eastern Daily Press,* January 21[tst]

EDP (2017b) Norwich City of Ale 2017 to kick off with a bang at beer festival launch party, *Eastern Daily Press,* May 8th

Ekinci, Y., Riley, M. and Fife-Shaw, C. (1998) What school of thought? The dimensions of the resort hotel quality. *International Journal of Contemporary Hospitality Management,* **10**(2), 63-67.

Fakeye, P. and Crompton, J. (1991). Image differences between prospective, first time and repeat visitors to the Lower Rio Grande Valley. *Journal of Travel Research,* **30**, 10-16.

Gallarza, M., Gil, I. and Caldero, H. (2002). Destination image: towards a conceptual framework.  *Annals of Tourism Research,*  **29**(1), 56–78.

Gartner, W (1989) Tourism image: Attribute measurement of state tourism products using multidimensional scaling techniques, *Journal of Travel Research* **28** (2), 16-20.

Gartner, W. (1993). Image formation process. In *Communication and Channel Systems in Tourism Marketing,* M. Uysal and D. R.Fesenmaier, eds., 191-215. New York: Haworth Press.

Gartner, W. C. and J. D. Hunt, (1987). An analysis of state image change over a twelve-year period (1971–1983). *Journal of Travel Research,* 26(2), 15–19.

5

Gartner, W, and Shen, J. (1992). The impact of Tiananmen Square on China's Tourism image. *Journal of Travel Research*, 3 0 (Spring), 47—52,

Gunn, C. (1988). *Tourism Planning*, 2nd ed., New York: Taylor and Francis.

Gunn, C. (1994) *Tourism Planning*, 3rd ed., London: Taylor and Francis.

Hall, C. M. (2000). *Tourism Planning*, London: Prentice Hall.

Heely, J (2011) *Inside City Tourism: A European Perspective* Clevedon: Channel View.

Holloway, C (2009) *The Business of Tourism*, 8th ed., London: Prentice Hall

Kozak, M. and Rimington, M. (2000) Tourists' satisfaction with Mallorca, Spain as an off-season holiday destination, *Journal of Travel Research*, **38**(3), 260-269.

Laws, E. (1993) *Tourist Destination Management: issues, analysis and policies*, London: Routledge

Mackay, K. and D. Fesenmaier, (1997). Pictorial element of destination in image formation. *Annals of Tourism Research*, **21**(3), 537-565.

Mason, P. (2016) *Tourism Impacts, Planning and Management*, 3rd ed., London: Routledge

Medlik, S. (1993) *Dictionary of Travel Tourism and Hospitality*, Oxford: Butterworth-Heineman

Murphy, P., Pritchard, N. and Smith, B. (2000) The destination product and its impact on traveller perceptions, *Tourism Management*, **21**(1), 43-52.

Ooi, C. (2010) Brand Singapore; the hub of New Asia, in Morgan, N., Pritchard, A. and Pride, R. (eds.) *Destination Branding*, Oxford: Butterworth Heinemann, 242-260.

Page, S. (2003) *Tourism Management*, Oxford: Butterworth Heinemann

Ritchie, J. and Crouch, G. (2003) *The Competitive Destination: a Sustainable Tourism Perspective*, Wallingford: CABI

Smith, S. (1994) The tourism product, *Annals of Tourism Research* **21**(3), 582-595.

Swarbrooke, J. (1999). *Sustainable Tourism Management*. Wallingford: CABI Publications.

UNESCO (2014) http://www.writerscentrenorwich.org.uk/unesco-city-of-literature/ accessed February 10th, 2017

Weiping, L (2010) Unpublished PhD thesis, Bedfordshire University, Luton.

White, C., (2005). Destination Image: to see or not to see? Part II. *International Journal of Contemporary Hospitality Management*, **17**(2), 191-196.

Woods, S. (2016) *The 50 Greatest Road Trips*, London: Icon Books.

Zimmer, M. and Golden, L. (1988). Impressions of retail stores: A content analysis of consumer images. *Journal of Retailing*, **64**(3), 285-293.

# Tourism Impacts

This section is concerned with tourism impacts. These are conventionally subdivided under sub-headings such as economic impacts, socio-cultural impacts and environmental impacts. It is also usually the case that impacts are grouped together using terms such as 'positive' and 'negative'. Although impacts can occur at any location in the tourism system (see Figure 1.1), it is within the tourism destination that these impacts are particularly noticeable, and this is at least partly to do with the fact that many destinations are concentrated spatially, so the geographical dimensions of the impacts are easy to observe and record. In reality, tourism impacts are not neatly subdivided under convenient headings, but are often multi-faceted. It is also the case that tourism impacts are usually set within a wider context of other socio-economic effects of human activity. Nevertheless, in an attempt to understand their importance here, tourism impacts are classified under headings and discussed in separate chapters in this section.

# 6 An Introduction to Tourism Impacts

## Introduction

Tourism, as a significant form of human activity, can have major effects on people and places, and these effects are commonly referred to as tourism impacts. Tourism always takes place in a context, which we usually refer to, in a broad sense, as the environment. This environmental context is made up of both human and natural features. The human environment comprises economic, social and cultural factors and processes. The natural environment is a combination of inorganic components such as rocks and water, and inorganic processes such as the erosion of rocks, and with organic elements, which comprise plants and animals and organic processes such as those within an ecosystem.

## The human and natural environments

When discussing impacts of tourism, it is possible to make a distinction between the human environment and the natural environment and this is the convention followed by most writers on tourism impacts. However, it is important to note that, in a real setting, the human and the natural environment are not separate, but interlinked, and human activity is both affected by and has effects on the natural environment.

Most writers and researchers consider the impacts of tourism under the following headings: socio-cultural, economic and environmental impacts. This convention is followed in the chapters that follow, but it should be remembered that in a real world context, tourism impacts are generally multi-faceted, often having a combination of economic, social and environmental dimensions, although tourism researchers, and others such as planners and politicians may concentrate on one type of impact and largely ignore the others. Nevertheless, when considering each type of impact, it should be noted that the impacts are multi-dimensional, not as easily compartmentalized as is often portrayed and frequently problematic. Hence, tourism impacts cannot easily be categorized as solely social, environmental or economic, but tend to have several interrelated dimensions.

Although it is conventional to subdivide tourism impacts under those three headings, it is also normally the case that the discussion follows a pattern in which the economic impacts are considered before the others. In this text, we divert from the norm, and the environmental impacts are discussed first. The rationale for this in summary is as follows:

- The environment is a key resource for tourism
- The environment is to a large extent the geographical context for much tourism
- The environment is a combination of both natural and human aspects
- There is a great range of environmental attractions that encourage tourism
- Environmental impacts of tourism are often easy to discern as their visual nature is very evident. These impacts are dynamic and change continually.
- As environmental impacts are frequently visual in nature they can significantly influence the image of a destination
- The environmental impacts of tourism can be either positive or negative
- Not only does tourism have an effect on the environment, but the environment can have effects on tourism.
- The environment is being affected by human activity (including climate change which is discussed Chapter 11) and this has effects on tourism.

The environment can be regarded as a key geographical resource for tourism. It is also the case that the variation in geographical factors, particularly spatial factors, are very obvious in relation to the environment. The environment is conventionally subdivided under both human and non-human components, which is either a natural or, as is more likely, a semi-natural environment. Environmental effects of tourism are also very apparent in terms of their visual nature, such as the existence of hotels, theme parks or marinas. Tourism can have significant negative impacts on the environment in terms of, for example, pollution, crowding and congestion, but can also give positive effects through, for example, raising awareness of the need to conserve threatened landscapes or species, as well as helping to raise money from visitors to support conservation measures.

Tourism impacts can be recorded in a number of locations. This can be in relation to tourists leaving an area of generation, usually the tourists' home locations, and moving towards, before arriving at, an area of attraction. Hence, impacts can be considered in relation to an area of origin, and the transport route and transport type used by tourists. However, tourism impacts tend to be most obvious in specific locations where tourists congregate, and in particular it is in the destination area that the impacts can often be seen most clearly. It is in the destination that impacts are particularly obvious, because it is here that tourists interact with the local environment and the local economy, as well as the local culture and society. Nevertheless, it is frequently the impacts on the environment in terms of the creation of hotels, and a related tourism infrastructure that is an immediate indication of the significance of tourism in a particular area, location or, as it is commonly referred to, the tourism destination.

# Impact as change

Many texts book on tourism have sections on tourism impacts. In these texts usually the approach is an initial division under different headings as indicated above, and this is then often followed by a concern with specific impacts. However, the discussion so far has assumed, through the use of the term *impact*, that tourism has some form of effect on society, the environment or the economy. But the term *impact* has been viewed as problematic by some researchers (see Hall and Page, 2014, for more discussion on this). However, as Hall and Page (2014) indicate, the term impact really is a short-hand way of indicating that there has been a *change* in something over time as a result of tourism visitation. In fact, it would probably be better to use a term such as 'tourism-related change' than impact (Hall and Lew, 2009).

There is another problem with the term impact – it implies a *one-way* process. This one-way process can be summarized as 'A has an effect on B', or using a specific example 'tourism has an effect on the environment'. The problem of using the term impact in this way is that it may hide the fact that 'B also has an effect on A' or referring again to the example 'the environment has an effect on tourism'. Hence, using the term impact may imply solely a one way process – a form of cause and effect in which only 'A has an effect on B'. In reality, it is very likely that 'A and B' have effects on each other – so it is a *two-way* process. In the real world, it is in fact even more likely that, not only do 'A and B' have effects on each other, but are found within a wider context in which there are other factors that affect both 'A and B'. Additionally, 'A and B' are very likely to have effects on certain aspects of this wider context.

The discussion in the previous paragraph indicates that the term impact is really a short-hand way of indicating tourism-related change (Hall and Lew 2009). Hence, the term impact is strictly speaking limited and not completely accurate, but it is the word that is in common use, so as Hall and Page argue (2014:140) 'we are stuck with it!' This book also follows the convention of using the term *tourism impact* when discussing what can be considered to be tourism related change.

# Positive and negative impacts

The impacts of tourism can be positive or beneficial, but also negative or detrimental. Whether impacts are perceived as positive or negative depends on the value position and judgment of the observer. This can be illustrated through the use of the following example, which is concerned with environmental effects, and is used here to help with an understanding of the importance of attitudes and value positions in relating to tourism impacts. One observer may suggest that creating a new footpath through a national park can be viewed as a way of routing tourists and therefore limiting damage to the wider area of the national park. This would be considered by the observer as a positive impact. Another observer may claim that this new footpath will lead to an increase in tourist numbers and therefore the likelihood of more damage to the environment, in other words it is viewed by this observer as a negative impact. Therefore, any discussion of tourism impacts needs to consider the value positions of observers and commentators and should be set within considerations of the wider context of tourism.

However, it is conventional for researchers and policy makers to note a number of both positive and negative effects of tourism. Positive environmental effects of tourism may include the revenue generated from visits to sites of natural attraction being used to protect or restore the attraction. Additionally there may be increased interest from visitors in the importance of the natural environment and this in turn may contribute to a greater willingness to support attempts at environmental protection. Positive economic benefits often include financial contributions to the local economy, the generation of more tax revenue and job creation. Positive social impacts of tourism can include types of cultural revival evident through traditional art or handicrafts, which are a result of tourist demand.

Negative environmental consequences include tourists' vehicle pollution, disturbance to habitats, damage to landscape features and litter. Negative economic effects of tourism include price increases, such as for houses and food in tourist destinations during the tourist season. An example of negative socio-cultural impacts is referred to as the 'demonstration effect'. This can be summarized as the loss of cultural identity, which can occur when tourists come from a wealthy part of the developed world and the hosts are located in a developing country. This effect occurs when the local residents imitate the behavior of the visitors from developed countries. This may start off as little more than the desire to wear brand-name clothes and consume branded fast food and drink. In more extreme examples, this effect may take the form of far more undesirable activities such as drug taking and prostitution.

Early commentators on the impacts of tourism in the 1960s and up to approximately the mid-1970s, suggested that tourism brought more benefits than costs. However, there was growing concern via evidence of more negative consequences of tourism from the mid-1970s (see for example, Young, 1975) and much research work on tourism impacts in the period since the late 1970s has tended to suggest that negative impacts outweigh positive impacts (Jafari, 1990; Wall, 1997). Nevertheless, many residents of destination areas have continued to want tourists to come (Wall, 1997) and this desire can be very great. Jobs, higher incomes, increases in tax revenues and better opportunities for children are frequently stated reasons for wanting more tourists (Wall, 1997), which also means that politicians, councillors and some planners may additionally desire large numbers of tourists. Those residents in tourism destinations may be prepared to put up with some negative impacts in return for what they regard as positive impacts. This introduces the concept of trade-offs, which are frequently involved in relation to tourism impacts. Here, as has been noted earlier in this chapter, it is important to be aware of the multi-dimensional aspects of tourism impacts and not see them as one dimensional. The trade-off aspect here is that a negative environmental impact of tourism, in the minds of destination residents, may be balanced with a positive economic effect. It also frequently the case that tourism impacts are viewed within a context of wider societal considerations. As Wall (1997: 2) stated:

> *Impacts are often desired, are extremely difficult to assess, may require the acceptance of trade-offs and in a policy context, may involve the development of strategies to mitigate undesirable impacts.*

There is a significant geographical aspects to the nature of tourism impacts and this helps reinforce the importance of studying these impacts in the destination area. In stressing the importance of the 'where' factor, Davison (1996) claimed the geographical influences set tourism's impacts apart from those of other industrial sectors. In relation to tourism being spatially concentrated (the important geographical dimension), Davison indicated that tourism production and consumption take place in the same location. This is unlike many other industrial activities, such as the car industry, where a single factory in one country may produce hundreds of thousands of vehicles which are sold to consumers all over the world. Hence, in tourism the tourist consumes the product where it is produced, which is the tourist destination. Therefore tourism impacts are largely spatially concentrated in the tourism destination.

It is also the case that tourism impacts are unlikely to be static over time. Hence, there is also an important temporal aspect to tourism impacts. In fact, impacts are likely to change as a destination area develops (see Butler, 1980, and the discussion of his destination area theory in Chapter 15). Key factors, contributing to the changing nature of the impacts over time, are the type of tourism activities engaged in, the characteristics of the host community in the destination region and the nature of the interaction between the visitors and residents (Wall, 1997). These factors are discussed in more detail in Chapter 14.

Not only are tourism impacts likely to change over the long term, but there is also a regular pattern of different impacts at different times of the year. This is related to the seasonality of much tourism, and as Davison (1996) suggested, it is the seasonal nature of tourism activity that makes the temporal dimension very important. The seasonality of tourism is largely due to two major factors: one is the key tourism resource of climate, as has been noted in Chapter 4, and the other is related to demand factors (as outlined in Chapter 2), particularly the case that in many countries there are set holiday periods (Burton, 1992; Davison, 1996). Climate is a significant factor in that it greatly influences important resources for tourism, such as hours of sunshine or amount of snow cover at particular times of the year. Tourists' ability to visit a destination at a particular time of the year, for example, during school holidays, tends also to make tourism a seasonal activity.

In terms of the geographical dimension, some of tourism's impacts also occur beyond the destination. Transport from the tourist's home to the destination – the transit zone, as shown in Figure 1.1 (Leiper's tourism system) – has an effect on the transit zone itself. Tourism also has impacts in the tourists' origin areas. If a tourist buys a package tour in their home region, then this is likely to benefit the tour operator based there, rather than one in the destination.

Tourism also has an impact on tourists themselves. These effects may be noted in their behavior in destinations and there may be evidence of this in relation to the local community, the local environment and the local economy. The impacts on the touriss may also become apparent when they return from a visit. For example, the tourists' experiences may affect their decision on a future visit to the destination. Some of the experiences gained would be in the destination, although the reflection on that experience and its effects on future choices could take place elsewhere. As Maher (2011) indicated a tourist experience can be profound and may not just lead to a desire to return, but change the tourists' views on the environment of the region visited and even generally about environmental issues.

# Factors influencing impacts

Major factors influencing tourism impacts have been synthesized and summarized below in Figure 6.1. These factors are based at least in part on the work of Davison (1996) and Wall (1997) and are set out in the form of questions, with some comment following the questions as examples or to provide explanation.

☐ **Where is tourism taking place?**
(e.g. rural/urban location, coastal/inland location, developed/developing country?)

☐ **What is the scale of tourism?**
e.g. How many tourists are involved?)

☐ **Who are the tourists?**
(e.g. What is their origin? Are they domestic or international visitors? Are they from a developed or developing country?)

☐ **In what type of activities do tourists engage?**
(e.g. Are these passive/active? Are these activities consumptive of resources? Is there a high/low level of interaction with the host population?)

☐ **What infrastructure exists for tourism?**
(e.g. Roads? Sewage system? Electricity supply?)

☐ **For how long has tourism been established?**
(see particularly Butler's (1980) theory of the destination life cycle)

☐ **When is the tourist season?**
(Time of year? Importance of rainy/dry seasons?)

**Figure 6.1:** Major influences on tourism impacts

Well over 20 years ago, McKercher (1993) argued that, despite the fact that impacts have been noted for many years, little research has been conducted into why tourism impacts appear to be inevitable. He claimed that there is a number of what he referred to as *structural realities*, although he used the term *fundamental truths*, which explain why the various effects, are felt, regardless of the type of tourism activity. McKercher 's fundamental truths can be considered even today as major influences on tourism impacts and hence are presented in Figure 6.2 (with comments added under the headings that McKercher employed) and there are a number of questions about these in the student activities.

1   **Tourism consumes resources and creates waste.** Tourism is essentially a resource-based industry and the resources are natural, man-made or cultural. It is a voracious consumer of resources. These are typically part of the public domain and hence tourism can be very invasive. Tourism is an industrial activity that creates waste, with sewage, rubbish and car exhaust common by-products.

2   **Tourism has the ability to over-consume resources.** The resources that tourism relies upon are liable to be over-consumed. If threshold limits have been reached, adverse effects over large areas can occur.

3   **Tourism competes with other resource users and needs to do this to survive.** Tourism and other, non-tourism but leisure-related activities often share the same resources. Two people may be doing precisely the same activity with one (a non-resident) classified as a tourist, and the other (a local) classified as involved in recreation. Tourism may also compete with other non-leisure activities such as agriculture and forestry in rural locations.

4   **Tourism is private sector dominated.** The profit motive therefore is the key one. Investment is far more likely in profit centres (e.g. a swimming pool) than a cost centre (a sewage system). Governments have had a key role in promoting and developing tourism, but have been little involved in controlling it.

5   **Tourism is multi-faceted and is therefore almost impossible to control.** Tourism is a very diverse industry including suppliers, producers, and government agencies as well as a very large number of consumers. Typically, many of the suppliers and producers have been independently owned family businesses. This makes controlling tourism extremely difficult.

6   **Tourists are consumers, not anthropologists.** Most tourists are consumers and pleasure seekers, and except for a minority they are not anthropologists. They tend to over-consume and are generally not interested in modifying their actions in relation to the host community or environment.

7   **Tourism is entertainment.** Most tourism products have to be manipulated and packaged to satisfy the needs of tourists to be entertained. This can lead to the commoditisation of local cultures and traditional activities. Products such as dances, and even religious activities, may need to be altered to satisfy the tourist demand. This will raise questions of authenticity.

8   **Unlike other industrial activities, tourism imports the clients rather than exports a product.** Tourism does not export products, but brings clients to consume the product in situ. This means tourism cannot exist in isolation from the host community. Tourism consumption usually takes place in concentrated geographical spaces, causing stress on the physical and social environment. Host communities also need to be aware that tourism is likely to cause a wide range of impacts.

**Figure 6.2:** McKercher's Fundamental truths about tourism. Adapted from McKercher (1993).

Gossling (2002), largely echoing the ideas of McKercher, suggested five important environmental aspects in relation to tourism impacts:

- Globally tourism contributes significantly to land use (e.g. hotels, theme parks airport)
- Tourism uses energy, particularly through transport/travel
- Tourism leads to damage to and possible extinction of wild species
- Tourism contributes to the spread of diseases
- Tourism can lead to changes in perception of the environment to that extent that it is regarded as a resource that can be exploited for tourism as part of an experience.

More recently, Cooper and Hall (2008) have indicated why assessing the consequences of tourism impacts has proved so difficult and these factors have significant environmental dimensions. They indicate nine factors in relation to the difficulties of assessing tourism impacts, and these are set out in Figure 6.3 under the nine headings used by Cooper and Hall with added explanatory comments.

**Figure 6.3:** The difficulties of assessing tourism impacts

☐ **Definition.** Tourism is often inextricably linked to leisure and recreation, hence separating tourism impacts from related impacts is often very difficult.

☐ **Differentiation.** Linked to the point about definitions, in many contexts, separating tourism impacts from other industrial, cultural and societal impacts can be difficult.

☐ **Scale.** Tourism has impacts at many different scales. Individual tourists may be affected by their experience, whole communities may be affected as can destinations. At an even bigger scale, countries use macro-economic data to compare their tourism industry with other countries, and we frequently talk about tourist regions that cross country boundaries, such as the 'Mediterranean coast' or 'South East Asia' or 'Pacific Islands'.

☐ **Relational effects.** Tourism is often discussed as if it has a one-way effect, i.e. tourism affects the local community, when the reality is that it is at least a two-way process, in which the local community affects tourists. That it is a two-way process is important in the understanding of how tourism works in reality.

☐ **Baseline information.** In order to understand the impacts of tourism, it is necessary to know what a destination/location was like before the arrival of tourism. Unfortunately, in all but a few cases, the baseline information is unknown.

☐ **Monitoring.** To understand the impacts of tourism, ongoing monitoring of tourism needs to occur. It is relatively unusual for this to happen. Even when this monitoring does occur, there is little use of 'control' sites (those where tourism is not occurring) to compare with the location of tourism activity.

☐ **Fragmentation.** Our knowledge of tourism activity and related impacts is very fragmented. This is partly to do with some of the points above (e.g. Definition, Differentiation), but also because tourism research is focused on some locations and environments

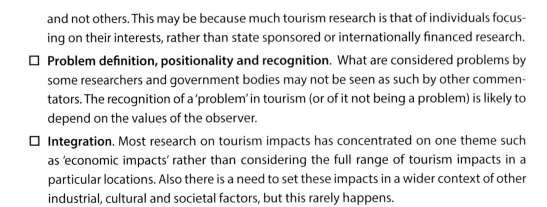

and not others. This may be because much tourism research is that of individuals focusing on their interests, rather than state sponsored or internationally financed research.

☐ **Problem definition, positionality and recognition.** What are considered problems by some researchers and government bodies may not be seen as such by other commentators. The recognition of a 'problem' in tourism (or of it not being a problem) is likely to depend on the values of the observer.

☐ **Integration.** Most research on tourism impacts has concentrated on one theme such as 'economic impacts' rather than considering the full range of tourism impacts in a particular locations. Also there is a need to set these impacts in a wider context of other industrial, cultural and societal factors, but this rarely happens.

## Summary

This chapter has provided an introduction to the study of tourism impacts. It has indicated that, although tourism impacts tend to be multi-faceted, it is usual for them to be subdivided under the following headings: economic, socio-cultural and environmental. It is conventional to discuss impacts in a sequence, with economic impacts nearly always presented first. This chapter has provided a rationale for a change in this sequence, with environmental impacts discussed in detail prior to a consideration of the other impacts. However, it is also conventional to present tourism impacts as either positive or negative. This chapter has indicated that such categorisation depends upon the value position of the observer, and has also suggested that the term 'impact' is, in reality, a short hand version of the concept of 'tourism-related change'. As impacts tend to be multi-faceted, often having a combination of economic, social and environmental dimensions, it may be not that straightforward to classify impacts at one particular tourism destination under the heading of either solely 'positive' or 'negative'. It is quite likely that there is a combination of impacts of tourism in relation to a destination and some of these impacts may be viewed as positive, while others are seen as negative.

The nature of particular tourism impacts is related to a variety of factors, including what type of tourism is under discussion, where it is happening, when it is happening, as well as the infrastructure for tourism. Ideas put forward by McKercher (1993) on the commercial and entertainment aspects of tourism have also been introduced and these have been considered in relation to tourism impacts. As has been discussed, Gossling (2002) largely concurred with McKercher (1993), whilst Cooper and Hall (2008) suggested a number of reasons why tourism impacts are difficult to assess.

## Student activities

1  What are the major influences on tourism's impacts?

2  How do McKercher's 'Fundamental truths', affect your views on tourism impacts?

3  To what extent do you agree with McKercher's 'Fundamental truths'?

4  McKercher's 'Fundamental truths' were created in 1992. What changes have there been since then to affect the 'Fundamental truths'?

5  Working in small groups (3/4 students) consider a tourism activity/business in your local area and the impacts of this activity:

   a) Make a list of the impacts under the headings 'positive' and 'negative'.

   b) Which of the two types of impacts are more important in relation to your example.

   c) Consider the points made in Figure 6.3 and discuss which apply to your particular tourism activity/business.

   d) Look again at the list and consider your own value position and indicate which of the impacts could be regarded in a different way, from your own assessment by another commentator, and how these impacts could be viewed.

# References

Burton, R. (1992) *Travel Geography*. London: Pitman.

Butler, R. (1980) The concept of a tourism area cycle of evolution. *Canadian Geographer*, **24**, 5-12

Cooper, C. and Hall, C.M. (2008*) Contemporary Tourism: An International Approach*, Oxford: Butterworth Heinemann.

Davison, R. (1996) The impacts of tourism. In *Tourism Destinations* (R. Davison and Maitland, eds), pp. 18–45. London: Hodder and Stoughton.

Gossling, S. (2002) Global environmental consequences of tourism, *Global Environmental Change,* **12**(4) 283-302.

Hall, C.M. and Lew, A (2009) *Understanding and Managing Tourism Impacts: An Integrated Approach*, London: Routledge

Hall, C.M. and Page, S. (2014) *The Geography of Tourism and Recreation,* 4th ed., London: Routledge

Jafari, J. (1990) Editor's page. *Annals of Tourism Research*, **16**, 3.

McKercher, B. (1993) Some fundamental truths about tourism: understanding tourism's social, and environmental impacts. *Journal of Sustainable Tourism*, **1**, 6–16.

Maher, P (2011) Antarctic human dimensions: Ambassadors for the experience, in Maher, P., Stewart, E. and Luck, M. (eds) *Polar Tourism: Human, Environmental and Governance Dimensions,* New York: Cognizant Communications, 121-141.

Wall, G. (1997) Rethinking impacts of tourism. In *Tourism Development* (C. Cooper, B. Archer and S. Wanhill, eds), pp. 1–10. Chichester: John Wiley and Sons.

Young, G. (1975) *Tourism, Blessing or Blight?* London: Penguin Books.

# 7 Environmental Impacts of Tourism

## Introduction

The environment is made up of both natural and human features. Human settlements set in the countryside may contain a large number of attractions for tourists. Often the natural environment is referred to as the physical environment. The natural or physical environment includes the landscape, particular features such as rivers, rock outcrops, beaches and also plants and animals (or flora and fauna), many of which are tourist attractions and have been discussed in Chapter 3. This chapter is concerned with the impact of tourism on the environment.

## Key perspectives

The environment is being increasingly recognized as the major resource for tourism. It has been noted that tourism depends ultimately upon the environment, as it is a major tourism attraction itself, or is the context in which tourism activity takes place (Holden, 2008). However, tourism–environment relationships are complex. There is a mutual dependence between the two, which has been described as symbiotic. Williams (1998) explains this relationship as one in which tourism benefits from being in a good quality environment and this same environment should benefit from measures aimed at protecting and maintaining its value as a tourist resource. Whether or not the relationship is beneficial, what is clear is that the environment is affected by tourism and the environment also has effects on tourism.

As we have seen earlier in this book, Hall and Page (2014) refer to the limitations of the use of the term tourism impact, when it is considered as just a one-way process. Hence, it is the existence of a two-way process between tourism and the environment that makes the relationship so important in any discussion of the geography of tourism and the case study at the end of this chapter, focusing on the Norfolk Broads, provides more details on the complexity of this relationship.

In the post Second World War period and especially since the beginning of mass tourism in the 1960s, it has become clear that the relationship between tourism and the environment has become unbalanced, meaning that in the past 50 or so years, tourism has become a major cause of environmental damage to the environment, rather than a force for enhancement and protection.

Despite a general awareness of the impacts of tourism on the environment, there is very limited in-depth knowledge and long-term understanding of these impacts due to a number of factors:

- Research into the environmental consequences of tourism tends to be reactive (in other words after a problem has occurred), so there is a lack of baseline information to compare with and then monitor any changes.
- It is often not easy to separate the environmental impacts that are attributed to tourism from other commercial/industrial activity and even non-human induced natural environmental changes.
- It can be difficult to separate changes made by tourists from those made by locals.
- The impacts of tourism may occur over a long period and can be cumulative and incremental rather than being evident through a sudden change.
- Spatial displacement of impacts is relatively common in tourism; for example, aircraft emissions contribute to climate change, but the effects are felt in locations distant from the place of emissions.

(after Holden, 2016).

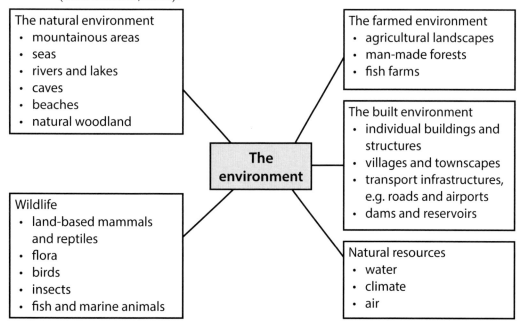

**Figure 7.1:** The scope of the environment (source: Swarbrooke, 1999)

The term *environment* is often assumed to mean no more than the physical or natural features of a landscape. However, as Figure 7.1 shows, according to Swarbrooke (1999), there are five aspects of the environment. These are: the natural environment, wildlife, the farmed environment, the built environment and natural resources. Figure 7.1 indicates the components of each of these five. It should also be remembered that these five aspects are not separate entities, but linked. For example, a fox (wildlife), may live in a woodland (the natural environment), will certainly consume water – a natural resource, is likely to visit farmland in search of live prey, and increasingly will go to a town (the built environment) in search of food, some of which may have been thrown away by humans.

# Factors affecting impact

Chapter 6 indicated the main factors influencing tourism impacts and it is advisable to reconsider these again. However, in relation to environmental impacts the following are particularly significant:

- The 'where' factor: some environments are more susceptible to tourism impacts than others.
- The type of tourism activity will affect the nature of impacts.
- The nature of any tourist infrastructure will also be important.
- When the activity occurs is important, particularly any seasonal variation.

In relation to the 'where' factor, a rural environment is likely to be affected differently, in comparison with an urban environment. A rural environment may be more fragile than an urban one, because it comprises a natural or semi-natural landscape, which could have rare plants and/or animal species. Even a farmed, rural landscape may be susceptible to damage by tourists because it is not designed to cope with significant numbers of visitors.

However, an urban environment, being a largely built one, can usually sustain far higher levels of visiting than most rural environments. This is not just because a city has, for example, roads and paths, which minimize the direct impacts of tourists' movements, but it is also the result of the nature of the organisational structure such as the planning process in urban areas (Williams, 1998). However, tourists are also particularly attracted to sites that are coincidentally fragile, such as cliff-tops, coasts and mountains (Ryan, 1991; Williams, 1998).

The nature of the activities tourists are engaged in will greatly influence the impacts they have. Some activities lead to minimal impact on the environment and are not resource consumptive, whilst others can be very resource consumptive and damaging to the environment. The scale of activity and numbers involved in tourism can be very important in terms of effects. However it is not always the case that the more visitors there are, the greater the impacts will be. For example, 50 sight-seeing tourists on a bus are likely to have relatively little effect on the actual environment travelled through (although the bus may contribute to pollution and traffic congestion). However, five visitors in an off-road vehicles in a mountain or dune environment may well have far more direct impact.

Similarly, the nature of the infrastructure that exists for tourism is significant in relation to impacts. For example, it would seem to be the case that the effects of those involved in mass tourism on Spanish Mediterranean coastal areas are potentially far greater than a small number of walkers in the Himalayas. However, if the coastal mass tourism is well planned and the groups controlled, it can limit impacts to a minimum. Paradoxically, a small group of trekkers visiting a relatively remote area of Tibet, where there is little preparation for tourists, could be far more damaging to the environment (see Holden and Ewen, 2002).

In many parts of the world, tourism is a seasonal activity. Under these conditions, tourism will only affect the environment for part of the year. During the rest of the year the environment may be able to recover. However, in some areas, despite only seasonal tourism affecting the environment, this impact is so serious that there is little chance for recovery. For example, there are certain areas of the Swiss Alps that are so heavily used for ski tourism that they cannot recover fully during the summer period. Over time, the inability of a slope to re-grow sufficient vegetation means it is more susceptible to erosion (Krippendorf, 1987; Hopkins and MacLean, 2014).

## ■ Ecology and ecosystems

In relation to tourism's impacts on the physical environment, an important term is *ecology*. Ecology is the study of the relationships between animals and plants. The relationships are often complex, involving soil, water, microorganisms, plants and animals. The individual components and the links between them are referred to as *ecosystems*. There is a huge range and number of ecosystems across the globe, ranging from, at the small scale, a pond, up to those covering thousands of kilometres, such as the tropical rain forest.

In some ecosystems particularly those in remote areas, humans are of relatively minor importance. However, increasingly all ecosystems are either directly or indirectly affected by human activity, and this activity of course includes tourism (Mason, 1990; Holden, 2000). At the relatively small scale, ecological impacts of tourism include the effects on plants of trampling by visitors and as a result of humans being present in their habitat, modifications to animal behaviour. At a global scale, an example of human impacts is atmospheric pollution caused by commercial passenger planes. This activity may also contribute to global climate change and affect both terrestrial and marine ecosystems.

It is possible to sub-divide environmental impacts under the headings 'positive' and 'negative'. Nevertheless, the value position of the observer, or commentator on environmental impacts, will affect their assessment of whether these impacts are classified as positive or negative.

The following are usually regarded as positive impacts:

■ Tourism may stimulate measures to protect the environment and/or landscape and/or wildlife;

- Tourism can help to promote the establishment of protected areas such as National Parks and/or Wildlife Reserves;
- Tourism can promote the preservation of buildings/monuments (this includes for example UNESCO's World Heritage Sites);
- Tourism may contribute to the generation of revenue, for example, via entrance charges, to maintain historic buildings, heritage sites and wildlife habitats.

Nevertheless, it is worth remembering what Holden (2016:112) claimed about the supposed positive effects of tourism on the environment, when he argued that:

> It is unlikely that any human activity has beneficial effects on the natural environment it interacts with, other than to protect it or conserve it from other more damaging forms of human behaviour.

Holden further indicates that when we refer to positive effects of tourism on the environment, we are really discussing tourism being used, not only as a way to protect the environment from damage, but also as an alternative to a less sustainable form of activity.

The following are usually regarded as negative environmental impacts:

- Tourists are likely to drop litter;
- Tourism can contribute to congestion in terms of overcrowding of people as well as traffic congestion;
- Tourism can contribute to the pollution of water courses and beaches;
- Tourism may result in footpath erosion;
- Tourism can lead to the creation of unsightly human structures such as buildings (e.g. hotels) that do not fit in with vernacular architecture;
- Tourism may lead to damage and/or disturbance to wildlife habitats.

**Figure 7.2:** Balance sheet of environmental impacts of tourism (adapted from Hunter and Green, 1995)

| Area of effect | Negative impacts | Positive impacts |
|---|---|---|
| Biodiversity | Disruption of breeding/ feeding patterns. Killing of animals for leisure or souvenir trade. Loss of habitat and species composition. Destruction of vegetation. | Encouragement to conserve animals as attractions. Establishment of protected or conserved areas. |
| Erosion and physical damage | Soil erosion. Damage to sites through trampling. Overloading of key infrastructure. | Tourism revenue to finance ground repair and site restoration. Improvement to infrastructure prompted by tourism demand. |
| Pollution | Water pollution through sewage or fuel spillage and rubbish from pleasure boats. Air pollution (e.g. vehicle emissions). Noise pollution (e.g. from vehicles, theme parks, bars discos). Littering. | Cleaning programmes to protect the attractiveness of location to tourists. |

| Resource base | Depletion of ground and surface water. Diversion of water supply to meet tourist needs (e.g. golf courses). Depletion of local fuel resources. Depletion of local building material sources. Land transferred to tourism (e.g. from farming). | Development of new/improved sources of supply. New uses for unproductive land. |
|---|---|---|
| Visual/ structural change | Detrimental impacts on natural/ non-natural landscapes through tourism development. Introduction of new architectural styles. Changes in urban functions. Physical expansion of built up areas. | Landscape improvement (e.g. to clear urban dereliction). Regeneration and/or modernisation of built environment. Re-use of disused buildings. |

Figure 7.2 shows a number of impacts of tourism on the environment and it indicates a somewhat more complex situation regarding the effects of tourism than the two lists of positive and negative above. By comparing the positive and negative effects of tourism in Figure 7.2 in relation to particular key themes, a form of balance sheet has been created. As this indicates, there are a far greater number of negative effects than positive effects. Nevertheless this does not necessarily mean that negative effects are more important, as the quantity of impacts does not necessarily equate with the quality of impacts.

# Carrying capacity

One of the key concepts in relation to environmental impacts of tourism is *carrying capacity*. This is usually regarded as a scientific term, and it is therefore considered possible to measure carrying capacity. When used in a scientific sense it may relate to, for example, a plant or animal species that is threatened by the damage caused by visitors, and any increase in visitor numbers will lead to more damage. In this way, it can usually be regarded as a threshold measure, beyond which damage and possibly irreversible change may occur.

Carrying capacity also has a less scientific meaning, as it can be viewed as a term linked to perception. In this sense, the perceptual carrying capacity is a much more subjective term. For example, what one observer views as a landscape virtually free of human activity, for another may be already too full with the evidence of people. This point about varying perceptions of carrying capacity is important in relation to damage/disturbance in the environment. One commentator may perceives damage, or perhaps unsightliness, while another does not 'see' these impacts. Whatever the nature of perception by different individuals, some landscapes are more susceptible to damage from tourism than others and carrying capacity is a particularly useful concept to assess the potential change to a landscape as a result of tourism.

It is conventional to separate environmental or physical impacts from ecological ones when discussing carrying capacity. As noted above, there is also perceptual carrying capacity. These three forms of carrying capacity are summarized below:

**7**

- *Environmental (or physical) carrying capacity* usually refers to physical space and the number of people (or the number of cars) in a particular place.

- *Ecological carrying capacity* is a threshold scientific measure, which if exceeded will lead to actual damage of plants/animals habitat.

- *Perceptual carrying capacity* is the level of crowding that a tourist is willing to tolerate before he/she decides a particular location is too full and then goes elsewhere. This is an individual, subjective concept.

The first two terms refer to scientific measures. Ecological carrying capacity would be used in a scientific approach to assess the environmental impacts of tourism. Equipment can be used to scientifically measure both environmental carrying capacity and ecological carrying capacity and these two are both likely to be significant measures in determining the point at which negative environmental impacts will occur. As perceptual carrying capacity is a subjective assessment of environmental effects, requiring individual views, it is not a strictly scientific term. However, the ways in which perceptual carrying could be assessed in a given context is through the use of interviews and/or a questionnaire survey.

# ■ The Glow Worm Cave

Waitomo Caves, located in the North Island of New Zealand, provides a good indication of the importance of different types of carrying capacity, how these are related and the complexities involved in the concept of carrying capacity. Waitomo Caves are a part of a system of limestone caves and underground rivers and the key attraction is the Glow Worm Cave. This cave, and the surrounding site, is regarded as of particular aesthetic and ecological significance and is one of the most important attractions in New Zealand, with over half a million visitors per year in the early 21st century (Doorne, 2002).

Tour groups are guided through various parts of the cave system and the intended high point of the visit is viewing of the glow worms from a boat on an underground river in almost complete darkness. As the glow worms hang from the roof of the cave they look like overhead stars in the night sky. Tours of the Glow Worm Cave lasts approximately 40 minutes and visitation is subject to diurnal and seasonal fluctuations. The major international groups in the early 21st century were, in descending order of importance: Japanese, Koreans, Taiwanese and Australians, with New Zealanders comprising approximately 8% of visitors.

An important environmental problem of the cave is carbon dioxide (most of this originating in exhalations by visitors), as excessive amounts of it may contribute to dissolving of the limestone that makes up the caves. In relation to carbon dioxide, in the early part of the 21st century, the cave license specified that the maximum number of visitors should be 300 people per hour. Although there was a lack of accurate measurement of visitor numbers, anecdotal evidence suggested that the limit of 300 people per hour was regularly exceeded. However, it appeared that the glow worms were not affected by actual visitor numbers. Nevertheless it seemed that the use of flash photography could change their behaviour.

With mounting concern about conditions in the caves, the New Zealand Department of Conservation carried out research, which focused on visitor experience in relation to crowding. The results indicated a number of differences between New Zealanders and the various international visitor groups in terms of perceptual carrying capacity. New Zealanders revealed the highest perception of crowding, although they were generally not dissatisfied with the visit. Koreans registered amongst the lowest levels of crowding, but were dissatisfied with the number of groups in the cave at any one time and having to wait for other groups. Almost three quarters of visitors in summer registered some form of crowding, although this dropped to 40% in winter. Australian and Japanese visitors tended to view the cave system as relatively crowded, more so than the Korean visitors, but less so than the New Zealanders.

The Waitomo study indicates that perceptual carrying capacity is difficult to assess. However, even in relation to ecological and environmental carrying capacities, measuring is far from straightforward. Capacities are also likely to vary according to whatever management strategies are in place. To overcome this problem, other measures have been created.

The limits of acceptable change (LAC) technique, was developed in the United States and has been used in relation to proposed developments. The timing of the use of LAC is important as it begins before a development has taken place. It involves establishing an agreed set of criteria before the development and the prescription of desired conditions and levels of change after development (Williams, 1998). Such an approach can be very useful as it can establish what existed before the proposed change – this is known as a baseline study. Without some form of baseline study it can be very difficult to assess the nature and importance of change. However, the LAC approach suffers from technical difficulties in agreeing some of the more qualitative aspects of tourism development. The LAC approach also assumes the existence of rational planning, which may not necessarily be occurring in any given context. This concept of rational planning is discussed more detail in Chapter 14

Another technique is that of the environmental impact assessment (EIA), which has become a particularly common process in the last 30 years or so. In relation to assessing tourism's impacts, the EIA is similar to the use of the LAC and the key principles of EIA are summarized in Figure 7.3. EIAs are also used in relation to other industries than tourism and they provide a framework for informing the political decision-making process. A number of different methods and techniques can be used in an EIA, including impact checklists, cartographic analysis simulation and predictive models (Williams, 1998).

LIVERPOOL JOHN MOORES UNIVERSITY
LEARNING SERVICES

**Figure 7.3:** Key principles of EIA (adapted from Hunter and Green, 1995)

☐ Assessments should identify the nature of the proposed and induced activities that are likely to be generated by the project.

☐ Assessments should identify the elements of the environment that will be significantly affected.

☐ Assessments will evaluate the nature and extent of initial impacts and those that are likely to be generated via secondary effects.

☐ Assessments will propose management strategies to control impacts and ensure maximum benefits from the project.

Discussion of carrying capacities, LACs and EIAs raises one of the key factors in relation to environmental impacts. This is the importance of scale. Footpath erosion, for example, can be viewed as a small-scale impact and may easily be alleviated by re-routing. In such a context, impacts and attempts to deal with the impacts will be limited to a small area. However, in the case of raw sewage being pumped into the sea from a hotel complex at one location, although the source is relatively small and localised, the impacts are likely to be recorded over a large area as the sewage spreads widely. In addition, attempts to alleviate this problem may require access to an extensive area.

## ■ Marketing New Zealand

As the discussion of Waitomo Caves above indicates, the environment is a key tourism draw in New Zealand. This is linked to the idea of the 'clean green image', which is used in the marketing of New Zealand to international tourists. For a relatively long period until the early 1980s, New Zealand felt sheltered from negative impacts of tourism on the environment. However there has been growing concern about environmental impacts of tourism in New Zealand over the past 30 years or so. This is particularly significant as the country needs to maintain its 'clean green image' to sell holiday experiences.

In the early 1990s almost 30% of all visits to New Zealand were to natural attractions and over half of the international tourists visited a national park (New Zealand Tourist Board, 1992). The continuing importance of this aspect of New Zealand tourism can be seen in figures that indicate almost one-third (31 per cent) of all visits to New Zealand in 2003 (New Zealand Tourism Board, 2004) and 29% in 2012 (Tourism New Zealand, 2013) were to natural attractions.

Contributing to the number of visitors to natural attractions are two important ideals in the relationship between tourism and the environment in New Zealand – first, the concept of wilderness and second, the view that there should be equality of access to the countryside.

Over 20 years ago a number of locations – coastal areas, offshore islands, lakes and rivers, and the high country and mountain areas – were identified as the most environmentally sensitive areas in New Zealand (New Zealand Tourism

Board, 1996). These, however, tend to be areas that are particularly attractive to both domestic and international visitors. Much of the land in these sensitive areas of New Zealand is owned by Maori, the indigenous people of the country. However, many Maori people have traditionally seen the growth in environmental concern as being largely a western concept and detrimental to their attempts to make a living from their land and there has been conflict as a result of different Maori attitudes to the environment compared with white New Zealand views. Nevertheless, there is evidence in New Zealand that tourism can assist with environmental preservation and, of particular relevance to Maori values, tourism can help promote protection of sites of cultural significance (New Zealand Tourism Board, 2013).

In Chapter 6 there was discussion of the meaning of the term impact. It was stated that an issue with the term impact is that it may imply a one-way process, a process in which for example, A has an effect on B. This understanding of the term can be rather simplistic and therefore misleading, as it could be that, in reality, not only does A have an effect on B, but B also has an effect on A. It is also possible that A and B not only affect each other, but are set within a wider context in which a number of other factors affect (or have impacts on) both A and B. Such a complex interrelationship of factors and their impacts is discussed in the case study below, which focuses on a wetland area in the UK, with protected area status (protected areas are discussed in detail in Chapter 13), and is called the Norfolk Broads.

## Case Study: The Norfolk Broads

**Figure 7.4:** A photograph of the rare swallowtail butterfly used to promote The Broads

The Norfolk Broads are a series of waterways and shallow lakes in the eastern area of England. As the whole area is relatively flat and low lying there are also tangled woodlands and marshes. However, the rivers and many of the shallow lakes (the actual 'broads' i.e. wide areas of water) are navigable by small boats. The specific Broads area is located mainly to the east of the city of Norwich and stretches over four river valleys, the Yare,

Bure, Waveney and Wensum and contains 700 hectares of lakes and 200 km of navigable rivers (Mason, 1990). As three of the rivers meet at different ends of a tidal estuary known as Breydon Water (see Figure 7.5) near the town of Great Yarmouth, in terms of tourism potential, the Broads are part of an interconnected waterways system.

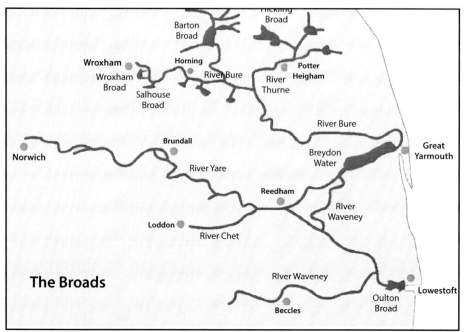

**Figure 7.5:** A map of the Norfolk Broads

It was believed until only just over half a century ago, that the Broads were a natural phenomenon. However, important research in the 1950s revealed the lakes to be the flooded remains of medieval peat diggings. The area of what is now the Broads was relatively densely populated in comparison with other parts of Britain, in the period from the 9th the 14th century, and agriculture, particularly sheep rearing, leading to the production of large amounts of wool, made some residents very wealthy and offered a good number of locals relatively secure work. Significant numbers of settlers from outside the region, in combination with an expanding local population, led to continued population growth. However, this put pressure on the local resources, particularly timber for house building but, of great importance, wood for heating in winter. When most trees had been cut down, peat (decayed vegetation) from the edge of the rivers was dug out. Although the peat turves were wet when dug they were dried out and became good, slow-burning, heating fuel. Huge amounts of peat were dug – for example, research has revealed that Norwich Cathedral used over 300,000 peat turves in one year in the 1190s. However. at the end of the 1200s and then in the early 1300s, a series of high tides and storms led to flooding and within a few years the peat diggings filled with water and the Broads were created. Eventually an area like no other in Britain, and one that has been recognised for its rare plants and often unique animals, was produced.

One important dimension of the realisation that the Broads are not natural is that since their creation they have gradually been disappearing over the past 700 years. They are shallow, being on average only just over one to one and a half metres in depth. This means plants, such as reeds and other small marsh plants, but eventually water loving trees will colonise the edge of a broad and over many years move the vegetation boundary from the edge of the lake towards the middle. Without human interference (and therefore management) the lake will disappear and be replaced by marsh and areas of dry land with trees. In fact, as old maps reveal, many former broads have disappeared over the past 500 years.

The history of the creation of the Broads and that they are a combination of natural and human induced processes means that they are unusual. Of particular significance is that they are lakes linked by navigable waterways. The linking together of the main rivers of the Broads meant that they became very important for transporting goods during the period from at least 1500 until the early 1900s. These goods, often heavy materials such as coal, sand, gravel, wheat and barley were transported by special vessels, known as wherries. These wooden sailing boats were specially designed, partly for the shallow water of the lakes and also to be able to pass easily under the low bridges of the area.

By the mid-1800s there was a realisation by locals and those from further afield that the Broads could be used for leisure as well as transporting goods. Lakes are a common place for water-based, leisure activities to take place, but lakes joined by natural waterways are relatively unusual and offer the prospect of tourism. Although a relatively small area, the Broads provided the opportunity to make a circular journey, travelling by boat for several days, stopping overnight at different locations on the way and then returning by a different route to the starting point.

A tourism industry developed from about 1850. The railways were a key catalyst, particularly when a line reached the town of Wroxham (a crossing point of the River Bure). The railway linked Wroxham to Norwich and from there lines went to London and the Midlands, enabling those from these areas to reach Wroxham in just a few hours. Wroxham developed as the key Broads location in the late 19th century. The main activity was sailing or, as the Victorians described it, yachting. Sailing boats were expensive to buy and so, initially, as with many other forms of tourism, it was the wealthy who participated. However, Wroxham and other places such as Horning and Potter Heigham (see Figure 7.5), soon had boatyards which hired sailing boats for periods of a few days, a week or longer. Many of these boats provided accommodation in the form of sleeping berths as well as a kitchen or galley area for cooking. By the 1920s, in addition to sailing boats, it was possible to hire motor boats, or cruisers as they became known. These were easier to manoeuvre for most non-sailors, and by the 1950s there were far more motor boats than yachts. By the early 1980s motor boats out-numbered sailing boats by 20:1 and there were just under 3,000 hire craft, in addition to 8,000 privately owned boats on the Broads (Mason, 1990). At this time, there were over 90 boatyards in the Broads area.

Nevertheless, during the early 1980s there was growing concern about the Broads area and some of this concern was directed at the tourism industry (Broads Authority, 1988). In summary the concern was focused on the following areas:

### Water quality

In the 19th century the water was generally clear and healthy with low growing water weeds on the bottom of the rivers and the lakes. Here there was a rich and diverse ecosystem of water plants, insects, fish, amphibians, birds and mammals. By the 1950s the water was becoming cloudy. Intensive agriculture, through the use of fertiliser, was adding phosphates and nitrates to the water, as it was washed off the land, and an increasing human population added effluent. The combined results was enriched water which encouraged the rapid growth of microscopic algae. Then in turn, the algae killed many plants and animals, as it spread out near the water surface, blocking out light and stopping plant growth. When the algae died, it sank to the bottom creating a black mud, which turned what was once a heathy, diverse ecosystem into largely lifeless water. However by the late 1980s/early 1990s there was pressure on agriculture to reduce the use of artificial fertilisers and untreated human waste was no longer pumped directly into the water. Nevertheless, conditions were not helped by the motor boats as they stirred up the mud at the bottom of the rivers and lakes, which added to the problems of cloudy water through which little light could penetrate. Initially, there was only a slow response to this, as the boat-based tourism industry was not greatly affected by these changing conditions and generally tourism was not viewed as the cause of the problems.

### Bank erosion

As the ecosystem of the rivers and lakes became less diverse, plants that had once protected the edges or banks of the rivers and lakes no longer grew. This coincided with an increase in the number of motor cruisers. These boats often travelled too fast (despite speed limit signs) and the wash (or waves) from the boats damaged the banks. The birds that once fed on the plants growing under the water at edge of the rivers and lakes, instead started to eat the plants on the banks themselves. This in turn contributed to weakening the banks, making them liable to further erosion.

### The Fens

The Broads vegetation is called fens and is composed of a variety of plants, but particularly reeds and sedge. For at least 500 years the reeds and sedge were regularly cut, with the reeds being used as house roofing material known as thatch. This landscape was unique in the UK and was the home of rare plants, such as the fen orchid, insects such as the swallowtail butterfly (see Figure 7.4) and unusual birds including the bittern. From the middle of the 20th century, the cutting of reeds and sedge declined and by the end of the century had almost stopped. The result was a change in the landscape, as trees and shrubs began to invade the edges of the lakes, as the reed areas expanded and created better conditions for their growth. This means that the Broads, as areas of open water, were gradually disappearing (and would continue to do so today without management) with the subsequent effects on wildlife and plants, as well as the water-based tourism industry.

### Grazing

Traditionally, for several hundred years the low-lying landscape was farmed with fields created for animal grazing. Many of these were liable to regular flooding and contained unusual plant and animal species. Following the UK's entry to the European Union (EU) in the 1970s, farmers were given incentives to grow arable crops such as wheat and barley and the traditional agriculture of beef and dairy cattle, which prior to UK entry into the EU was already being regarded as not particularly profitable, became even less attractive. Hence, very large areas of marshland grazing were drained and planted with arable crops. These crops required fertiliser, some of which was subsequently washed off the land by rain and added to the problems of changes in water quality.

### Tourism

Tourism developed in a piecemeal, generally unplanned way from the mid-19th century. Most Broadland villages until the mid-20th century were largely self-contained. They were usually built of local materials, including red clay bricks for house walls and pantiles, reeds for thatched roofs, wood for boatsheds and stone and flint for churches. These buildings were viewed as blending into the landscape. The tourism development was often out-of-character and out-of-scale, frequently using non-traditional material such as concrete, asbestos, plastic and corrugated iron. Therefore, this development was often unsightly, disturbing the aesthetic quality of the area. In terms of the waterways of the Broads, early tourism in the 19th century opened up the area and provided visitors with enjoyable experiences, contributed to the local economy, and caused relatively little in the way of negative impacts. However, by the 1980s, the motorboats caused bank erosion, pumped human effluent into the water and there was frequently conflict with other visitors, in particular sailing boat users, as well as those fishing.

In the 25 years or so since the assessment of conditions on the Broads, there have been some improvements to the environment. Farmers have been more cautious and careful in their use of fertilisers and other chemicals, and they have also responded to EU directives to 'set aside' some land for conservation purposes. Some land has been taken out of intensive arable farming and has reverted to pasture. A number of small broads have been separated from the navigable waterways. These have been dredged to remove the black mud and attempts have been made, with some success, to re-establish the original plants and wildlife. The motor cruiser based sector of the tourism industry has stopped pumping sewage into the waterways and additionally the industry was in decline from the late 1980s up to approximately 2010, so there have been fewer boats to cause bank erosion. Board walks have been created around some broads to enable visitors to develop awareness and understanding of the landscape and also, if fortunate, see the rare plants and animal species. Organisations such as the Royal Society for the Protection of Birds and the Norfolk Wildlife Trust have also raised awareness of the real and potential dangers to the unique wetland environment.

At the end of the first decade of the 21st century, the issues of the Broads could be summarised under the following headings:

- ☐ Water quality – particular problems relate to increased salination, partly as a result of rising sea levels due to climate change, and also sewage issues and lack of oxygen in the water
- ☐ Invasive plant species
- ☐ Siltation – increased silt on the bed of broads and river beds making them shallower
- ☐ Lack of depth of water for navigation purposes
- ☐ Excessive water removal mainly for agricultural purposes
- ☐ The need for continual ditch management for water drainage
- ☐ Tree management
- ☐ Grazing management
- ☐ Shoreline management – particularly in areas close to the broads near the sea, to prevent flooding.

In 2015, in recognition of its national significance, the Broads area became, in effect, a national park, although it does not have the precise status of other UK national parks, largely, because unlike other parks, it has navigable waterways within it. Nevertheless, it shares the two main aims of other UK national parks, which are to conserve plants and wildlife and to act as a place of enjoyment for visitors. The current importance of the Broads can be seen in the fact that although it covers only one thousandth of the area of the UK, it has more than a quarter of its rarest wildlife.

(Based on Mason, 1990, Moss, 2001, the Broads Authority, 1988, Broads Authority, 2009, Broads Authority, 2015, Broads Forum, 2017, Broads Plan, 2017)

To provide further confirmation of the importance of seeing tourism within the context of environmental issues, the most recent plan for the Broads, created in 2017, sets out a long-term vision for this protected area, and shorter-term strategic actions under eight themes:

- ■ Managing water resources and flood risk
- ■ Sustaining landscapes for biodiversity and agriculture
- ■ Maintaining and enhancing the navigation
- ■ Conserving landscape character and the historic environment
- ■ Offering distinctive recreational experiences

- Raising awareness and understanding
- Connecting and inspiring people
- Building 'climate-smart' communities (Broads Plan, 2017)

However, not only should tourism be set within the context of wider environmental issues in the area, but events during the summer of 2017 indicate that tourism there also needs to be seen in relation to socio-cultural factors. As indicated in the case study, a major tourism activity of the Broads is the hiring of motor boats, but during the 2017 summer season, there was increasing media attention focusing on the behaviour of some of the visitors on hired cruisers. In particular, stag parties (usually young men accompanying the bridegroom-to-be, on his last night as an unmarried man) getting drunk, becoming excessively noisy, being abusive to locals and other visitors, urinating in public and engaging in various types of obscene behaviour (EDP, 2017). These, and other, types of socio-cultural impact of tourism are discussed in detail in the next chapter.

# Summary

The environment is a key resource for tourism. It is possible to subdivide the environment into the human (or built environment) and the natural environment. The environment provides some of the significant attractions for visitors. Hence, any damage to the environment may contribute to a reduction in visitor numbers.

Tourism can have important negative impacts on the environment, including footpath erosion, river and marine pollution, litter, traffic congestion, overcrowding and the creation of unsightly structures. It can seriously affect ecosystems. However, it can have beneficial impacts by contributing to an awareness of the need to conserve valued landscapes and buildings and revenue generated from visitor charges can be used to preserve and maintain threatened sites.

In relation to planning and management of environmental impacts, the concept of carrying capacity is particularly useful. Environmental and ecological carrying capacity are scientific terms and hence lend themselves to scientific forms of measuring. The concept of perceptual carrying capacity is no less important, although it may be more difficult to assess in a given context, as it is more subjective.

Although tourism has impacts on the environment, the environment can also affect tourism development. In fact, there is often a complex relationship between tourism and the environment and this relationship also needs to be seen within a wider context of other issues, as has been discussed in the case study of the Norfolk Broads.

## Student activities

1  In relation to your own area, identify parts that are particularly susceptible to environmental impacts of tourism and indicate why this is the case.

2  What are the major types of environmental impact of tourism in your country/region?

3  How can tourism negatively affect ecosystems in your area?

4  How might environmental impacts on a heavily visited small island vary from those on a remote mountain environment?

5  Why is carrying capacity a problematic concept?

6  In relation to the case study of the Norfolk Broads:

a) Why should such an area become a national park?

b) What is the importance of tourism on the Norfolk Broads?

c) In your view, should tourism be allowed on the Norfolk Broads?

d) Consider the eight themes of the 2017 Broads Plan. Where does tourism fit within the themes? Do you expect that the eight themes will work together in harmony, or is there the likelihood of conflict? Explain your response.

# References

Broads Authority (1988), *The Broads - Last enchanted land?*, Norwich: Broads Authority.

Broads Authority (2009), *Broads Plan*, Norwich: Broads Authority.

Broads Authority (2015), *Broads Plan*, Norwich: Broads Authority.

Broads Forum (2017) *Meeting of the Broads Forum*, Yare House, July 25th, Norwich.

Broads Plan (2017), *The Broads Plan*, Norwich: Broads Authority.

Doorne, S. (2000). Caves, culture and crowds: carrying capacity meets consumer sovereignty. *Journal of Sustainable Tourism*, **8** (4), 34–42.

EDP (2017) Broads Stag Parties, Boat Firms Speak Out: For or Against? *Eastern Daily Press*, July 12, Norwich, http://www.edp24.co.uk/news/environment/broads-stag-party-debate-boat-firms-argue-for-and-against-1-5101892.

Hall, C.M. and Page, S. (2014) *The Geography of Tourism and Recreation* 4th ed, London: Routledge.

Holden, A. (2000) *Environment and Tourism*, London, Routledge.

Holden, A. (2008) *Environment and Tourism*, 2nd ed., London: Routledge.

Holden, A. (2016) *Environment and Tourism*, 3rd ed., London: Routledge.

Holden, A. and Ewen, M. (2002). Understanding the motivations of ecotourists. *International Journal of Tourism Research*, **4**, 435–46.

Hopkins, D. and MacLean, K. (2014) Climate change responses and perceptions in Scotland's ski industry, *Tourism Geographies*, **16**(3), 400-414.

Hunter, C. and Green, H. (1995). *Tourism and the Environment: A Sustainable Relationship?* London: Routledge.

Krippendorf, J. (1987). *The Holiday Makers.* London: Heinemann.

Mason, P. (1990) *Tourism: Environment and Development Perspectives,* Godalming: WWF.

Moss, B. (2001) *The Broads,* London: Harper Collins.

New Zealand Tourism Board (1992). *Residents Perception and Acceptance of Tourism in Selected New Zealand Communities.* Wellington: Ministry of Tourism.

New Zealand Tourism Board (1996). *Tourism in New Zealand: Facts and Figures.* Wellington: Ministry of Tourism.

New Zealand Tourism Board (2004). *Tourism in New Zealand: Facts and Figures.* Wellington: Ministry of Tourism.

Ryan, C. (1991). *Recreational Tourism.* London: Routledge.

Swarbrooke, J. (1999). *Sustainable Tourism Management.* Wallingford: CABI Publications.

TourismNewZealand, (2013). *New Zealand Tourist Board,* accessed November 10 2014.

Williams, S. (1998) *Tourism Geography,* London: Routledge.

**7**

# 8 The Socio-cultural Impacts of Tourism

## Introduction

When discussing the socio-cultural impacts of tourism there is a need to first understand the terms *society* and *culture*. The concept of society is studied, in particular, within the subject of *sociology*. Sociology is largely concerned with the study of society and focuses on people in groups and the interaction of those in groups, their attitudes and their behaviour. *Culture* is a similar concept to society and is about how people interact as observed through social interaction, social relations and material artefacts. According to Burns and Holden (1995), when discussing culture within the context of tourism, they indicate that it consists of behavioural patterns, knowledge and values which have been acquired and transmitted through generations. Burns and Holden (1995:113) provide more detail when they indicate that "culture .... includes knowledge, belief, art, moral law, custom and any other capabilities and habits of people as members of society'"

## Key perspectives

The focus in this chapter is on the study of the impacts of tourism on people in groups. The specific groups are those who are residents of tourism areas (such people are usually referred to as *hosts*), but also the tourists themselves. Socio-cultural impacts are concerned, in addition, with impacts on the culture of the local residents, (or host population) and also with any effects on the culture of the visitors themselves. The study of socio-cultural impacts also involves ways in which culture can be used to promote tourism, and this frequently involves reference to how aspects of culture are packaged to 'sell' to tourists. The resulting effects this has on the culture itself are also topics investigated.

There are a significant number of cultural factors that can act as tourism attractions. Of particular importance, according to Ritchie and Zins, (1978) are:

- Handicrafts
- Traditions
- Gastronomy
- Art and music

- History of the area/including visual reminders
- Types of work engaged in by residents
- Architecture
- Language
- Religion (including visible manifestations)
- Education systems
- Dress
- Leisure activities.

# The nature of the impacts

Before proceeding with a discussion of specific socio-cultural impacts, it is worth considering once again the influences on the impacts of tourism which were presented in Chapter 6. All the factors discussed there are important in relation to socio-cultural impacts, however, of particular importance are the following:

- Who is involved
- What activities are engaged in
- Where tourism is taking place.

The scale of tourism can also be an important factor in terms of socio-cultural impacts, and the length of time tourism has been an activity in a particular location may significantly affect the nature of this type of impact.

8

However, in addition, the nature of both the visitors and the host population can be very influential in relation to the nature and extent of these types of impacts. For example, the culture of each of these two groups may be very similar, or very different. Visitors may come from, for example, a wealthy European country and the local population be poor residents of a Pacific island. These two groups may or may not speak the same language. They may, or may not, have the same religion, share the same beliefs, enjoy the same food or like the same music. Whether there are similarities or differences, the interaction of the two groups will be a major issue in affecting the types of impact. Nevertheless, as Burns and Holden (1995) argued, if there is a large contrast and major differences between the culture of the receiving society, or host population, and the origin culture of the tourists, then it is likely that socio-cultural impacts will be greatest. Page (2003) concurs with the point about impacts being particularly significant when cultural differences are great. Drawing on the work of Douglas and Douglas (1996), Page (2003) states that the interaction between the two groups is dependent on the following:

- The nature and extent of social, cultural and economic differences between tourists and hosts
- The ratio of visitors to residents
- The distribution and visibility of tourist developments
- The speed and intensity of development
- The extent of foreign and local employment

As with the environmental impacts and economic impacts of tourism, it is possible to categorize these effects as positive or negative. The more major positive impacts of tourism on society and culture include the following:

- The creation of employment
- The revitalisation of poor or non-industrialized regions
- The rebirth of local arts and crafts and traditional cultural activities
- The revival of social and cultural life of the local population
- The renewal of local architectural traditions
- The promotion of the need to conserve areas of outstanding beauty which have aesthetic and cultural value (Mason, 1995).

It is also the case that in some developing countries in particular, tourism can encourage greater social mobility, through changes in employment from traditional agriculture to service industries, and may result in higher wages and better job prospects.

However, tourism has had, for at least 40 years, a reputation for major detrimental effects on the society and culture of host areas. So for example, where there are very large numbers of visitors, tourism can cause overcrowding in destinations. This is likely to result in stress for both tourists and residents. Douglas and Douglas (1996) claim the ratio of tourists to locals is important in terms of negative effects. Hence, it is usually the case that the larger the number of tourists to locals, then the higher this ratio and the greater likelihood of perceived and possibly actual detrimental impacts. As noted in Chapter 7, in relation to Waitomo Caves, New Zealand, assessment of overcrowding is a subjective activity, but when tourist number greatly exceed numbers of local residents, then negative consequences of tourism are likely to be recorded.

Where tourism takes over as a major employer, traditional activities such as farming may decline. In extreme cases, regions can become over-dependent on tourism, and this effect is considered in more detail in Chapter 9 which focuses on the economic aspects of dependency on tourism.

## The reactions of the host community

Residents may find it difficult to co-exist with tourists who may not only have a different set of values to theirs, but also unlike them, are involved in leisure activities, while they are working. This problem can be made worse where tourism is a seasonal activity and residents have to modify their way of life for part of the year. In countries with strong religious codes, altered social values caused by a tourist invasion may be viewed as nationally undesirable.

In the mid-1970s, at the time that there was growing concern about both the potential, and real, negative impacts of tourism on destination regions, an important theory was put forward on the possible effects that increasing numbers of tourists could have on a host population. Doxey (1975) proposed what was termed an 'Irritation Index', or, in its shortened form, *Irridex.* Doxey's Irridex considered the relationship between tourists and locals. The main idea in Doxey's Irridex is that, over time, as the number of tourists increases, a greater hostility from locals towards tourists will emerge. The process by which this occurs is summarized in Figure 8.1.

Doxey's theory is built upon the premise that destinations will develop and grow over a period of time, although the length of time may vary from place to place. Nevertheless, Doxey suggested that whatever the time period it was likely that the process of locals' views changing from euphoria to antagonism would occur. An important implication of Doxey's theory, is that destinations may not have the ability to grow without check. Doxey's Irridex suggests that, over time, as locals become more hostile to visitors, visitor numbers will not continue to grow at the same rate as previously and may actually decline. Although regarded at the time as important, and still seen as adding to our understanding of tourist–host interactions, Doxey's Irridex was not based on any detailed empirical research, but mainly on conjecture at a time when researchers and commentators were considering seriously for the first time, the negative consequences as well as the benefits of tourism.

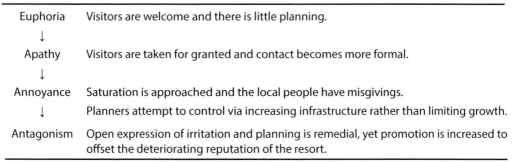

Figure 8.1: Doxey's Irritation Index

Several pieces of research have been conducted on socio-cultural impacts of tourism to apply major theoretical perspectives. One important study was conducted, in the Scottish Highlands, by Getz, who attempted to apply, in particular, Doxey's theory. The study is unusual, in that it is one of the relatively few attempts in tourism to conduct a longitudinal study. In reality, it was two 'snapshots' taken at different dates, as Getz investigated the Spey valley, in Scotland, in the late 1970s and then again in the early 1990s. As return visits to the same location are uncommon in tourism, the findings are particularly important. The sample size and questions used for Getz' studies of 1978 and 1992 were fairly similar, but the actual respondents involved on each occasion were different. Each of the studies used a sample of 130 households and the main findings were as follows:

- Residents were generally supportive of tourism on both occasions.

- Although on each occasion there were positive views on tourism, by 1992 there was much more of a negative feeling. This was attributed to tourism being perceived as less successful than had been hoped in the 1970s.

- Those directly involved in tourism were more likely to be positive about the activity.

- Although there was some support for Doxey's theory that, over time, locals become more negative towards tourism, the change in attitudes seemed more linked to a general feeling of economic depression than concerned solely with tourism. The surveys indicated that residents were particularly concerned that there were few viable alternatives to tourism in the area, so despite the lower satisfaction with tourism's impacts by 1992, it was still believed to be the best alternative.

- Over the 14-year period between 1978 and 1992, the number of tourists did not appear to have gone beyond a threshold in Speyside, so the there was little evidence of the views of residents as indicated in the latter stages of Doxey's theory.

In summary, the research by Getz (1978, 1994) suggested that, unlike the theoretical statements of Doxey, in the context of the Scottish Highlands, the attitudes of residents did not appear to change greatly over time. Although Getz noted some increase in negative attitudes to tourism in this time period, he discovered that locals' attitudes to tourism were closely linked to economic fluctuations, as well as to an awareness of the lack of viable alternatives to tourism in the local region.

## ■ The demonstration effect

One of the more significant socio-cultural impacts of tourism is referred to as the 'demonstration' effect. This depends on there being visible differences between tourists and hosts (see Burns and Holden, 1995 and Douglas and Douglas, 1996). Such a situation can occur in some contexts, particularly developing countries. In the demonstration effect, it is theorized, that simply observing tourists will lead to behavioural changes in the resident population (Williams, 1998). The demonstration effect can arise when local people note the superior material possessions of the visitors and the locals then aspire to have these possessions themselves. This may have positive effects, in that it can encourage residents to adopt more productive patterns of behavior.

However, more frequently the demonstration effect can be disruptive, in that locals become resentful of the tourists, because they are unable to obtain the goods and the accompanying lifestyle as demonstrated by the visitors (Burns and Holden, 1995). It has been noted that young people are particularly susceptible to the demonstration effect (Burns and Holden, 1995). Tourism may then be held responsible for generational divisions in society between the young and old. The demonstration effect may also encourage the brighter, more able, more motivated younger members of a society to migrate from rural areas in search of the 'demonstrated' lifestyle in urban areas or even overseas. It seems most likely that the demonstration effect will occur where the contacts between residents and visitors are relatively superficial and short lived (Williams, 1998), which is the case in many forms of tourism. Under these conditions, the local residents may not have the time to gain perspectives on the possible negative aspects of the tourist culture, but respond only to what they perceive as positive factors.

## ■ Acculturation

Another process, known as acculturation, may occur when the contact is for a longer period and is deeper. Williams (1998) noted that when two cultures come into contact for a period of time there will be an exchange of ideas and probably products. If this time is sufficiently long, then there will be a tendency for the cultures to converge and in this way they will become more alike. However, as one culture is likely to be stronger than the other, this process will not necessarily be balanced. As with the demonstration effect, it is in the relationships between the developed world and developing world, particularly, where the process is most likely to occur. The USA has one of the most powerful cultures, and it is most frequently American culture that predominates over one from the developing country in any such meeting of cultures. This particular process of acculturation has been referred to as the 'MacDonaldisation' or 'Coca-colaisation' of global cultures (Mason, 2003; MacCannell, 1995). Hence, one of the perceived negative effects of this acculturation process is the reduction in the diversity of global cultures and increasing homogenisation of cultures.

Less than 20 years after the end of the Second World War, in the early 1960s, prior to the age of mass tourism, a number of researchers and commentators viewed the relationship between tourists from the developed world and residents of destinations in developing countries as a potentially positive one (see Tomlejnovic and Faulkner, 2000). These writers believed that tourism could act a positive force in helping with international understanding. For example, the Swiss writer Hunzicker (1961) suggested that tourism was the 'noblest instrument of this century' for achieving international understanding. Hunzicker claimed that irrespective of language, race, creed, political beliefs and economic standing, tourism could bring people together and the contact between tourists and local residents would lead to a better understanding of the attitudes of each group and help overcome differences between them. This process would enable individuals to develop international friendships and benefit international relations.

However, approximately a quarter of a century later, views on tourism's potential to contribute to greater international understanding had changed. Writing after at least 20 years of mass tourism, another Swiss author Krippendorf (1987) suggested that tourism contributed to misunderstanding and the reinforcing of stereotypes, rather than to greater international understanding. Krippendorf considered this process would occur, in particular, where there was a large differences between cultures. In this context, tourists from developed countries would be likely to view the local residents of a developing country as 'primitive natives' and the local residents would view the tourists as very rich, never having to work and therefore as 'unrestrained foreigners'.

Acculturation, and hence homogenisation of cultures, became an important process towards the end of the 20th century. Nevertheless, the desire of many

**8**

tourists to experience a different culture is still a major motivation for tourist visits (Ryan, 1997). Tourists wish to see and experience at first hand, the actual culture and its manifestation, in terms of art, music, dance and handicrafts, of a destination. One beneficial effect of this desire has been a revival of traditional crafts as well the development of new activities, in a number of locations, including, for example, Bali (Cukier and Wall, 1994; Mason, 1995). In Bali, as in other countries where this process has occurred, there has been a related growth of a souvenir trade that has made a significant contribution to the local economy.

## ■ Authenticity

However there can be negative consequences of this desire of visitors to actually experience the supposed 'real' culture of a destination, as it has brought into question the authenticity of the tourist experience. In some developing world locations, for example, Bali and the Solomon Islands, and a number of developed world locations with indigenous cultures, such as Arctic Norway and Finland, and Northern Canada, there has been a high demand for cultural artefacts and cultural performances. This has meant that 'experiences' have become packaged for convenient consumption by visitors. Such commoditisation has led to questions concerning the authenticity of the experience for tourists. The commoditisation has contributed to the creation of pseudo-events that may be based on a 'real' local activity, but have been packaged for tourists. These events tend to share the following characteristics:

- They are carefully planned and choreographed, rather than being spontaneous;
- They are designed and packaged to be performed to order, at times that are convenient for tourists;
- They hold, at best, an ambiguous relationship to real elements on which they are based (Mason, 1995; Williams, 1998).

If such pseudo-events are successful in terms of gaining a large enough visitor audience and generate sufficient revenue, there is a danger, as Williams (1998) noted, that they eventually *become* the authentic events and replace the original events or practice.

One such example of the creation of events for tourist consumption is the *keechak* dance of Bali. As Mason (1995) reported, this dance, part of a traditional Hindu religious ritual, was performed in Bali originally only on special occasions. However, it has been shortened, taken out of its religious context and performed on a frequent, often daily basis, to paying tourist groups for many years. It is possible that tourists who know and understand the origins of the dance, when observing an inauthentic pseudo-event, may feel cheated. However, this assumes that there are tourists who have the knowledge to comprehend the local traditions, and it is likely that many may not even be aware that they are watching a pseudo-event. Whether tourists realize that the event is authentic (or not) may not necessarily affect their enjoyment of the experience and it can be argued that this type of performance may actually relieve pressure upon local communities, provide them with an income and even help to protect the performances' real cultural basis (Mason, 1995). However, there is danger that the local performers in a tourist-orientated activity, may eventually forget the true meaning and importance of the practice or event (Mason, 1995).

Much of the preceding discussion has focused on the interaction between tourists and residents of tourist destinations, with an emphasis on the effects on the resident population. However, contact between tourists and residents is also very likely to have an impact on the tourists themselves. There is increasing evidence that the impacts of experiences on tourists can lead to, not only changes in their thinking and attitudes, but may also result in behavioural changes. For example, a growing number of tourists visited the Antarctic continent in the last decade of the 20th century. However, the continent still remains relatively inaccessible and expensive to visit and so for many who travel there it is a once in a lifetime journey (Maher, 2011). Those who visit often have a deep interest in the natural world and in particular the wildlife of the continent. It would appear that those who have visited, return with not only increased knowledge, but also a greater awareness of the need to conserve Antarctica's wilderness environment (Mason and Legg, 1999). The effects of visiting the Antarctic on tourists is discussed in more detail in Chapter 13.

**8**

## Researching socio-cultural impacts

A significant problem in recognizing and therefore assessing socio-cultural impacts is that it is not easy to differentiate these from other impacts and hence particularly difficult to measure them. This partly explains why these impacts have been regarded in the past as less significant than for example, economic impacts. The research into socio-cultural impacts has frequently involved residents completing questionnaire surveys or being interviewed to assess the impact on themselves, or on others. This form of research tends to be more qualitative and subjective in comparison with the more quantitative approaches used to assess some types of environmental impacts such as carrying capacity or to measure economic impacts of tourism. This qualitative approach is less acceptable, for some commentators, than quantitative approaches, as it is argued that such an approach is less scientific. However, a number of criticisms of a quantitative approach can also be made, as those who support the more qualitative approach may argue their techniques are generally more flexible, can achieve a higher response rate and the 'data' is likely to be richer, in depth and hence more meaningful (see Tribe, 2000).

In the mid-1990s, research using both quantitative and qualitative techniques was conducted into resident attitudes to tourism growth on the Greek island of Samos (Harlambopolous and Pizam, 1996). The research involved a 20% sample of the resident population of one town, Pythagorean, on Samos. The results from this research, which involved a questionnaire survey and interviews, provide a particularly good example of the attitudes to tourism, and are summarized below.

- In terms of the sample, as many as 71% of those questioned were involved in a tourism-related business and 59% had a family member involved in tourism.
- In general, residents were strongly supportive of tourism.
- Over 80% indicated that the image of Pythagorean had improved since tourism developed.
- Respondents were in favour of increasing visitor numbers.
- Almost 90% of the residents perceived that tourists were different from them.
- The major positive factors resulting from tourism were: employment, personal income and standard of living.
- The negative factors resulting from tourism, were, in order of importance: drug addiction, fighting/brawls, vandalism, sexual harassment, prostitution and crime in general.
- The researchers found that those with direct involvement in tourism had more positive views on it.
- Even those with no personal involvement indicated that tourism had positive effects, but were generally less keen on it than those directly involved.
- The young were generally more in favour of tourism.
- The older respondents were less in favour of tourism.
- Better educated residents were more likely to have positive attitudes to tourism.
- Increasing sexual permissiveness was the only factor seen negatively by all groups except the young.

A significant issue with regard to the social impacts of tourism, as referred to above, is that it can be difficult to separate socio-cultural impacts from other impacts. However, it may also be a problem to distinguish between impacts of other socio-economic activities and the impacts of tourism on society. In other words, changes may not result from the direct effects of tourism, but broader societal change which is not actually directly related to tourism. This can be the case when tourism has been an important activity for a lengthy period, such as in the case of Samos discussed above, and also in relation to changes discussed in Getz' studies of Scotland. However, if tourism has not been a significant activity in a particular location, and is then introduced, it may be easier to assess any changes, and then investigate these, to reveal if they can be attributed to tourism. The following case study provides a context of this kind, in that it discusses a tourism development before it actually occurred, in an area where tourism was prior to the development, of relatively little importance.

## Case study: Local residents attitudes to tourism development in the Pohangina Valley, New Zealand

The Pohangina Valley is a North Island New Zealand rural backwater, which has generally remained off the beaten track. The location could be described in tourism marketing language as 'undiscovered and unspoiled'. The area was settled by Europeans from the late 19th century onwards. A number of small scattered settlements of fewer than 100 people grew up and the region reached its peak population in the 1930s. The population then declined for almost 50 years until the early 1980s, when a number of new migrants moved into the area, but it remained sparsely populated, at the start of the research on which this case study is based, in the late 1990s.

The development, which is the focus of this study, caused much local interest and controversy. It originally involved a proposal to develop an old school house in the township of Pohangina into a café/bar for the use of locals, but also to attract tourists. Although this first proposal was withdrawn after opposition to the private use of a communal facility, a new proposal was submitted involving the establishment of the cafe/bar using an existing private house just outside the Pohangina township. However, this proposal was strongly opposed and even led to death threats for some of the intended developers, a group of eight local individuals. This reaction contributed to much media interest, particularly from the local evening paper, which for several days ran front-page stories about the proposal and related issues. The proposal was submitted to the local district council and after a one month objection period had elapsed, it was granted planning permission. A questionnaire survey, which was the main research instrument from which the material for this study has been derived, was distributed within a few days of the granting of planning permission. The results of the survey, completed by 47% of local residents, were:

☐ As tourism was at such an early stage, residents could not even be considered to be at the euphoria stage of Doxey's (1975) Irridex theory. Generally, residents were in favour of the proposed development, but a significant minority (approximately a quarter), were opposed to it. The study indicated that the community, like many others, was heterogeneous not homogeneous in its views on tourism, in relation to the perceived impacts of tourism.

☐ The respondents' views were based on perceived impacts, as the development had not yet occurred and respondents tended to view these impacts from their own perspective, without necessarily any reference to tourism, which is probably not surprising given the general lack of tourism development in the area at the time. Residents believed positive impacts would be the establishment of a meeting place, provision of a place close to home to obtain a meal and drink and the related reduction in travelling time to such locations. Some responses made reference to tourism when indicating the proposed development would create jobs, attract

8

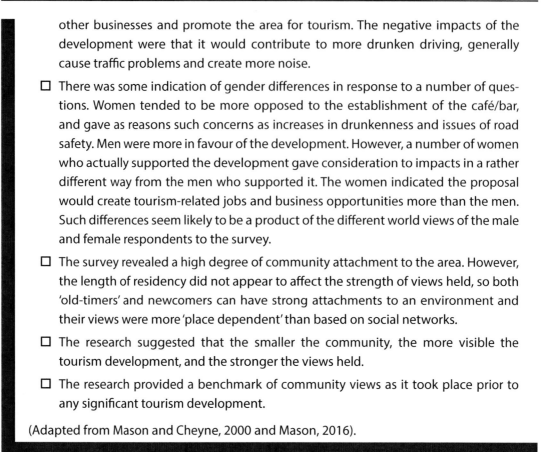

other businesses and promote the area for tourism. The negative impacts of the development were that it would contribute to more drunken driving, generally cause traffic problems and create more noise.

☐ There was some indication of gender differences in response to a number of questions. Women tended to be more opposed to the establishment of the café/bar, and gave as reasons such concerns as increases in drunkenness and issues of road safety. Men were more in favour of the development. However, a number of women who actually supported the development gave consideration to impacts in a rather different way from the men who supported it. The women indicated the proposal would create tourism-related jobs and business opportunities more than the men. Such differences seem likely to be a product of the different world views of the male and female respondents to the survey.

☐ The survey revealed a high degree of community attachment to the area. However, the length of residency did not appear to affect the strength of views held, so both 'old-timers' and newcomers can have strong attachments to an environment and their views were more 'place dependent' than based on social networks.

☐ The research suggested that the smaller the community, the more visible the tourism development, and the stronger the views held.

☐ The research provided a benchmark of community views as it took place prior to any significant tourism development.

(Adapted from Mason and Cheyne, 2000 and Mason, 2016).

As noted above, research on the Greek island of Samos suggested that socio-cultural effects tend to be unbalanced in relation to different groups in society. In the Samos example, those who were more actively involved in tourism were more likely to be supportive of it. The case study of the Pohangina, New Zealand also indicated that there can be gender differences in relation to attitudes to tourism, with women generally more opposed to tourism development than men. There is also a major gender dimension to some socio-cultural impacts of tourism.

## ■ Sex tourism in South East Asia

There is now significant evidence to indicate that women are on the receiving end of different effects of tourism, particularly within the context of the developing world. The exploitation of mainly women (but also children – both male and female) through prostitution in some developing countries was a feature of the last three decades of the 20th century and has continued into the 21st century. Prostitution is only one form of sex tourism (massage parlours, sex shops, sex cinemas are other examples), but it is particularly strong in developing countries. Although sex was identified as one among several motivations for tourism by Ryan (1991) (see Chapter 2), sex tourism is the activity of 'travelling with express intent of engaging in sexual activity' (Page and O'Connell, 2009:647).

In a number of Southeast Asian countries, prostitution and some form of sex tourism have been in existence for a long period. Such areas include Thailand, the Philippines, Korea, and Taiwan. In these countries, traditional attitudes means that the use of female prostitutes by males is a relatively common practice. Therefore this activity does not carry the same stigma as it would in a Western society. Although prostitution is not necessarily legal in most countries of Southeast Asia, the laws tend not to enforced and it has become institutionalized in countries such as Thailand and the Philippines.

What has been unusual in the past 50 years or so, compared with the more distant past, has been the growing scale of sex tourism and that it increasingly involved international tourists. The great majority of these international tourists originate in developed countries (O'Grady, 1980; Hall, 1992; Mason, 2016). One of the reasons for this has been the cost differential for sexual services in the developing world compared with the developed world (Hall, 1992). Other reasons include the difference in attitudes to women in Southeast Asian societies compared with Western societies, and the actual status of women in Western societies and Southeast Asian societies, respectively (Mason, 1995). Additionally, until the late 1990s, sex tourism in, for example, the Philippines and Thailand was strongly promoted and marketed to mainly male tourists from Australia, the United States and Europe.

**8**

In attempting to trace its history, Hall (1992) suggested that sex tourism in Southeast Asia passed through four stages. The first stage was indigenous prostitution, in which women were subjugated within the patriarchal nature of most Southeast Asian societies and this dates back several hundred years. The second stage came about as a result of economic colonialism. An example of this was American military personnel engaging in sex with prostitutes in Thailand during 'rest and relaxation' from the Vietnam War. This was made possible as a result of the infrastructure that existed for indigenous prostitution. The third stage involved international tourists replacing the military personnel. Hall suggested that the authoritarian nature of many Asian political regimes meant that sex was often considered as an important commodity that could be traded in an attempt to achieve economic growth, with little regard actually given to individuals involved in providing the sexual services. This attracted media condemnation from Western societies, but also is likely to have stimulated increased sex tourism, as potential customers noted that the attitudes of the authorities were not condemnatory of the tourist's activities. In the early 1990s, in the fourth stage, Hall suggested that standards of living in Southeast Asia had been improved, meaning less dependency on sex tourism as a means to economic development.

In the last decade of the 20th century, there was growing awareness of the spread of AIDS via prostitutes in developing countries (Mason, 1995). This, coupled with the attempts of some politicians and influential members of Thai society to move the image of the destination away from one where sex tourism is a key activity, appears to be reducing the dependency on sex tourism, in the early part of the 21st century.

However, sex tourism is not confined to South East Asia and neither is it the case that it is men who are always those seeking sex, and women providing it. For example, in The Gambia in West Africa and Barbados in the West Indies, since at least the early 1990s, 'beach boys' have been performing sexual services for female travelers, many of whom are from Europe and North America, for financial, or some other form of, reward.

During the first years of the 21st century it is becoming clear that there are significant numbers of pa edophiles, mostly from developed countries, who are seeking to have sex with children. For these people (almost always men) this activity would be a criminal offence in their own country in the developed world, so instead they turn to locations where they believe they will not face punishment and the developing world has been the setting for this, largely because authorities in developing countries, such as Thailand, Vietnam and Cambodia, have rarely prosecuted the foreign tourists involved. However, more recently, partly through campaigns run by pressure groups, such as Tourism Concern in the UK, and as a result of sectors of the developed world media applying pressure on their own governments, as well as closer liaison between the authorities in the origin and destination countries, those involved are being prosecuted – either where the men have committed the offence, or on their return home. Nevertheless, this form of 'cultural imperialism' (Page and O'Connell, 2009:541) has not yet been eradicated and seems likely to continue until attitudes change and economic conditions in developing countries improve. The following case study provides more details on this form of activity, through a discussion of the nature and causes of, as well as those involved in, child sex tourism in Thailand.

## Case study: Child sex tourism in Thailand

### The background

International sex tourism in Thailand can be traced back to the presence of American military in the early 1960s on rest and recreation leave during the Vietnam War. Today it is part of a large sex industry that includes prostitution, pornography and human trafficking. It is important to realise that local men make up the majority of the purchasers of sex, but foreign tourists are a significant proportion of these.

As child sexual abuse takes place largely behind closed doors and is therefore hidden from public scrutiny, reliable figures are difficult to compile and cases of the activity problematic to document. However in the first decade of the 21st century, available figures estimate that some 30,000 to 40,000 children under eighteen years of age, not including foreign children, were being exploited as prostitutes. However, the number of Thai children in the sex industry has been falling largely as a result of improvements in the economy, better educational opportunities and changes in the law.

In fact, many of the children being exploited have been more recently from neighbouring countries that have been trafficked into Thailand. Some of the exploited children are ethnic hill tribe children trafficked within the country from the north of Thailand. The trafficking from here has been organised by criminal networks that operate much of the sex tourism industry. These criminal gangs have been involved in drug smuggling and they have used pre-existing drug smuggling routes for trafficking people. According to the US State Department's Trafficking in Persons Report (2005), "the widespread sex tourism industry in Thailand encourages trafficking for commercial sexual exploitation". The US report noted that the government is failing to protect child trafficking victims, because it continues to treat them as illegal immigrants and deports them, instead of providing them with protection or investigating the abuse that they have been subjected to.

Procuring children for sex is illegal in Thailand, so the transactions generally take place off-street in bars, brothels or hotel rooms, although sex tourists have been known to openly pick up children on the streets. Although pimps, who act as mediators between women and customers, are not that common (as in some developed countries), they are often involved in the exploitation of children. Relatives and acquaintances also play a role in coercing or persuading children to 'help' the family economically by prostituting themselves. The main areas where sex tourism thrives, in addition to Bangkok and Patpong, are the beach destinations resorts, especially in Phuket and Pattaya, where there are large numbers of international tourists.

Thailand signed the UN Convention on the Rights of the Child in March, 1992, and accepts the definition of a child as anyone not over 18 years of age. However, under domestic law there are different ages of consent depending on the crime committed. Those committing forms of indecent assault or rape will be treated differently if the age of the victim is between 15 and 18 compared with one under the age of 15, with those committing a crime against a child under 15 in theory receiving a longer prison sentence.

The lengthier sentences are reserved for the procurers, seducers and traffickers of children into prostitution who face up to 20 years in prison. Parents who allow a child to enter into prostitution also face punishment. The law also has provisions to protect witnesses and victims in court, although these are not widely used. There are also detailed provisions for punishing traffickers. Although these laws have been used, relatively few of those accused have been sentenced to long terms in prisons and very few foreign tourist who have been arrested have subsequently been imprisoned.

While British tourists who commit sexual offences in Thailand can be prosecuted there, they can also be prosecuted in the UK for crimes committed while abroad. Under the UK Sexual Offences Act, 2003, people can be prosecuted for a crime that is viewed as a criminal offence in both countries. Therefore if a tourist sexually abuses a child in Thailand, they can be tried in the UK as both countries have laws against this offence.

### Who are the children and how do they become involved?

Children from various backgrounds are being sexually exploited in the country. While there has been a general reduction in the number of Thai children in the sex industry, since 2000, this is not true for all groups. The northern hill tribe children are especially vulnerable to internal trafficking due to government policies, but the majority of trafficked children have come from Burma, Laos, China and Cambodia.

The major reasons why and how children are commercially sexually exploited are:

☐ **Poverty:** A third of the population lives on less than US$2 a day and in the agricultural northeast one in six people lives on less than US$1 a day.

☐ **Ethnic hill tribe children:** There are approximately 800,000 to 900,000 hill tribe people in the border region of northern Thailand. They suffer from high levels of poverty in relation to the general population and most lack citizenship cards. This means that they do not have access to health care or primary school, which limits their education and employment opportunities. This discrimination makes the children and women especially vulnerable to trafficking and other forms of sexual abuse.

☐ **Trafficked children:** Many children are trafficked into or within the country through criminal networks, acquaintances, former trafficking victims and corrupt border police and immigration officials who transport them to brothels across Thailand. Because foreign children are unable to speak the Thai language and are often considered illegal immigrants, they are particularly vulnerable to physical abuse and exploitation. Some of these children have been lured into the country with promises of jobs as waitresses, bar workers or cleaners, but end up working as prostitutes.

☐ **Sense of duty:** According to traditional customs, the first duty of a girl is to support her family in any way she can. Due to this sense of duty (and often because of the need to pay off family debts), many girls have been forced into prostitution.

☐ **Wealthy tourists:** The sex tourism industry hinges on the profits made from wealthy tourists, and children seeking to escape poverty are often lured into sexual activity. Street children are easily picked up by sex tourists and abused in hotels. Relatives are also known to coerce young girls into sex with tourists in private homes or hotels.

☐ **Foreign child sex offenders:** Reportedly, some foreign sex offenders who live in Thailand have taken up jobs giving access to children or are involved in trafficking children, or organising sex tours for others.

### Who are the abusers?

Male sex tourists from Europe and North America, as well as men from neighbouring countries, fuel the child sex industry. However, local men are also involved. But, it is the economic power of foreign tourists that makes the sex industry so lucrative for organised criminal gangs. These men include both the opportunistic and the paedophile sex tourists who are to be found mainly around the well-known beach resorts, such as Pattaya and in Bangkok. There have been allegations that foreign paedophiles living in Thailand who traffic and continually rotate children around the country's tourist destinations so as to avoid detection by the police. There are also reports of foreign paedophiles setting up residence in the country and abusing children either in their own residences or at places of work allowing access to children.

According to research, British men who frequent prostitutes and who may sexually abuse children in Thailand can be characterised within three different categories: the 'Macho Lads', 'Mr. Average' and the 'Cosmopolitan Men'. Macho Lads are in their early twenties, travel in groups and seek sex with many girls or women and congregate around the resort of Pattaya. 'Mr. Average' is generally older, on a second or third trip to Thailand and seeks a longer-term relationship with a prostitute. 'Cosmopolitan Men', well-read and travelled, fail to see any similarity between themselves and other male sex tourists. However, what all these men have in common is their denial of the exploitative nature of their activities. They may indeed rationalize their behaviour as providing benefits for the women or child prostitutes and the local economy. Overwhelmingly these men have been attracted to Thailand because sexual services are readily availability and choice is immense and they are cheaper than in many other countries.

**How is the tourism industry involved and what can it do?**

According to the Tourism Authority of Thailand (TAT) there were twelve million tourists in 2004 and this had risen top over fourteen million in 2013. Tourism is a major foreign currency earner, accounting for as much as 6% of GDP. Sex tourism is an integral part of this. The government has been trying for 20 years or so to reverse the image of Thailand as a haven for sex tourists and paedophiles. In 1996, it identified the trafficking of children for sexual purposes as a priority issue and framed a national policy and action plan to prevent it. In 1999, together with NGOs and intergovernmental organisations, the government came up with a *"Memorandum of understanding on common guidelines of practices for agencies concerned with cases where women and children are victims of human trafficking"*. This is meant to aid police officers in filing charges against those suspected of trafficking offences and protecting victims. Since 2003, child protection officers have been monitoring offences against minors in Pattaya, and carrying out awareness-raising campaigns to encourage people to report abuses. However, arrests and prosecutions of offenders remain relatively low, despite all these and previous measures, and hill tribe children remain excluded from many of the prevention programmes and victim services.

The government is also working with the tourism industry, non-governmental and international organisations to provide young people with skills and employment opportunities to widen their options. The TAT has worked with tourist police in detecting and prosecuting sex tourism operators found guilty of organising sex tours. UNICEF has teamed up with 18 hotels to provide job training in hotel work for young people from poor rural families.

Adapted from ECPAT UK - End Child Prostitution Pornography and Trafficking, (undated).

# Summary

There is a range of both positive and negative socio-cultural impacts of tourism. Much has been written about the supposed negative impacts, including the demonstration effect, cultural damage, authenticity and specific issues such as increases in sex tourism, drug taking and crime in general. The negative consequences have been noted, particularly where there is a major cultural difference between the tourists and the local population. Assessing and measuring socio-cultural impacts is not straightforward. Most research has relied on the attitudes of a range of respondents, particularly local residents, but also tourists themselves and other players in tourism, and this information has frequently been gathered via questioning of a sample of respondents. As local communities are not homogeneous, socio-cultural impacts are perceived differently by different individuals.

A significant amount of research has also been conducted in an attempt to apply various theories, such as that of Doxey (1975) to specific contexts. Empirical research tends to suggest that local residents in many locations are willing to accept some negative consequences as long as tourism is perceived as bringing some benefits. This is particularly so where tourism is one of a small range of choices. One finding of this research is that men and women often view the socio-cultural impacts differently. There is also a gender difference in relation to the exploitation of women as prostitutes, as part of the sex tourism industry in many countries, both developed and developing. A relatively recent aspect of the sex tourism industry, particularly in developing countries, has been the exploitation of children and this has been discussed via a case study focusing on Thailand.

## Student activities

1   In relation to tourism activity in your area, identify the main types of socio-cultural impact. Arrange these impacts under the headings of 'positive' and 'negative'.

2   What aspect of your own culture, that is currently not being used, could be packaged and commoditized for tourist consumption. What could be the impacts of this commoditisation on your culture?

3   Under what conditions would Doxey's theory apply?

4   What would you suggest are the main reasons for the responses obtained in the survey conducted on the Greek island of Samos?

5   Getz's findings from his research in the Spey Valley, Scotland were not closely related to Doxey's theory? What reasons would you give for this?

6   Why has sex tourism become so important in society in countries such as the Philippines and Thailand? What factors make it difficult to stop sex tourism being a prominent tourism activity in countries?

7   Why has Thailand become a significant location for child sex tourism?

8   If you were a politician in Thailand, what would you try to do about child sex tourism?

# References

Burns, P. and Holden, A. (1995). *Tourism: A New Perspective*. London: Prentice Hall.

Cukier, J. and Wall, G. (1994). Tourism and employment perspectives from Bali. *Tourism Management*, **14**, 195–201.

Douglas, N. and Douglas, N. (1996) The social and cultural impacts of tourism in the Pacific in C.M. Hall and S. Page (eds) *Tourism in the Pacfic: Issues and Cases,* pp 49-64, London: International Thomson Business Press.

Doxey. (1975). A causation theory of resident visitor irritants. In *The Sixth Annual Conference Proceedings of the Travel Research Association*, pp. 195–8.

Getz, D. (1978). Tourism and population change: long term impacts of tourism in the Badenoch and Strathspey District of the Scottish Highlands. *Scottish Geographical Magazine*, **102**, 113–26.

Getz, D. (1994). Residents' attitudes to tourism. *Tourism Management*, **15**, 247–58.

Hall, C. M. (1992). Sex tourism in South East Asia. In *Tourism in the Developing World* (D. Harrison, ed.). Chichester: John Wiley and Sons.

Hunzicker, R. (1961). Human relations in tourism development, *Revue de Tourisme*, **1**(3),90.

Krippendorf, J. (1987). *The Holiday Makers*. London: Heinemann

MacCannell, D. (1995). *The Tourist Papers*. London: Routledge

Maher, P (2011) Antarctic human dimensions: Ambassadors for the experience, in Maher, P., Stewart, E. and Luck, M. (eds) *Polar Tourism: Human, Environmental and Governance Dimensions*, New York: Cognizant Communications, 121-141.

Mason, P. (1995)*Tourism: Environment and Development Perspectives*, 2nd ed Godalming: WWF

Mason, P. (2003) *Tourism Impacts, Planning and Management*, Oxford: Butterworth-Heinemann

Mason, P. (2016) *Tourism Impacts, Planning and Management*, 3rd ed., London: Routledge.

Mason, P. and Cheyne, J. (2000). Resident attitudes to tourism development. *Annals of Tourism Research*, **27** (2), 391–412.

Mason, P. and Legg, S. (1999). Antarctic tourism: activities, impacts, management issues and a proposed research agenda. *Pacific Tourism Review*, **3**, 71–84.

O'Grady, R. (1980). *Third World Stopover*. Geneva: Risk Books, World Council of Churches.

Page, S. (2003) *Tourism Management*, Oxford: Butterworth Heinemann

Page, S. J. and O'Connell, J. (2009) *Tourism: A modern synthesis*, 3rd ed. Andover: South Western Cengage Learning

Ritchie, J. and Zins, M. (1978). Culture as a determinant of the attractiveness of a tourist region. *Annals of Tourism Research*, **5**, 252–67.

Ryan, C. (1991). *Recreational Tourism*. London: Routledge.

Ryan, C. (1997). *The Tourist Experience*. London: Cassell.

Tomlejnovic, R. and Faulkner, B. (2000). Tourism and world peace: a conundrum for the twenty-first century. In B. Faulkner, G. Moscardo and E. Laws, eds., *Tourism in the Twenty First Century*. London: Continuum.

Tribe, J. (2000). The philosophic practitioner. *Annals of Tourism Research*, **27** (3), 437–51.

Williams, S. (1998) *Tourism Geography*, London: Routledge.

# 9 The Economic Impacts of Tourism

## Introduction

For approximately 40 years from the early 1960s, the 'impacts of tourism' was the most researched topic in tourism, and economic impacts were more researched than any other type in this period. When, in the late 1980s, Pearce discussed research on tourism impacts, he stated that the geographical focus of this research, was the tourism destination. As Pearce (1989:2) indicated:

> Studies of the impact of tourist development on a destination or destinations have been the largest single element of tourism research … and has concentrated on the effects of income and employment.

Despite this quotation coming from nearly 30 years ago, and taking into account the development of many different research areas in tourism since then, it is still the case that economic impact studies are a key focus in tourism research. Although, as has been stated in Chapter 6, economic impacts of tourism are linked to, and cannot easily be separated from, other types of impact, largely in an attempt to assist with understanding, economic impacts are discussed in this chapter separately from other tourism impacts.

## Key perspectives

Chapter 6 provided a general indication of the key influences on the impacts of tourism, but of particular importance in relation to economic impacts are:

- Scale of tourism activities
- When tourism occurs (particularly whether tourism is a seasonal activity)
- The historical development of tourism (with a particular emphasis on infrastructure for tourism) (Mason, 2016).

Measuring the economic impacts may appear at first sight to be an easy process. If, for example, a tourist buys an ice cream at an ice cream parlour in a tourism destination, then it should be obvious that the owner of the shop will financially benefit. They will receive the price of the ice cream (in economic terms they will derive revenue) and, simply stated, will make a profit, if the price exceeds the cost of producing and selling the ice cream. However, the amount of revenue gained may depend on a number of factors, including where the ingredients come from and how easy they are to source, be they local, from another part of a country or overseas, the cost of the ingredients, where the ice cream is made, whether the staff selling the ice cream are part-time or full-time, seasonal or permanent, and if the ice cream parlour is open all year, or just during the tourist season. It is therefore likely that the revenue and hence profit will vary according to different combinations of these factors.

The focus on an ice cream parlour is an example of micro-economics, and as should be clear in the discussion above, it affects just one individual business. However, data and statistics on economic aspects of tourism are usually expressed in what are known as macro-economic terms. These are factors that affect a whole economy. Hence they will be, for example, at the national or possibly regional level. Such information can be then compared internationally and an indication of the importance of tourism, (or any other economic activity) to a specific country's or region's economy, be gained. Such economic factors will include jobs (or employment), regional development and what is known as Gross Domestic Product (GDP).

These macro-economic activities are particularly important economic measures as they add together, or *aggregate,* individual economic activities. Hence, GDP is an aggregate of the total productivity of a country's economy and provides an indication of the size of the economy. GDP is the value of goods and services produced domestically and is usually indicated over a specific time period, such as a year (Tribe, 2011). The International Monetary Fund defined GDP :

> GDP measures the monetary value of final goods and services - that is,
> those that are bought by the final user - produced in a country in a given
> period of time (say a quarter or a year) (IMF, 2014).

GDP may be given as a total figure, using a currency such as dollars, euros or pounds. Alternatively it may be the total figure in monetary terms, divided by the total number of people living in a country. In this way it as expression of productivity per inhabitant, or *per capita.*

There is a great variation in GDP geographically, partly because some countries are spatially very large, including the USA, China and India, while others are small, including islands such as Fiji and Mauritius. GDP also varies because some countries produce manufactured goods, others make agricultural products, and yet others have an economy dominated by services, including banking and insurance. Tourism would be included as a service industry. In the past, economies where manufacturing is important would have high *per capita* GDP. However, in the past 30 years or so, economies with a significant proportion of service industries have had high *per capita* GDP. The stage at which an economy is found can also affect the amount of GDP, with some countries having a history of several hundred years of significant economic activity accompanied by high manufacturing activity, whilst others are at a far earlier stage of such development.

In relation to GDP and tourism there are great variations in tourism's share of this economic measure internationally, but in 2014 when taking all countries into account, it exceeded 3% of total global GDP (WTTC, 2015). Several European countries obtain at least 5% of their GDP from tourism, which makes it particularly significant in these countries (WTTC, 2015).

# Positive economic impacts

As was discussed in Chapter 6, different forms of tourism impacts can be considered under the headings of either positive or negative. In relation to economic impacts the following have been considered to be positive effects (Lickorish, 1994):

- Contribution to government revenues;
- Contribution to foreign exchange earnings;
- Generation of employment;
- Contribution to regional development.

In relation to these effects, **contribution to government revenues** is particularly important. This can be recognized and measured, for example, in relation to the amount of taxes paid by businesses that are directly involved in tourism, such as hotels and airlines. Government revenues can also be the result of, for example, value added tax that is paid by tourists who buy food and drink in a bar or public house. However, depending on the circumstances, it may be difficult to assess whether the revenue has come from local residents or visitors. It may also be a problem to separate revenue gained from international visitors from that obtained in relation to domestic visitors.

The **contribution of tourism to foreign exchange earnings** is usually regarded as the amount of money obtained by governments, and input to the economy, from international visitors. It may be represented in government accounts as an export, as it is in effect a sale of a home-produced commodity to an overseas buyer. The difference between this form of export and conventional exports is that the commodity has not been purchased overseas, but the international buyer (the tourist) has travelled overseas, visited the country and made the purchase as a tourist. However, as tourism is usually recoded as an export, it can be very important in what is known as the balance of payments. The balance of payments is the relationship between what a country exports and what it imports. If a country sells more products and services overseas than the goods and services it imports from overseas, then it will have an economic surplus. If, however, it imports more than it exports then it will have an economic deficit.

**Generation of employment** appears a straightforward economic impact to understand and, therefore, measure. However, this may not necessarily be the case, as some jobs may be part-time rather than full-time. Also as we have already noted earlier in the book, tourism is a seasonal activity and therefore a significant number of tourism jobs are likely to be only available for a part of the year. Calculating the number of jobs created by tourism is yet more complicated because not all jobs are solely tourism related. For example, a waiter in a bar or café may serve both locals and tourists. This means that those assessing the effects of tourism on jobs use terms such as direct effects and indirect effects, where direct effects are in relation to purely tourism jobs. The case study of the importance of tourism to the Spanish economy below, discusses the nature of direct and indirect effects in more detail.

As indicated earlier in the book, tourism takes place in specific locations which are referred to as destinations. These places that attract tourists can act as locations that provide revenue, taxes and jobs to a local area. This means that they may be important in helping areas that have suffered from recent economic decline recover. Or tourism can help open up remote areas and in this way **contribute to regional economic development**.

**Figure 9.1:** Employment in Tourism in Great Britain in local areas, as a percentage of all employment (source: World Travel and Tourism Council, 2015)

Figure 9.1 shows the distribution of employment in tourism within Great Britain. The map indicates areas where a relatively high percentage of those in work are employed in tourism and those areas where this is not the case, in other words, in these areas the percentage working in tourism is relatively low. Note that Figure 9.1 does not show the total number of those in work in tourism in any one area, but the percentage of the entire working population who are employed in tourism in the local area. The map shows that relatively peripheral areas of GB, such as the Scottish Highlands, North and Central Wales and South West England have high percentages of the working population employed in tourism. Figure 9.1 also shows that some coastal areas have high percentage involved in working in tourism. In contrast many urban areas have relatively low percentages working in tourism.

The positive impacts of tourism that have been discussed above can be assessed at a variety of scales including the local and regional, particularly in relation to regional development. However, in terms of the importance of tourism to revenue generation, foreign exchange earnings and employment, it is frequently the case that these are measured at the national level. This enables them to be compared with contributions from other sectors of an economy.

Spain has one of the most important tourism industries of any European country, particularly in terms of the positive economic impacts of its contribution to GDP and employment. The case study below discusses the importance of tourism to Spain's economy and refers to a number of important economic measures.

## Case study: Tourism's contribution to Spain's economy

Spain has one of the most important tourism industries of any European country and, in fact, of the world. For at least the last 15 years, Spain has been the major destination in Europe for international visitors, with earnings of 69bn Euros from these visitors in 2014, and the number of international arrivals has averaged over 60m annually since 2006.

This case study initially indicates and explains in more detail, the particular terminology in relation to the impacts that tourism can have on an economy and focuses in particular on Gross Domestic Product (GDP), and then provides actual figures from Spain.

The *direct* contribution of tourism to GDP is concerned with the 'internal' spending on tourism. This is the total spending within a country on tourism by residents and non-residents for business and leisure purposes. Therefore it covers domestic and international tourism. This contribution relates to the following sectors of the industry: hotels, airlines, airports, travel agents, and leisure and recreation services that deal directly with tourists.

There is also what is known as the *indirect* effect of tourism on the economy. This has wider impact and includes what are usually referred to as the indirect impact and the induced impact. The indirect impact includes tourism investment spending, that could involve activity such as the purchase of new aircraft and construction of new hotels. This indirect impact usually includes government activity, such as tourism marketing and promotion, aviation, administration and resort area security services. This indirect impact also includes domestic purchases of goods and services by the sectors dealing directly with tourists, including, for example, fuel and catering services by airlines and purchases of food and cleaning services by hotels. The 'induced' impact or economic contribution measures the contribution to GDP in relation to jobs supported by the spending of those who are directly or indirectly employed by the tourism sector. Money spent by foreign visitors to a country is referred to as *visitor exports* and is a key component of the direct contribution of tourism to GDP.

☐ The direct contribution of tourism to GDP in Spain represented 5.6% of total GDP in 2014, and was forecast to rise to 5.7% of total GDP in 2025. The total contribution of tourism to GDP was 15.2% of GDP in 2014, and forecast to rise to15.4% in 2025.

☐ Tourism generated 870,000 jobs directly in 2014, which represented 5.0% of total employment and this was forecast to grow to 1,023,000 by 2025, which would represent almost 5.5% of employment.

☐ The total contribution of tourism to employment, in other words including the wider impacts as indicated above, was 2,652,500 jobs in 2014. This represents just over 15% of total employment. The total contribution to employment was forecast to rise to 2,995,000 jobs by 2025, representing 15.7% of total employment.

☐ In 2014, Spain generated Euros 52.2bn in visitor exports and there were just over 66 million international tourist arrivals. By 2025, international tourist arrivals were forecast to total 85.4 million, generating expenditure of Euro 70.7bn.

☐ Tourism investment in tourism in 2014 was Euros13.5bn, or 6.9% of total investment. It was forecast to rise by 3.5% per annum over the period from 2015-2025 to Euros 19.6bn in 2025, representing 7.2% of total investment.

Table 9.1 summarises the figures presented above and also shows an indication of percentage growth forecasts. Table 9.2 shows the same information for Europe as a whole .

**9**

**Table 9.1:** The Spanish economy and tourism, 2014

| Spain | 2014 of total GDP | 2025 of total GDP | 2015-2025 growth |
|---|---|---|---|
| Direct contribution to GDP | 5.6% | 5.7% | 2.3% |
| Total contribution to GDP | 15.2% | 15.4% | 2.1% |
| Direct contribution to employment | 5.0% | 5.4% | 1.3% |
| Total contribution to employment | 15.3% | 15.7% | 0.9% |
| Visitor exports | 15.4% | 14.5% | 2.7% |
| Capital investment | 6.9% | 7.2% | 3.5% |

**Table 9.2:** Europe's Economy and Tourism, 2014

| Europe | 2014 of total GDP | 2025 of total GDP | 2015-2025 growth |
|---|---|---|---|
| Direct contribution to GDP | 3.4% | 3.6% | 2.8% |
| Total contribution to GDP | 9.2% | 9.8% | 2.6% |
| Direct contribution to employment | 3.6% | 4.1% | 1.6% |
| Total contribution to employment | 9.0% | 9.9% | 1.2% |
| Visitor exports | 5.6% | 5.8% | 3.8% |
| Capital investment | 4.7% | 5.0% | 3.2% |

In both Table 9.1 and 9.2 the 'Total contribution to GDP' includes the 'Direct Contribution to GDP' and goods and services which are related to tourism, but are not included in 'Direct contribution to GDP'. Similarly 'Total contribution to employment' includes employment related to, but not included in, 'Direct contribution to employment'. 'Visitor exports' are, in effect, the percentage of GDP received from international visitors. The growth figures in both Table 9.1 and Table 9.2 for the period 2015-2025 have been adjusted for inflation.

(Source: World Travel and Tourism Council, 2015)

The negative consequences of tourism in general terms include the following:

- inflation
- opportunity costs
- over-dependence on tourism.

(Pearce, 1989; Mason, 1995)

Such negative effects of tourism were not always measured in detail in some early studies of the impacts of tourism. This is partly to do with the difficulty of measuring/assessing, for example, the role that tourism has, as a separate economic activity, on inflation. However, in addition, the political stance of some early studies, which indicated that tourism had far more positive contributions then negative effects, meant that the negative impacts tended to be regarded as less important and played down.

However, there is evidence that inflation is a negative consequence of tourism and relates to the increases in prices of land, houses and food that can occur as a result of tourism (Mason, 2016). Prices for these commodities can increase when tourists place extra demands on local services at a tourism destination. This can occur at different times of the year, particularly when tourism is a seasonal activity. Hence, prices of, for example, food and drink may rise during the summer season in some tourism destinations, as the demand increases with the large number of tourists at the location. It is likely that local people buying these goods in the same place as the visitors will have to pay these higher prices. This may be a temporary increase, rather than a permanent one and, hence, in this form of inflation, prices may return to a lower level outside the tourist season. Nevertheless, the price rises may recur at the onset of the next tourism season. However, land and property price increases are much more likely to occur, year-on-year, for a period of many years and even decades.

The term *opportunity costs* refer to the cost of engaging in tourism rather than another form of economic activity. For example, in a coastal area, which is located on the edge of fertile farmland, opportunity costs refers to investing in tourism instead of in arable farming, market gardening or fishing. Tourism has often been viewed as a cheap development option in comparison with, for example, manufacturing industry (Mason, 2016). However, if the infra-structure for fishing, for example, exists already in a coastal location, the cost of developing tourism as an alternative may be high in comparison to this activity.

Over-dependence on tourism can occur and has happened in some small states and a number of islands. Such locations often have governments which view tourism as the best method of development. A major reason tourism is viewed in this way is because of the lack of resources for other forms of development. Under these circumstances, over a period of time, tourism becomes the main form, if not the only form of development. As a result, the country becomes dependent on tourism revenue. This dependency is such that any change in demand for tourism is likely to lead to a major economic crisis. The following case study indicates the 20 countries most reliant on tourism in 2014, as well as referring to those countries which are least dependent on tourism.

## Case study: Top 20 countries most reliant on tourism and the 20 least reliant on tourism

A significant number of countries are very reliant on tourism. The World Travel and Tourism Council (WTTC) published a list of the most reliant and least reliant countries in 2014.

The world's island nations are typically the most reliant on income from tourism. According to the WTTC 2014 data, nine of the ten countries that rely most heavily on tourism are islands, including the Maldives and the Seychelles in the Indian Ocean, and the British Virgin Islands, the Bahamas, Aruba and Anguilla in the Caribbean. The value of tourism to the Maldivian economy in 2014 was $1.03bn, which amounted to 41.5% of its GDP. The British Virgin Islands – a British Overseas Territory – relies on the tourism trade for 33.5% of its GDP. Other destinations, that are particularly reliant, are those that are traditionally popular with European tourists, and these include countries such as Thailand. Macau, which is a special administrative region of China (in some ways similar to Hong Kong) relies more heavily on overseas visitors than any other place in the world, with 44% of its GDP stemming from the tourism and travel industries.

**9**

The 20 places most reliant on tourism in 2014

1.  Macau
2.  Maldives
3.  British Virgin Islands
4.  Aruba
5.  Seychelles
6.  Anguilla
7.  Bahamas
8.  Vanuatu
9.  Former Netherlands Antilles
10. Antigua and Barbuda
11. Cape Verde
12. Belize
13. Malta
14. Palestinian territories
15. St Lucia
16. Fiji
17. Cambodia
18. Croatia
19. Mauritius
20. US Virgin Islands

Although absolute figures for travel and tourism's value were highest in other countries in 2014, including China ($263bn), and the USA ($458bn), these countries rank lower on this index because other industries than tourism generate even more wealth.

The 20 countries least reliant on tourism are shown below. It is important to note that no data was available for many countries in Africa, with unstable political situations, such as Eritrea, Somalia, and South Sudan. Figures for Afghanistan come from the World Bank and are based on receipts from international tourism in 2013, and its GDP from the same year. The WTTC also acknowledges that they have had to use alternative sources of information for some of the countries in this list (such as Tajikistan), where no reliable government level data was available.

According to the WTTC data, countries with little reliance on tourism as part of GDP also include Chad and Suriname: tourism makes up just 1.1% of total income in each.

The 20 countries least reliant on tourism

| | | | |
|---|---|---|---|
| 1. | Afghanistan | 11. | Niger |
| 2. | Papua New Guinea | 12. | Kyrgyzstan |
| 3. | Moldova | 13. | Macedonia |
| 4. | Uzbekistan | 14. | Burkina Faso |
| 5. | Gabon | 15. | Russia |
| 6. | Tajikistan | 16. | Kuwait |
| 7. | Chad | 17. | Paraguay |
| 8. | Democratic Republic of the Congo | 18. | Republic of Congo |
| 9. | Suriname | 19. | Brunei |
| 10. | Canada | 20. | Sierra Leone |

Source: WTTC, 2015, and The Daily Telegraph, UK, 2016.

A significant factor when discussing economic impacts of tourism, whether they are positive or negative, is scale. Although similar processes may operate in a number of destinations, effects can be different, because they are operating at different scales. The global economic importance of tourism has been briefly referred to above, with discussion of employment and gross domestic product. In addition to this data, is the projection that jobs in tourism are likely to increase steadily over the next ten to fifteen years. This contrasts with jobs in a number of other economic sectors, such as in some manufacturing industries. These macro-economic level figures, however, hide the unbalanced nature of global tourism, and this can be discerned at different scales. Hence, at the level of continents, Europe was the single most important tourism destination with over half of all international visitor arrivals in the early part of the 21st century and most international arrivals of tourists in Europe were visits from other European countries (Mason, 2016).

In a similar manner, the United States and Canada are both important destination areas and tourism generating regions. Hence, Americans travel to many overseas destinations, but also North America acts as a major tourism attraction region.

Over the past 40 years or so with increasing access, Asia has become an important destination for tourists from Europe, North America and Australasia, but is also becoming increasingly important as a source of tourists. These tourists, coming in particular from Japan, Korea and Taiwan, but increasingly from India, Indonesia and Malaysia are visiting other parts of Asia and the Pacific Rim but are also making visits to Europe and North America.

Two continents, in particular, indicate the great variations in the scale of tourism in different locations and this provides further evidence of the uneven balance of international tourism. These two continents are South America and Africa. South America is a growing destination for tourists, but produces relatively few international visitors, on a global scale, that travel beyond the continent. Africa shows this to an even greater extreme with increasing numbers visiting, but the number of world tourists originating in Africa is still very low.

## ■ Bali: An island example

Reference to Africa and South America leads to the view that economic impacts of tourism can be particularly marked in developing countries and can be seen at both the micro-economic and macro-economic level (Mason, 1990). Historically, the Indonesian island of Bali provides a good example of both the benefits and problems that can arise from tourism development in destinations located in a developing country. If Bali was a country, rather than one of many islands in the country of Indonesia, it would be high on the list of places reliant on tourism, as shown in the case study above. Bali has been a tourism destination for wealthy European and North American visitors since the 1930s, but tourism as an important industry began to grow in importance in the 1960s, and since then a significant number of jobs have been created. These have been in tourism sectors found in other areas of the world, such as in hotels, bars and cafes, but also in perhaps less obvious forms of employment, such as boat hire, cycle hire, cycle repair, car hire, food and drink selling, and souvenir making and selling. Tourism is also viewed as a significant contributor to the revival of the arts and crafts activities of painting and wood carving, as well as promoting the introduction of new activities, including batik making (Mason, 1995).

Many residents of Bali have tried to benefit from tourism over the past 50 years or so. Some have been engaged directly in hotel, restaurant and guiding jobs, and others through the manufacture and sale of craft products, the involvement in cultural performances and food production to feed tourists (Wall, 1997). As Wall (1997) stated some Balinese have benefited from tourism via the provision of home-stays and the increase in those providing informal services to tourists. Home-stays are the Balinese equivalent of the Western 'bed and breakfast'. The great majority of home-stays have traditionally run by local residents, and not outsiders. In these circumstances almost all of the economic gain from the activity has gone directly to the local population (Cukier and Wall, 1994).

A significant number of young males (aged 15–25) have traditionally worked as street and beach vendors in Bali. These men generally lack formal education, but have good language skills. Although they worked long hours, and believed they had few alternative work opportunities, most of them were happy with their lifestyle and by Indonesian standards were well remunerated (Cukier and Wall, 1994). Tourism grew very rapidly in Bali between 1970 and 1995, and along with the associated craft industries, it contributed over 30% of GDP (Wall, 1997).

On the negative side, however, Bali provides evidence of tourism promoting inflation. Tourism began to grow fairly rapidly from 1968, but before this land prices had been fairly constant for about 20 years. During the 20 years after 1968, land prices rose by an average of 100%, but in tourist areas by over 150% (Mason, 1995). Although opportunity costs are difficult to calculate, there is some evidence from Nusa Dua, a large-scale tourism development on the southern coast of Bali, which received funding from the World Bank, that it may well have been better to spend money on a smaller, less intrusive hotel complex (Mason, 1995). Not only would this form of development have cost less, but it also would have been more in keeping with local values and would probably have contributed more to the local economy. The Nusa Dua development was targeted at up-market international tourists, but it has been argued that the money would have been better spent on local farming or forestry, or even retailing, rather than this form of tourism (Mason, 1995).

The future of tourism in Bali was brought into question after the terrorist bombings at Kuta, in October 2002, and the second bombings in almost the same area in October 2005. Over time, Bali has become heavily dependent on tourism, and although it appears to have largely recovered from the two terrorist bombing events, what happens in the longer term may indicate whether the island has become economically over-dependent on tourism.

## ■ Nepal and international tourism

One of the few places in the world that has developed international tourism only in the past 50 years is the Himalayan state of Nepal. It has had similar tourism issues to those of Bali. In Nepal, not only was tourism relatively unimportant until the second half of the 20th century, but similar to Bali, tourism grew quite rapidly to become very significant to the economy of Nepal. At the end of 20th century Nepal was the fourth poorest country in the world. As a landlocked Himalayan kingdom it has relied largely on access to imports via India. Throughout the period of European global exploration, dating from about 1400 until as recently as the 1950s, Nepal was unusual in not being colonized by a European, or any other, country. It was almost inaccessible to outsiders, particularly westerners. As a result of this isolation, it has become particularly attractive for some potential tourists. International tourism began slowly in the 1960s, but grew rapidly in the 1970s as travel by wide bodied jet aircraft made Nepal much more accessible to western tourists. By 1999, there were in approximately 500,000 tourists annually, despite fluctuations due partly to the political instability in the country since then, had risen to over 800,000 annually by 2012 according to the Nepalese ministry responsible for tourism (MOTCCA, 2013).

Particularly rapid growth took place in tourism during the 1980s. There was a 60% increase in tourist numbers and foreign earnings from tourism went up by 75% between 1977 and 1988. In the capital city Kathmandu, in the same period there was an almost 50% increase in those employed in tourism (up from 2,800 to 4,100) and an over 60% increase in tourist rooms (Department of Tourism, 1990).

Nepal also shares some other similarities with Bali, in that violence there has had a negative effect on the numbers of international tourist and hence an adverse effect on the contribution of tourism to the economy. Many tourists have been dissuaded from visiting Nepal by Maoist rebels who have become particularly active since the mid-1990s. They have not targeted tourists directly (as the terrorists in Bali have done) but created an unstable situation, which is far from attractive to tourists. Hence, in early 2005 a state of emergency was declared in Nepal after an intensification of the Maoist activities. This did little to entice tourists to the country in the numbers that were visiting in the late 1990s (IRIN, 2007). However, it appears since the latter part of the first decade of the 2000s, tourist numbers have been rising steadily again.

Many jobs in Nepal's tourism industry have been in the informal sector and difficult to measure accurately. They include part-time tour guide work and this has frequently been done by those with language and presentational skills such as lecturers, teachers, and students. The state pay for such government employees has traditionally been very low, while guiding work not only pays more, but usually means those doing these jobs receive their money immediately and this may be accompanied by tips. Souvenir producing and selling is also important in terms of job creation, and once again as these are in the informal economy may not appear in government statistics.

Many local people in Nepal have attempted to derive economic benefit from tourism, but this has led to negative effects. In addition to the Himalayan landscape, a key motivation for many tourists is the evidence of Nepal's culture, and the Buddhist and Hindu temples have become major attractions. However, these are not just tourist attractions but are used for religious activities. Those who wish to use the temples for religious activities may be confronted by the crowds of tourists who are contribute to the wear and tear of buildings, and they are also likely to have to put up with those who have become economically dependent on tourism. These include souvenir and food and drink sellers, but also beggars who are there because of their increasing reliance on tourist handouts (Mason, 1991).

# The Santa Claus industry in Lapland

Some parts of Europe have similar issues to developing countries, in terms of being resource frontiers for tourism development. In the far north of Europe is the unlikely setting for the 'Santa Claus Industry'. This industry, a focal point for domestic and international tourism, is located in Finnish Lapland and is centred on the Santa Claus Village. The village opened in 1986, using the concept of it being the home of Santa Claus.

Lapland is the northern-most province of Finland and is the most remote from the more densely populated southern area of the country. It is also the least populated region of the country. Traditionally, the region has attracted two major types of tourists: those who enjoy wilderness landscapes, and those who are interested in the indigenous culture of the Sami (Lapp) people.

The economy of Lapland has become increasingly dependent on tourism and despite the success of encouraging more domestic tourism during the 1980s, overseas tourist numbers fluctuated up to the early 1990s. The main overseas generating countries were Germany, the Netherlands, Switzerland, Italy and France. Most tourists from these countries visited in summer and many were journeying to the North Cape, the most northerly point of mainland Europe. Tourists from Britain and Japan come in winter to experience a white winter, take part in winter sports or see reindeer.

In the late 1970s and early 1980s, the Finnish Tourism Board indicated that the natural and cultural attractions of Lapland were not enough to attract sufficient numbers of tourists and decided that a new attraction had to be created. The idea of promoting Santa Claus as an attraction was viewed as appealing. The region around the town of Rovaniemi, the capital of Lapland, was declared 'Santa Claus Land' and the showpiece of Santa Claus Land became the Santa Claus Village. This is located exactly on the line of latitude, the Arctic Circle, a few kilometres north of Rovaniemi. The site was chosen as, prior to the establishment, tourists had stopped at the Arctic Circle sign to have their photograph taken. The village was opened in 1985 and contains Santa's workshop, where he may be visited at all times of the year, Santa's Post Office, a reindeer enclosure, several restaurants and many gift and souvenir shops.

The impacts on the local economy have been greatly assisted by the existence of Rovaniemi international airport, which can take large jet aircraft. The most famous international flights to the airport were the regular flights by British Airways Concorde at Christmas between 1986 and 1992.

There have several significant economic impacts of the establishment of the Santa Claus Village. In 1985, 225,000 visitors came to the village and this reached 277,000 in 1989. Despite falling visitor numbers, due largely to the world recession in the early 1990s, in the second part of the 1990s, numbers once again increased and reached over 300,000 in 1995. In 1996, there were 1.6 million international and domestic visitors to Lapland and 325,000 visited the Village. In excess of

300,000 tourists visited the village each year in the period between 1995 and 2005 (Finnish Tourist Board, 2007). In 2012 the number of international visitors to the Village exceeded 500,000, accounting for one third of the 1.5 million overseas visitors to Lapland (VisitFinland, 2014). The contribution of the Village to revenue and employment can be seen in the following information. Visitors to Lapland increased by 22% between 1986 and 1994 and foreign earnings were up by 29% and this was attributed mainly to the Santa Claus Village. The Village employed 290 people, which in 1990 was 7% of total tourism employment in Lapland.

The Santa Claus Village is a totally artificial creation, but has been an attempt to bring tourists to an area perceived as relatively remote, lacking many natural attractions and generally inhospitable to tourists, but has been regarded by many as an economic success, which has also not resulted in serious environmental or social damage (Pretes, 1995).

## ■ New Zealand and Asian tourism

Other relatively peripheral areas in terms of the global reach of tourism have also seem an increase in tourists in the past 30 years, or so. For example, although New Zealand received only 0.2% of international tourists in 1996, this percentage increased in the last decade of the 20th century and the economic impacts were highly significant. According to the New Zealand Tourism Board, from 1993 to 1996, the number of visitors increased by an average of 6.5% per year. The average spend per trip rose from NZ$ 2,041 in 1993 to NZ$ 2,776 in 1996 and by 2000, had risen to NZ$ 3,222. Visitor spend continued to rise in the early 2000s and the 2006 figure was up by 4% on that for 2005, indicating that international visitors spent $NZ 6.4 billion in 2006 (NZTB, 2007).

In terms of the main groups of tourists, Australia, United Kingdom, Japan and the United States were the major origin areas for international visitors to New Zealand in the period 1996-2010. However, new markets areas were opening in this period and particularly significant were Taiwan and South Korea. In March 1996 these two areas made up 15% of total visitors. In this period, Japanese, Taiwanese and South Koreans were the biggest spenders, averaging over NZ$ 200 per day. The importance of this expanding market can be seen in the following figures: there were 216,162 visitors from Japan, Taiwan and Korea in 1996 with an estimated spend per head of NZ$ 234. By 2000, the average spend per head had increased to NZ$ 330 for Japanese visitors, which was the largest daily spend of any visitor group and NZ$ 221 for Koreans (Hall and Kearsley, 2001).

The economic crisis in Asia that occurred in late 1997/early 1998 meant a fall in Asian visitor numbers. However, by 2002 visitors from Asia exceeded 500,000 for the first time, with Korea (104,000 in 2002) and China (71,000 in 2002) growing particularly rapidly in the first years of the new millennium. This trend of increasing visitor numbers from Japan and Korea continued throughout the first decade of the 2000s, although the rise in numbers was not as pronounced after 2008.

In relation to employment, in 1995 there were 155,000 jobs in New Zealand tourism and by the end of 2001 this had reached 176,000. This trend continued during the early years of the 21st century, so that as visitor numbers to New Zealand continued to increase and reached 2.4 million in 2006, there was an increase to 183,000 jobs in tourism (TIANZ, 2007). Despite the global recession of 2008-2012, when there was only slow growth in international tourism, visitor numbers exceeded 2.7 million in 2013, the number of jobs was slightly lower however at approximately 170,000 (TIANZ 2014).

# The multiplier effect

This book does not discuss the actual *techniques* for assessing economic impacts (or other impacts) of tourism in any detail. However, there has been reference to and discussion of a number of measures such as employment and investment. One common tool for assessing economic impacts of tourism is the known as the *multiplier*. It usually has a prominent place in government and international reports on the economic impacts of tourism. The multiplier effect takes place when spending is circulated throughout an economy. It is a form of 'knock-on effect' and can be used to distinguish between direct and indirect income derived from tourism (Lomine and Edwards, 2007). Hence, it is a very useful way of conceptualizing what happens when tourists spend money in a destination. The multiplier shows how the local (or regional/national) economy can be seen, not only to benefit directly from money that tourists spend, but also when staff employed in the tourism sector spend their wages on goods and services in the economy. This circulation of income derived from tourists is the secondary or indirect income.

Figure 9.2 shows, in relatively simple terms, the direct and indirect effects of tourism spend, within the context of the establishment of new hotels. Figure 9.2 indicates that the new hotels not only create jobs directly in these hotels, but that the wages of the staff who work in the hotels gets spent in the local area on products and services. Also, the new hotels will require supplies, so local (and probably non-local suppliers) provide these for the hotels. This generates more revenue for the supply companies involved. Additionally new jobs may be created in the supply organisations. Figure 9.2 also shows that there will be extra taxes generated. These can be spent on improving the infrastructure of the area. This, in turn, may make the area more attractive for tourists and will lead to an increase in demand by tourists, which could lead to greater profitability of tourism businesses and the re-investment of some of this profit in the local economy. Figure 9.2 indicates one other important economic dimension – leakage – which is usually considered a negative economic impact. Not all money generated by a local tourism business may stay in the local area. If, for example, much of the food and alcohol consumed in the hotels is imported from overseas, then it will be the overseas supplier that will benefit and not the local supplier. This is an example of leakage from the local economy.

In most real settings, multiplier analysis is more complex than shown in Figure 9.2 and involves various tools, data sources and statistical analysis. It enables the calculation of, for example, income multipliers, output multipliers and government revenue multipliers. There is a lack of agreement about precise values in much multiplier calculation, nevertheless, most commentators agree that although it is not an entirely accurate technique, it can provide a valuable framework for assessing economic impacts of tourism (Lomine and Edwards, 2007).

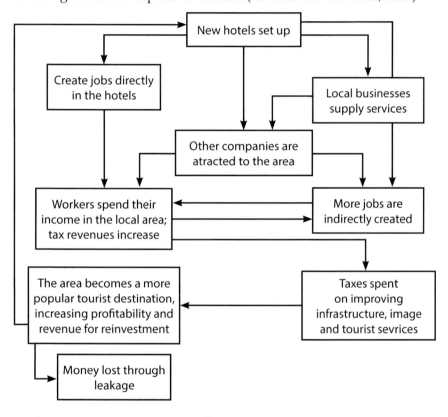

**Figure 9.2:** A diagrammatic representation of the tourism multiplier within the context of the establishment of a new hotel

## Summary

Economic impacts are one of the most researched areas of tourism. Traditionally, they have tended to be far more researched than other forms of impact, but like other impacts, economic impacts can be subdivided into both positive and negative groupings. Historically, countries have perceived positive economic benefits as more significant than negative effects and hence have been supportive of tourism development. Evidence suggests that a number of developing countries have selected tourism as part of their approach to development. Such countries desire the positive economic benefits; however they have tended to be less aware that their tourism may also bring some negative economic effects.

Tourism is often one of a range of development options facing both developed and developing countries and regions within countries. Tourism is often viewed as a preferred option, in relation to other possible choices. Hence, either where there are old, dying industries in areas in need of revitalisation, or in remote areas or relatively unexploited locations, but where there are few alternative choices, tourism can bring important economic benefits, although not all of the revenue generated may stay in the local area, and some may leave through leakages.

Some countries have become very reliant on tourism and these include several in Europe, in particular Spain. Many islands have become so reliant on tourism that they have developed an over-dependence on it, which is a problematic situation in these places, particularly in a changing world where external forces may have damaging effects on their economies.

An important technique for assessing the economic impacts of tourism (and other economic activities) is the multiplier and this has been discussed in this chapter within the context of the creation of new hotels.

## Student activities

1   In relation to a community affected by tourism that you know well, identify the positive and negative economic impacts of tourism.

2   Why do small islands often become dependent on tourism?

3   How might the economic impacts of tourism in small islands differ from those of larger mainland countries, in Europe or North America?

4   Why is tourism particularly important to the economy of Spain?

5   What factors acting (a) internally within a country; and (b) externally (beyond the country) could affect the economic impacts of tourism, particularly in a negative way.

6   In small groups (3/4 students) discuss how developing countries can overcome the problems of the negative economic impact of tourism.

7   How can countries maximize the economic benefits of tourism?

# References

Cukier, J. and Wall, G. (1994). Tourism and employment perspectives from Bali. *Tourism Management*, **14**, 195–201.

Daily Telegraph (2016) Mapped: The countries that rely most on your money, *Daily Telegraph*, UK, April 7th.

Department of Tourism (1990). *Tourism Statistics 1988–9*. Kathmandu, Nepal: Department of Tourism.

Finnish Tourist Board (2007). *Tourist Attractions in Finland*, Finnish Tourist Board, www.mek.fi/webs MekEng/publish.nsf Accessed July 10, 2007.

Hall, C. M. and Kearsley, G. (2001). *Tourism in New Zealand: An Introduction.* Melbourne: Oxford University Press.

IMF (2014) World Economic Outlook Database  http://www.imf.org/external/pubs/ft/ weo/2014/01/ weodata/index.aspx, accessed March 21, 2017

IRIN (2007). Humanitarian News and Analysis, *UN Office for the Co-ordination of Humanitarian Affairs*, www.//irinnews.org accessed October 19 2007

Lickorish, L. (1994). *An Introduction to Tourism.* London: Sage.

Lomine, L. and Edmunds, J. (2007). *Key Concepts in Tourism.* London: Palgrave Macmillan

Mason, P (1990) *Tourism: Environment and Development Perspectives*, Godalming: WWF

Mason, P. (1991). *Internal Report on the Annapurna Conservation Area Project.* Prepared for WWF UK, Godalming (unpublished).

Mason, P (1995) *Tourism: Environment and Development Perspectives*, 2nd ed., Godalming: WWF

Mason, P (2016) *Tourism Impacts, Planning and Management*,  3rd ed., London: Routledge

MOTCCA (2013) *Nepal Tourism News*, Autumn. Ministry of Tourism, Culture and Civil Aviation Nepal.

New Zealand Tourist Board (2007). *Tourism in New Zealand: Facts and Figures.* Wellington: Ministry of Tourism

Pearce, D. G. (1989). *Tourist Development.* London: Longman

Pretes, M. (1995). Post-modern tourism: the Santa Claus industry. *Annals of Tourism Research*, **22** (1), 1–15.

TIANZ (2007). Tourism Industry Association of New Zealand, www.tianz.org.nz/industry-facts/key-facts- figures.asp accessed October 19, 2007.

TIANZ (2014) Tourism Industry Association of New Zealand, www.TIANZ.com accessed 30/9/2014.

Tribe, J (2011) *The Economics of Recreation, Leisure Tourism*, Oxford, Butterworth Heinemann,

VisitFinland (2014) www.VisitFinland.com, accessed 2/10/2014.

Wall, G. (1997). Rethinking impacts of tourism. In C. Cooper, B. Archer and S. Wanhill, eds *Tourism Development*, pp. 1–10. Chichester: John Wiley and Sons.

WTTC (2015) *Travel and Tourism: The Economic Impact 2015 Spain*, London, World Travel and Tourism Council,

9

# Tourism Issues

The global climate is changing and this is having significant effects on tourism, while tourism is contributing to climate change. The combined effects of climate change on tourism and tourism's impacts on climate, may lead to a very different geography of tourism by the end of the 21st century. Disasters and crises have had significant effects on tourism. With natural processes such as earthquakes and volcanoes, where they may happen is generally known, but when and how damaging they will be is not predictable. Human activity can lead to crises, and an increasingly common and worrying trend is terrorism, as terrorists have frequently targeted tourists during the last 20 years or so. Despite such problems, over the past 50 years, tourist numbers have grown and this has put increasing pressure on the environment. As a result, some areas are being protected so that they can act as locations of conservation of flora and fauna, and continue to offer spaces for recreation and tourism. These two aims can be in conflict, creating a major global issue. The overall setting for many of the world's human induced issues, is a global context of uneven development, with global inequalities in wealth, health, education, access to clean water and adequate food supplies. Tourism is a part of this unbalanced world, having contributed to it and being affected by it and global development and the role of tourism within this, is the first issue discussed in this section.

# 10 Global Development

## Introduction

Global development is a process that has been occurring since human history began. However, a key aspect of this development, particularly within the last 250 years is that it is not even development in all places. Some countries developed manufacturing industries over 100 years before others. Many countries now have more important service sectors of their economies than manufacturing industry sectors. Nevertheless, a number of countries, even today, have developed relatively little in the way of manufacturing industry or services. This has resulted in a very uneven balance of development in global terms. This chapter looks at the processes that have led to global development, as well as important theories about this complex process. It also locates tourism within the context of global development.

## Defining and measuring development

Definitions of developing countries are usually based on economic measures, in particular GDP or *per capita* income (Lea, 1988). Using such measures means that some countries will be labelled 'high income countries' others as 'low income countries'. The low income countries (the poor ones) will then be considered to be 'developing countries' and in the past, until relatively recently, were labelled 'Third World Countries' (O'Grady (1980)). The concept of 'Third World' implies that there are two other worlds – the first and second. Conventionally the First World has been seen to include Western Europe, North America, Australasia and South Africa, whilst the Second World, until the fall of the Berlin Wall in 1989 was made up of the Soviet Union (now largely equivalent to Russia) and Eastern European countries. The Third World was all the rest of the countries of the world (Mason, 1990). Clearly this terminology is no longer applicable, mainly because the Soviet Union and the countries of Eastern Europe, which were strongly linked to the old Soviet Union, are no longer communist and the Eastern European countries are now independent states, many of which are members of the European Union.

However, the two-fold concept of *developed world* and *developing world* still remains. Although it is important to note that these concepts are not static but dynamic. Hence, several countries of Asia, including Korea and Malaysia, which 50 years ago would fit reasonably well within the Third Word and be considered developing countries are now much more like First World or developed countries. Parts of Brazil are very similar to developed countries, but other parts resemble many developing countries. Also some parts of American cities and some European cities are not that dissimilar from developing country cities. China and India have large areas, particularly the rural parts, which resemble developing countries, but the cities in each country have parts that closely resemble parts of European, Australasian and North American cities.

From the late 1980s, the terms 'North' and 'South' were frequently used where the North (roughly the Northern hemisphere north of the Tropic of Cancer) was seen as the more developed parts of the world, while the 'South' was the less developed. Clearly this categorisation is not entirely accurate as Australia and New Zealand, for example, are in the South. However the classification meant that the continent of Africa (except South Africa), all of South and Central America and much of Asia, south of the old Soviet Union, were in the South.

These classifications indicate that using geographical divisions alone may not be entirely satisfactory. Instead a number of criteria have been used to separate the world into 'developed' and 'developing'. Originally, as indicated above, these were primarily economic criteria. In addition to GDP, trade, industrial output and energy consumption, other measures such as economic growth, employment rate and food production have been used (Mason, 1990). Industrial structure has also been viewed as a way of separating the developed and developing worlds, with developed countries having a high proportion of those employed in manufacturing industries, whilst developing countries would have a high employment percentage in primary industries, such as farming, fishing and forestry. However, in the last 50 years, the service sector of the economy has become very important in developed countries. This sector includes banking and insurance, but also tourism. So another way of distinguishing a developed country from a developing country, has been to consider the percentage of the population working in the service sector.

Nevertheless, using solely economic criteria for measuring the level of development does not give a true indication of living conditions for the residents of a country. A major issue with economic measures is that they tend to be at the macro level – i.e. the national level or on some occasions the international level. Such measures may tell us very little about actual conditions for individual citizens in any one country. So in the past 40 years or so a number of social, political and environmental factors have also been used to designate a country as 'developed' or 'developing'. These include issues related to nutrition, food, health, access to clean water, sanitation, education and human rights. Hence, measures related to these factors include literacy rate, percentage of the population attending school

up to a certain age, infant mortality rate, calorie supply per head, various measures of environmental pollution and even the number of political prisoners in a
specific country.

# Development theories

There are a number of theories concerned with global development. Cooper *et al.*
(2005) suggest that there are six important groups of theories, with some that date
back over 20 years and others from within the last 50 years. These are as follows:

- English classical economic theory
- Marxist theory
- Rostow's stages of economic growth
- Vicious circles of supply/demand
- Balanced and unbalanced theories of growth
- Theories of dependence.

Each of these important theories is explained below and the role of tourism is
discussed in relation to the theories.

## ■ English classical economic theory

Malthus, Mill and Ricardo are important authors who were working during the
18th and 19th centuries. In summary, they each argued, although in different contexts, that there will always be a close relationship between resource availability
and the ability to produce more resources – this being something required by
human society. As one example of these theorist, Malthus' ideas focus on human
population growth but, although he made no mention of it, they have relevance
to tourism. Malthus argued that the human population would continue to rise
until food resources became scarcer. If food began to run out, then the population
would begin to decline and return to a position once again balanced against the
food supply. This seems a relatively simple concept, but Malthus indicated that it
was a more complex relationship, which he contextualised in 18th century England
farming communities and focused on agricultural labourers, and his theory was
linked to economic conditions and particularly wage levels. Malthus' economic
theory suggested that the agricultural workers would control and reduce population when the food supply began to become scarce (in other words, *before* it had
actually run out). The process can be summarised in the following way. With a
large number of working age citizens in a country, wages would fall as the supply
of workers exceeded the demand for them. The growing awareness of this by
the workers, over time, meant that population numbers would eventually fall, as
workers would reduce their family size to ensure there was enough food for them
and their family to stay healthy and survive. The means of population control
was a natural one (there was no effective birth control in the 1700s when Malthus
was writing). Malthus suggested that the control mechanism was that men would

delay getting married until they were older, (he lived in a male-dominated world) so they would produce fewer children to feed. With fewer people being born, in the next generation the supply of labour would be smaller, so wages would rise again and with a smaller population there would be sufficient food supply. This, in turn, would encourage men to marry earlier, and have more children. The result of more children would be greater demands on food and the next generation would receive lower wages, as the supply of labour had increased, and therefore men would delay getting married and hence have fewer children. Sometime later, once again there would be enough food and higher wages, as the pool of labour had shrunk. This system of checks and balances, rises and falls in wages and population, would continue *ad infinitum*, Malthus suggested.

Malthus formulated his theory and criticised the situation in Britain at the time that he was writing, as he could see no real incentive for workers to produce more food. He considered that although more food would make them healthy and encourage them initially to have more children, they would know from previous generations that this would soon be followed by a period of low wages and as there would be many more mouths to feed, a less healthy population. So Malthus wanted conditions to improve for the workers, but believed the system his theory postulated would prevent this.

A major criticism of Malthus is that he ignores technological change. In relation to Malthus' ideas and the introduction of new technology, it could mean that either there are higher food yields from the same area of land, or possibly that the population can be artificially controlled (as happens in many countries today) and hence this would reduce the size of families – or indeed both of these!

There may appear, initially, to be little in the way of a link between Malthus' theory and tourism. However, tourism is an economic activity that exerts considerable pressure on the resource of land. Land for use in tourism is not the same as land for food production, but nevertheless tourism creates extra demands on this limited resource, and this is likely to affect its economic value and its supply. As indicated in Chapters 8 and 9, this extra demand on land, if it is not possible to increase the supply, means that it will push up prices, causing inflation. As we noted in Chapter 6, McKercher considers the idea of tourism being a consumptive activity, and that the resources it uses – those making up the global environment – are finite. Even if we build in one of the aspects that Malthus largely ignored, that of changing technology, this is not necessarily beneficial in relation to resources for tourism, as the use of new technology could mean, for example, new modes of transport, and this could lead to the consumption of more resources as new destinations for tourism are likely to emerge.

## Marxist theory

Marxist theory is contextualised within a dynamic world, unlike the static one that Malthus and the other classical economist used in their theories. Marx indicated that the (European) world would go through a series of changes in socio-economic systems – from feudalism in the European Middle Ages to capitalism, at the time Marx was writing in the middle of the 19th century, and he projected into the future, socialism and then communism. When Marx was writing, the system was referred to as capitalism and for Marx, the capital in society could be individual workers' skills, but also entrepreneurs' money, or land, or a factory where goods are produced. He referred to all these forms of capital as the means of production. According to Marx, workers sell their capital (their labour) to employers in return for wages. The main driver for change in most societies, according to Marx, is the discontent of workers about their working conditions and wages, and this will lead them to eventually rise against their employers, in a revolution. According to Marx, successive revolutions will mean that society becomes, over time, more egalitarian, in other words where there is greater equality between workers and owners of the means of production. Following socialism in sequence, communism is the most egalitarian.

However, Marx suggests that the changes in the socio-economic system (feudalism to capitalism for example) occurs because of some form of catalyst in society. In feudalism, agricultural workers gave their labour to a landowner, in return for food, shelter and protection. The change from feudalism to capitalism occurred because of the catalyst of the Industrial Revolution, where workers moved from the countryside into towns and sold their labour in return for a wage from an employer, such as a factory owner.

Marxist theory has relevance, if tourism is considered as a catalyst for change in an economy. Tourism can speed up change and contribute to rapid development, for example from a primary-industry based economy, to one where service industries such as tourism become more important. In this way a developing country can change relatively quickly to become much more like a developed country. This process of rapid change may be as a result of what is termed globalisation. The process of globalisation is explained later in this chapter. The catalyst effect could mean, for example, that tourism helps move a society, over time, from capitalism to socialism.

## ■ Rostow's stages of economic growth

Rostow's (1962) theory has some similarities with Marx' and suggests that there are a series of economic stages that society passes through. However, although Rostow's theory has some similarities, it is different in many other ways, and it has a significant geographical, as well as an economic focus. Rostow argued that countries at different locations in the world are likely to be at different stages of economic development at the same time. Hence, at one specific point in time, for example, Country A in Europe may be far more developed than Country B in Africa. Rostow, like Marx, suggests that there are certain stages that any country will pass through and the sequence of stages will be the same whatever the country. Rostow indicates that there are five stages of growth of an economy:

1   The traditional society

2   Preconditions for take off

3   Economic take off

4   Self-sustained drive towards maturity

5   The age of mass consumption.

Rostow's theory is more a series of stages that he had identified through observation and research than a solely theoretical perspective. Rostow's traditional society is one where primary industry, such as farming or fishing is the major activity. The four stages that follow lead towards an economy where manufactured goods are produced and this has become the main economic activity. However, Rostow argues that there is often in traditional societies something that holds back their development – a natural tendency to inertia, meaning no change will occur. So similar to Marx' theory, Rostow's theory indicates that there has to be a catalyst for change, except the catalyst is not the same as for Marx. In his second stage (Preconditions for take off) and the third (Economic take off), Rostow argues that there needs to be three factors present: investment in infrastructure, particularly transport; improvements in agriculture; and imports of capital – and these three are in effect the catalyst for change. If the pre-conditions are present then the economy will eventually move to Stage Three. Over time, as manufacturing industry becomes the main activity, the economy moves towards 'Self-sustained growth'. In Stage Four people move from rural to urban areas and there is a developed labour force and a state system of political and economic stability. Eventually the 'Age of mass consumption' (Stage Five) is reached where much manufacturing is devoted to the production of goods, such as washing machines, refrigerators and cars – these are termed consumer goods.

Tourism can have a very important role in relation to Rostow's theory when it helps in the development of infrastructure, and particularly in the creation and development of transport. It can also be particularly important in developing countries where their economic development has been held back by inertia. In this scenario, the improvements in transport infrastructure help speed up development of other parts of the economy.

## ■ Vicious circles of supply/demand

In the Vicious circle of supply/demand theory, the main argument is that poor countries will remain poor because they are poor! What this means is that the people of a poor country (measured, for example, by income levels or GDP) will find it very difficult to be anything other than poor as they are unlikely to have a permanent paid job and hence they will not have enough income to save. As they have little or no income they will not pay taxes and there will not be investment in the economy. Under these circumstances, it will mean they are likely to remain poor. Hence this is a vicious circle of poverty, which is not easy to break out of. One way out of this, however, is to have an activity that provides jobs, income and investment. Tourism can be such an activity and can lead to an injection of investment into an economy and create jobs, which provide income, helping to lift people out of poverty.

# ◼ Balanced and unbalanced theories of growth

Balanced and unbalanced growth theories relate to whether the whole of an economy is developed at the same time or just separate sectors. In many developed countries separate parts of an economy developed at different times, so, for example, usually coal mining developed before steel production. Steel production may have been followed by car production, and this also allowed for the service industries of insurance, finance and marketing, in relation to car production, to then develop later. Applying the idea of balanced growth would mean attempts to ensure that all sectors (i.e. primary, manufacturing and service industries) are developed together. However it is not always possible to do this, as it may be very expensive and/or take a long period of time, so unbalanced growth is promoted instead. In this way one sector of industry is developed with the intention that it acts as catalyst for the development of other parts. Once again, as noted in relation to some other theories, tourism can act as an important catalyst, in either an 'unbalanced' or a 'balanced' approach. Tourism can be particularly good in this context because it is linked to many other sectors, such as hospitality, food production, transport, marketing and insurance, and therefore it can help develop these sectors as well.

# ◼ Theories of dependence

The dependency theory largely relates to countries that were once colonies, usually of European countries (Cooper et al., 2005). The theory argues that countries that were colonised by, for example, Britain or France in Africa or Asia, were deliberately prevented from having manufacturing industry sectors of their own, as this would have meant that they would be competing with the industries in the country that had colonised them. Instead, the colonised countries were kept underdeveloped in terms of the industry sectors by the colonializing country and they had to produce raw materials, such as sugar, cocoa, coffee, tea or rubber that would be exported to the colonializing country. Here, it would be manufactured into processed products and inevitably some of the manufactured products would be sold back to the colony. Tourism can be seen to fit within dependency theory, either because it has been set up in developing countries by companies from developed countries, so the tourism industry is then dependent on foreign suppliers, or, as noted in earlier chapters, that some countries or regions have become reliant or even too dependent on tourism. So, in relation to dependency theory, tourism can act as a stimulant to development, but in another setting can be seen as an inhibitor of development, when a country becomes too dependent on it.

In summary, almost all of the development theories discussed above have an important tourism dimension. Although the English classical economic theories appear to have little relevance to tourism, as they postulate a relationship between available resources and the way they are used by humans, there is a link to tourism as it is an activity that makes use of environmental resources, especially finite resources of land. However, it is the role of tourism as a catalyst for change that means it fits particularly well within almost all more recent theories of development. Nevertheless, it is worth noting that the changes are not necessarily for the better. As indicated in earlier chapters, a number of changes brought about by tourism can be negative as well as positive.

# Modernisation theory

The theories discussed in this chapter so far have had largely an economic perspective. However, there are also important theories relating to development which have a different background and hence perspective. Of particular significance is modernisation theory. Modernisation theory has some links to parts of Marx' theory and in many ways, it appears to be the sociological equivalent of Rostow's theory. It also has dimensions that relate to the vicious circle of poverty theory, notions of balanced and unbalanced growth and theories of dependency.

If Rostow attempted to indicate the main economic factors that will contribute to change from a traditional society to an industrial society, modernisation theory considers the social variables in this process. The theory looks at the social processes that occur as a country moves from a traditional society to a 'modern' society. Modern societies are seen by those who support the theory, as being ones where citizens are more wealthy, which leads to them having more power and hence are freer to enjoy a higher standard of living (Bernstein, 1971). The 'modern' society is one with new technology, better communication and transport and changes in methods of production. The sum of these changes is viewed, by those who support the idea of modernisation, as far more preferable than the status quo of a traditional society (Wagner, 2001).

Modernisation theory dates to the early part of the 20th century and is linked to the German sociologist, Weber. It was popularised in the middle of the 20th century, and is particularly associated with the American sociologist, Talcott Parsons.

Critics of this theory include socialists and others who argue that not all citizens are better-off as a result of modernisation, as it does not necessarily lead to an equal share of the supposed benefits for each citizen (Wagner, 2001). For some critics, modernisation also can result in dependency, as they argue those who benefit from modernisation can only do so if others are dependent on the countries with improving living standards. The process of modernisation also leads to cultural changes, where traditional beliefs and religions will become less important and will be replaced by new cultural and social structures (Bernstein,

1971). Modernisation is also likely to result in political changes, with relatively simple political structures and relationships replaced by more complex ones, but also more abstract ideas (Leroy and van Tatenhove, 2000). For those who support the idea of modernisation, democracy is one of the major political developments that results from the changes in social processes (Wagner, 2001). As the ideas of 'modern' were developed in the early and middle of the 20th century, the period since then has been referred to as the 'post-modern'.

Tourism can be viewed as both a product of modernisation and a contributor to it. As societies become more modern, if citizens become wealthier, then they are likely to have sufficient disposable income and probably the time to engage in tourist activities. Tourism can also be seen as an important part of the process of modernisation, as it can contribute to wealth, particularly of those who work in the activity, which then enables these citizens to have a higher standard of living compared with traditional societies. Modernisation can also be seen to be linked directly to the type of impacts discussed in Chapter 8, that of acculturation, in which cultures are becoming more similar. As noted in Chapter 8, tourism can contribute to acculturation, so if tourism is considered as a product of modernisation, this is a specific example of how it can also contribute to modernisation, by making societies become more similar.

# Globalisation

Perhaps the most important current theory relating to global development is that of globalisation. Globalisation is particularly important because it links together economic, social, cultural and political aspects of development. However, there are a large number of definitions of this process and it is a contested term. Although it is difficult to define precisely, it is generally agreed that globalisation is a process involving global markets, global production, global competition and global communication (Mowforth and Munt, 2016). In this way, globalisation is viewed as the way in which national and regional economies, societies, and cultures have become linked through a global network of trade, communication, immigration and transportation. So, globalisation involves the evolving interconnectedness of the world, reflected in the expanded flows of information, technology, goods, services and people (Dwyer *et al.*, 2008). However, globalisation can be considered as to some extent different from the processes discussed above, as it stems from commerce and industry and is not based or linked to a particular individual's theory or a political movement.

For some writers and researchers, globalisation is an inevitable process in which the developing countries of the world are closely linked to the developed countries and, in fact, follow the lead of the developed countries, and they will eventually become like them. For other writers, globalisation is a process in which the developed countries can maintain their level of development only by keeping the developing countries from reaching the same level as they have achieved. In this way the developed countries can only remain wealthy at the expense of the poor countries, who will forever remain poor, to ensure that the wealthy remain wealthy!

A major result of globalisation is that countries of the world are converging and becoming more similar in terms of their culture, business, politics, the products they make and what the people of each country want (which is mainly more consumer products) (Mason, 2016).

As a primarily commercial process, supporters of globalisation argue that it:

■ promotes global economic growth

■ creates jobs

■ makes companies more competitive

■ expands consumer choice

■ lowers product prices

■ helps spread technical knowledge and education

■ improves global communication and transport

■ creates new markets for firms and countries

■ generates innovation and improves product quality

■ spreads democratic ideals and cultural exchange and international understanding.

(Dwyer *et al.*, 2008)

However those who criticize globalisation suggest that it:

■ generates income inequalities

■ destroys local industries

■ creates greater dependency of developing economies on developed ones

■ destroys small business.

And at the local level:

■ increases prices of consumer goods and services

■ increases the price of land and housing so locals cannot afford to buy

■ increases demands on public services and facilities.

(Dwyer *et al.*, 2008)

Whether or not people agree with the benefits and costs of globalisation, it is a process that almost all commentators agree is occurring. What is driving the process of globalisation is a combination of economic, social, political and technological factors (Mowforth and Munt, 2016). The main economic factors are greater trade in goods and services that link national economic systems, the creation of trading blocks, (the European Union being such an example) and that generally the world's trade has been expanding for a quarter of a century. One major result of this is that the world's economy has been shifting eastwards towards Asia, particularly China and India, and southwards involving Brazil, Argentina, Australia, New Zealand and South Africa.

Globalisation of the economy, combined with technological change means the need for a more highly skilled labour force. As globalisation also means a more integrated and interrelated world market in terms of work, some (skilled) workers, such as those in computing, banking and finance, may be able to get jobs anywhere in the world (Dwyer *et al.*, 2008). However, while jobs are created in developing countries, globalisation is claimed to cause unemployment in developed industrialized countries as businesses 'outsource' work to developing countries where the cost of labour is low (Mowforth and Munt, 2016).

Developments in information and communications technology and transportation have increased the speed of globalisation, lowering operating costs and making it simpler for a firm to locate in different countries. Technology has made it possible to produce specially designed services on a large scale at low prices. Some developing countries have copied or modified technology providing opportunities for them to catch up with the developed economies (Dwyer *et al.*, 2008).

The Internet and related social media have been vital developments in almost all industries, as consumers use them to collect information on products and services and in relation to tourism, on destinations. The rise of social media, such as Facebook, Twitter, YouTube, WhatsApp, Instagram and Skype, have helped with cross-cultural communication (Dwyer *et al.*, 2008). Technological advances in transport particularly aviation, with larger jet aircraft that have over 500 seats, have enabled the continual rise in the ability to travel. It has become possible for people to travel greater distances, more comfortably and faster (Mason, 2016).

In relation to demographic factors, public health in developed countries has assisted in increasing length of life. With increasing life length, the growing world population is ageing, especially in rapidly expanding urban areas in developed countries. However the population is getting younger in developing countries. The world's population is also becoming increasingly urbanized (Mason, 2016).

At the same time as there have been changes in demography, there have been changes in people's values, aspirations and expectations. This has been accompanied by a general rise in income (in developed countries, at least) which means that it is possible for many to achieve what they aspire to. Over the past 30 years or so, many people have become more individualistic, but in what might appear to be a contradictory way, at the same time, more socially and environmentally conscious. People are also become more hedonistic or pleasure seeking. However, there are those employed with well paid jobs, who are seen to be 'money rich, but time poor' and others who are unemployed, who are 'time rich, but money poor' (Dwyer *et al.*, 2008).

In general, globalisation has produced a generation that is more international in its outlook than any before. There are far more members of international organisations than ever and more studying abroad. The movement of people – either from rural to urban environments within countries or migration between them – is a prominent feature of the process. In this way globalisation can be seen to provide better opportunities for people all round the world to gain access to jobs.

International organisations such as the World Trade Organization and the International Monetary Fund have helped globalisation by reducing trade barrier and deregulating world financial markets. The Organization for Economic Cooperation and Development and the World Bank are supporters of liberalisation of trade through lending and debt relief policies. In many developing countries, there is a new political pressure for higher living standards, with a growing global middle class creating a cycle of rising aspirations (Dwyer *et al.*, 2008).

Part of this globalisation process has also meant a growing concern for the environment and this has led to pressure to use resources more efficiently. At the same time, there has been development of consumer protection and consumer laws in many countries. This has given increasing certainty to many businesses as well as consumers as to their rights, expectations, responsibilities and obligations across all industries (Mason, 2016).

However, as we have noted above, there are negative aspects of globalisation as well as these positive changes. Nevertheless, the changes brought about by globalisation are frequently assessed at the national level and viewed as positive. In addition, much writing about global development and the processes of globalisation uses relatively complex socio-economic terms, as well as considering only macro-level (national and international) factors such as GDP, income level, international trade, industrial output and energy consumption. In the quotation following, Bennet (2010:83) not only indicates, as stated above, that globalisation is primarily a commercial process, but that it is important also to consider what the meaning of globalisation is from an individual's perspective:

> *Globalisation is the new form of empire. Despite its name it is largely unconcerned with territory. Its unit of organisation is not the nation state but the corporation. It has been enabled by the jet plane and more recently the internet. It originated in the (United) States, but has become a game played by all wealthy nations, with the American still in the lead, but with countless others at their heels. It's game of money. For the winners the rewards are absurdly generous. For the losers, the Filipina maids and the Indian labourers, well, they were losing before they began. Nothing much changes for them* (Bennett, 2010: 83).

Globalisation has major impacts on tourism. Rising income is a significant generator of tourism flows to the extent that globalisation generates a dynamic world economy, and creates the economic basis for continued growth in domestic and international tourism worldwide. In particular, strong income growth in Brazil, Russia, India and China is expected to drive the increase in international tourism worldwide as the 'new wealthy' seek new experiences (Dwyer *et al*, 2008).

However, if tourism income is not received equally, it can create much more inequality. This can be exacerbated if there are tourism expenditure leakages. This is when tourism revenue does not stay in the local community, but leaks back to countries who own parts of the industry, such as hotels. Also, the relationship between inbound tourism and economic growth may not necessarily lead to higher living standards in developing countries, as these are also dependent on the distribution of income and the quality of services such as health care and education (Mason, 2016). Hence, some studies suggest caution when generalizing the effects of tourism growth on poverty within a country (Mowforth and Munt, 2016).

As noted above, dependency can be a product of globalisation. In Chapter 9, it was stated that certain parts of the world, particularly islands and some developing countries can be dependent on tourism. The global financial crisis, beginning in 2008, has demonstrated the risks involved in tourism dependency arising from sudden downturns in demand from world markets. Too much reliance on tourism can result from dependence on specific origin markets, or possibly too much reliance on a particular tourism product, such as casino tourism or spa tourism. Given that people do not have to spend income on tourism, as it is not a basic necessity, the industry is extremely sensitive to crises of every type (Mason, 2016).

Tourism can result in new jobs and higher incomes than previously in developing countries. It may also mean that some people have long-term jobs and real career possibilities. However, the industry can also contribute to de-skilling of the workforce, where workers lose the ability to do a traditional job, when they transfer to tourism (Dwyer *et al.*, 2008). If a country becomes over-dependent on tourism and there is a crisis in which tourism no longer occurs, then not only may workers of a country have lost their current jobs, but they may not be able to take up their old traditional jobs, as they no longer have the knowledge and skills to perform them (Mason, 2016).

The following case study considers tourism within the context of global development. It focuses on a specific type of tourism, known as pro-poor tourism, which has the major aim of trying to benefit particularly poor communities in developing countries through the use of tourism (Mason, 2016). Pro-poor tourism is intended to provide jobs in tourism and hence income and also investment in communities that have traditionally had little tourism development or where there has been significant economic leakage from a developing country destination (Mowforth and Munt, 2016). The case study discusses how evidence of lack of development or uneven development in the form of slum areas in developing world cities can act as tourist attractions. As the case study indicates however, this type of tourism is not without controversial aspects.

# Case study: Slum tourism in Kenya

The idea of tourists visiting slums may be viewed as an unlikely activity. It would seem to fly in the face of what motivates tourists. However, for a tour operator in Kenya this is one type of tourism experience that they provide. Victoria Safaris' main activities in the past has been to provide wildlife safaris, but for half a dozen years or so, they have been offering guided tours of some of the poorest parts of Kenya. The country has a large number of poor people, with many living on no more than a dollar a day. These people live in the suburbs of the capital Nairobi, and in the same types of area in other large urban settlements such as Kisumu. Victoria Tours offers the possibility of interaction with local people in these suburbs. This enables tourists to see, at first hand, the nature of the day-to-day problems that residents of these areas have to deal with.

Victoria Tours has come up with the idea of this form of tourism to raise awareness, amongst both domestic and foreign tourists, of the conditions that the local people live in so that their lives can be improved and the slums actually wiped out. Tourism is the most significant business in Kenya in terms of foreign earnings and Victoria Tours wants local people in the slums to financially benefit from tourism. This type of pro-poor tourism should help local people to participate more effectively in gaining revenue from tourism. As the aims of this type of pro-poor tourism range from employing more local people to involving locals in decision-making, Victoria Tours has hired a number of slum residents to undertake a range of jobs. This includes those who are employed as tour bus drivers, others who act as guides and yet more who are part of the slum police and security team. A number of those employed are local community leaders, and they are very aware of living conditions in the slums as they live there.

The film *The Constant Gardener*, based on the John Le Carre novel, starring Ralph Fiennes and Rachel Weisz, was filmed in the Nairobi slum suburb of Kiberia. This has become one of the main centres for slum tourism in Kenya. Guided tours are organised by Victoria Tours. The General Manager of Victoria Tours, who comes from the same tribe that makes up the majority of Kiberia residents, claims that people are fed up with animal-based tours in Kenya and he decided to set up something different – slum tourism. He claims that his aim is to raise awareness of condition in Kiberia, to enable local people to benefit from tourism, and to ask tourists to donate money to community projects and charities operating in the slum area. However, his activities have caused controversy. A local paper the *Daily Nation,* has asked the question: 'What is the fascination with Kiberia for people who have no idea of the real meaning of poverty?' This question was followed up by another: 'More to the point: What do Kenyans think of this back-handed compliment, as the custodians of backwardness, filth, misery and absolute deprivation?'

The answer would seem to be 'Not a lot'. Although residents realise that the attention on Kiberia is potentially good, as it could help put pressure on the government to improve conditions, there had been relatively few benefits to date and the embarrassment factor was steadily growing. 'The tourists like to come and have a little walk and then tell their friends that they have been to the worst slum in Africa, but nothing changes for us', one resident indicated. 'If they want to come, well, let them do something for us, or even stay the night with us here, or walk around after rain, and see that the roads are like rivers', he continued. Some of those working in community projects in Kiberia have also been annoyed about the large number of high profile visitors to the slum, as their visits raised the expectations of locals that things would be improved, in addition to putting even more strain on the very limited resources of the area and annoying the usually hospitable local community.

**10**

The image of the slum has also caused controversy with some residents and other Kenyans. 'The image is one of unremitting misery' one resident stated 'It's poverty, poverty, poverty!' This is not fair as there are so many different stories in this area'.

But the publicity used by Victoria Tours has also annoyed some locals: 'After lunch, proceed to the Korochoko slum and you will be amazed by the number of roaming children' is one sentence in marketing material. There has also been sarcastic 'marketing' articles written by local newspapers journalists: "Kiberia is the rave spot of Kenya… see it all in one simple stop. The AIDS victim dying slowly on a cold cardboard bed. The breastless teenager….plastic-eating goats, fighting small children and, ah yes, the famous 'shit-rolls-downhill-flying-toilets'".   A government minister has been trying to promote the bright side of Kenya, but says: 'It is very sad when dignitaries come here, the first place they run to is Kiberia...the locals are getting tired of people coming and giving lip-service. Kiberia is the in-place, everybody wants to be associated with, whether they are doing anything about it or not.  People look at others who are poor and destitute and get a 'feel good' attitude about themselves, that they are above that'

Source: Mowforth and Munt, (2016), based on www.victoriasfaris.com/kenyatours/propoor.htm and 'Slum tourism stirs controversy in Kenya', Reuters, 9/2/07

# Summary

A number of important economic and sociological theories have been created over the last 200 years or so in relation to global development. Although several make no specific reference to it, they do have important implications for tourism, particularly the point that tourism can act as a catalyst for change.

Globalisation is a major process affecting the development of the world. It has important economic, social, cultural, political and environmental dimensions. Almost all countries have been affected by globalisation. Tourism is an important dimension of globalisation, both contributing to it and being affected by it. For many commentators, globalisation has a large number of benefits, and these can be measured at the national and international level, but also it is important to be aware that although there may be winners, globalisation can also create losers.

## Student activities

1  What do you understand by the term 'global development'?

2  What are the characteristics of:

    a) Developed countries

    b) Developing countries

3  What factors have contributed to countries being classified as either developed or developing?

4   What role does tourism have within the following theories:

   a) Dependency theory

   b) Rostow's stages of economic growth

   b) Vicious circles of supply/demand

5   What links are there between modernisation theory and tourism?

6   How is tourism affected by, but also contributes to, the process of globalisation?

7   Why is slum tourism in Kenya controversial?

8   Working in small groups (3/4 students) discuss why either

   a) you would like to visit the Kiberia slum in Kenya,

   or b) not like to visit the Kiberia slum in Kenya.

# References

Bennet, J. (2010), *Hello Dubai*, London: Simon and Schuster.

Bernstein, H. (1971). Modernisation theory and the sociological study of development. *Journal of Development Studies*, **7**(2), 141–60.

Cooper, C., Fletcher, J., Fyall, A., Gilbert, D. and Wanhill, S. (2005) *Tourism: Principles and Practice*. 3rd ed., London: Prentice Hall

Dwyer, L.M., Edwards. D., Mistilis, N.A., Roman, C., Scott, N. and Cooper, C., (2008), *Megatrends Underpinning Tourism to 2020: Analysis of key drivers for change*, Queensland: CRC for Sustainable Tourism Pty Ltd.

Lea, J. (1988) *Tourism and Development in the Third World*, London: Routledge.

Leroy, P. and van Tatenhove, J. (2000). Political modernisation theory and environmental politics, in Spaargaren, G., Mol, A.P.J. and Buttel, F. H. *Environment and Global Modernity*, London: Sage.

Mason, P. (1990) *Tourism: Environment and Development Perspectives*, Godalming, WWF.

Mason, P. (2016) *Tourism Impacts, Planning and Management*, 3rd ed., London: Routledge.

Mowforth, M. and Munt, I. (2014) *Tourism and Sustainability*, London: Routledge.

O'Grady, J. (1980) *Third World Stopover*, Geneva: World Council of Churches, Risk Publications.

Rostow, W.W. (1962) *Stages of Economic Growth: A Non-Communist Manifesto*, Cambridge: Cambridge University Press.

Wagner, D. (2001) *Theorizing Modernity. Inescapability and Attainability in Social Theory*, London: Sage.

10

# 11 Climate Change

## Introduction

Climate change poses a major threat to almost all forms of human activity on earth, including tourism. As Holden (2016: 227) argues:

> Of all the challenges facing tourism's relationship with nature, it is not an exaggeration to state that climate change represents the greatest.

Holden gives as his rationale for this statement that it is the stability and predictability of climate that is vital for the environments and ecosystems that are required for the continuation of current types of tourism, whether these are the traditional form of mass tourism, in terms of 'sun, sea and sand' holidays, or a niche activity which involves visiting a tropical rain forest with rare flora and fauna as the main attraction.

Climate change also presents opportunities for tourism. If areas currently experiencing cool winters and mild summers get warmer, then new types of tourism may be possible including beach-based holidays where at present these are of little importance. Climate change is likely to lead to modifications in the weather at different times of the year so 'seasonality' which is currently a very important dimension to many forms of tourism will be affected, probably to the extent that seasons when there is high tourism activity will get longer in some parts of the world.

Although tourism is likely to be significantly affected by climate change, it has also contributed to climate change through for example the burning of fossil fuels in transport for tourism as well through the use of power in hotel accommodation.

## Global warming

When we discuss climate change in relation to tourism and many other economic and social activities, most often the discussion is concerned with *global warming*. It is important to be aware that the process of regular daily and seasonal global warming is a natural occurrence and without it there would not be life on earth as we currently know it. However, when discussing global warming, we are usually talking about an unbalanced situation where global warming is occurring more quickly, on an annual basis, than previously.

The regular process of global warming is a result of natural processes. In Chapter 4, we saw that the earth is warmed by the heat from the sun, and discussed what happens in terms of the amount of heat available at different places on the earth's surface (the effects of latitude), the effects on temperature of increasing or decreasing altitude, and also the impacts of seasonality on temperature.

However, it is important to be aware of what happens to solar radiation when it reaches the earth's surface. As noted in Chapter 4, the atmosphere around the earth is not heated directly by the solar radiation – the gases that make up the atmosphere cannot absorb the short wave radiation from the sun. Instead, the short wave radiation hits the surface of the earth, warms the solid or liquid (if it is an ocean, sea or river) surface and is converted to long wave radiation which can heat the gases that make up the atmosphere. This means that the atmosphere is heated from below.

However, not all heat from the sun is available to heat the earth's surface and the atmosphere. This is because when the sun rays strike the earth, some rays are bounced back by reflectivity of the earth's surface. The term for reflectivity is *albedo*. The albedo varies, largely in relation to the nature of the surface of the earth. For example, a white, snow covered surface reflects a lot of solar radiation, so the albedo is high. A dark brown, ploughed field absorbs much more solar radiation, so the albedo is low. A liquid (water) surface reflects a significant amount of radiation and usually has a higher albedo than a solid surface.

On average, about 30% of the solar radiation is reflected back into space as a result of the albedo effect. This means, however, that about 70% of the sun's energy remains and is absorbed into the atmosphere by what we call the *Greenhouse Gases* (GHGs). The main GHGs are as follows: $CO_2$ (carbon dioxide), $N_2O$ (nitrous oxide), $CH_4$ (methane) and $O_3$ (ozone). There is also water vapour in the atmosphere, which absorbs heat. The greenhouse gases make up only approximately 1% of the earth's atmosphere, but they have a high capacity to absorb and release energy.

11

To understand the effects being discussed here, it is important to understand what is meant by a *Greenhouse Gas*. A greenhouse is in reality a glasshouse and this allows the sun's energy (the short wave radiation) through, but traps heat generated inside, because the short wave radiation has been converted, when it passes through the glass inside the greenhouse, to long wave radiation, once it reaches solid surfaces such as growing plants. The long wave radiation is then able to warm the air (the mixture of gases) inside the greenhouse, but is not able to pass back through the glass, and is trapped inside. So the temperature of a greenhouse will be higher (assuming the sun is shining) than outside the greenhouse. Gardeners and farmers have known this for a long time, so in winter greenhouses, or glasshouses, are warmer during the day when the sun shines and can be used to grow crops that will not grow outside at that time of the year.

We use the analogy of the greenhouse to explain what happens in terms of global warming. However, it is important to remember that the daily and seasonal warming of the lower atmosphere is a regular process and allows plants and animals (including us) to live on earth. Without this warming effect, the earth would be 30°C cooler and life on earth would be very difficult and, if it existed at all, very different from what it is now. However, the greenhouse gases act in the same way as a greenhouse in that they trap the heat from the sun and keep the atmosphere much warmer than it would be without them.

As just indicated, the warming is natural, but in the last 250 years, particularly since industrialisation began, humans have added to the amount of greenhouse gases in the atmosphere and so that average global temperatures have been rising. Hence, in the 20th century temperatures rose by an average 0.6°C and the predictions are that the rise by 2100, will be by another 1.4°C. This may not appear to be a very significant change but it is an average figure, and according to most scientists, enough to melt more snow and ice, which are found at the poles and high mountain ranges, than ever before. The melting of the ice and snow means there is more water in liquid form and this water will find its way into the seas and oceans causing seal levels to rise. In addition, the melting of snow changes the earth's albedo. Hence, if enough melts, this lowers the albedo which then raises the earth's temperature and this in turn causes more snow and ice to melt.

# The evidence that climate change is occurring

It is relatively easy for an individual to be aware and comment on what they consider to be unusual weather, be it extreme heat, stronger winds, bigger storms, more rain or heavier snowfall. But this is not climate change, this is merely unusual weather and could be occurring for many reasons and, within any time period, unusual weather will not be that unusual! In fact, deviations from average weather conditions are to be expected. However as we saw in Chapter 4, weather and climate are not the same. In brief, climate is average weather. What this means is that climate is weather over a relatively long period. The period of time for discussion of climate is at least 30 years and is frequently 50 years.

Collins (2004) when discussing the meaning of climate change in relation to weather and climate, summarises this relationship in the following way:

> Change in the climate of an area or the whole world over an appreciable period of time. That is, a single winter that is colder than average, does not signal climate change. It is the change in average weather conditions from one period of time (30-50 years) to the next (Collins, 2004:75)

The evidence for climate change is summarised below:

1   As humans have only been around for a relatively short period of time and have kept records of historical events for even less time, accurate written records of past climatic conditions do not exist. However, one source of information is ice. Because there is circulation of air masses between tropical and high latitude regions, tiny particles including seeds and volcanic dust, as well as air bubbles containing evidence of ancient gases frozen inside ice, are found in ice which dates back thousands of years. This ancient ice is obtained

by drilling deep into it in the polar regions and high mountain glaciers. This produces what is known as an ice core. So, for example, ice dating back 110,000 years has come from cores in Greenland, and in Antarctica ice cores going back almost 800,000 years have been dug out (Riebeek, 2005). These cores contain evidence of what climate was like in the past. As *The Guardian Scientist* (2011) put it:

> *Ice contains dust from volcanic eruptions and desert windstorms, pollen, microbes, meteorites, small trapped bubbles of "fossil air" and even changes in the concentrations of Beryllium-10, indicating changes in the strength of solar radiation. Combined, all of these data provide scientists with a surprisingly detailed look at past seasons, and can be used to reconstruct an uninterrupted and detailed climate record extending over hundreds of thousands of years.*

So, in this way a global climate record from the ice cores can be built up, and this can be supplemented by sediments found at the bottom of lakes (Riebeek, 2005). This record indicates that there have been numerous occasions when the earth's climate has changed in the past, and this has occurred because of variations in the sun's energy over time, but also because of increased (or decreased) amounts of material in the atmosphere, including dust from volcanoes. Atmospheric dust tends to reflect some heat back away from the earth (the albedo effect), so temperatures fall slightly, and this fall can cause average global temperatures to drop. Nevertheless, these changes in climate from hotter to cooler have traditionally taken many hundreds, if not thousands, of years according to the scientific research that has been conducted, and the evidence from ice cores. The changes that have been recorded in the 19th, 20th and so far in the 21st century have happened very quickly – far quicker than ever before. It is linked by most scientists to the burning of, in particular, coal and oil which has put far more $CO_2$ into the atmosphere in the past 200 years or so.

**2** In the 20th century the average temperature of the entire earth rose by 0.6° – this rate of increase exceeds anything recorded during the whole of the last 20,000 years (Holden, 2016).

**3** The amount of $CO_2$ had been constant at approximately 280 parts/million for 1000 years until the mid-18th century. However since approximately 1750 – the beginning of the Industrial Revolution – $CO_2$ levels have risen to 425 parts/million (CO2Now.org, 2015).

**4** The period from 1983-2012 (note this is a 30 year 'climate' period of time) has been the warmest 30 years in the last 1400 years (Holden, 2016)

**5** The highest recorded global temperature occurred in 2014, according to records going back to 1880. The year 2014 was the 38th consecutive year of the earth's temperature exceeding the global average and the odds on this occurring without human-induced change are 1 in 27 million (Goldenberg, 2014).

11

**6**   GHGs have increased in the period from 2000 to 2010 (IPCC, 2014). Some of these gases are more efficient at trapping the sun's heat. So for example the trace greenhouse gas methane is 23 times more efficient than carbon dioxide, and in the last 20 years, the amount of methane in the atmosphere has been increasing (Holden, 2016).

The way in which the GHGs in the atmosphere are being measured is through what is referred to as the *carbon footprint*. This can be considered to be the total set of GHG emissions caused by an individual, event, organisation or product, and is usually expressed as a carbon dioxide equivalent. However, this is not always easy to measure as there can be complex relationships and overlaps. For this reason, Wright *et al.* (2011:63), have defined the carbon footprint as:

> *A measure of the total amount of carbon dioxide ($CO_2$) and methane ($CH_4$) emissions of a defined population, system or activity, considering all relevant sources, sinks and storage within the spatial and temporal boundary of the population, system or activity of interest.*

Over the last 20 years, with the general acceptance that climate change has been occurring, there have been several attempts to achieve international agreement on what the response should be. The most recent of these, and probably the most successful, was the meeting that took place in December 2015 and produced the Paris Climate Accord. In total, 195 countries signed the first ever legally binding global climate deal in Paris. The agreement sets out a global action plan to put the world on track to avoid dangerous climate change by limiting global warming to well below 2°C. In more detail, in the Paris Climate Accord, countries agreed:

- a long-term goal of keeping the increase in global average temperature to well below 2°C above pre-industrial levels;

- to aim to limit the increase to 1.5°C, since this would significantly reduce risks and the impacts of climate change;

- on the need for global emissions to peak as soon as possible, recognising that this will take longer for developing countries;

- to undertake rapid reductions thereafter in accordance with the best available science.

(European Commission 2016)

Despite the fact that there is a very large amount of agreement amongst scientists around the world that global warming is occurring and has been doing so for many decades up to and continuing in the present and that human activity is a major cause of this, there are a (relatively small) number of people who do not accept the scientific evidence. Some of those who do not accept the scientific evidence have vested interest in continuing to support the use of fossils fuels, such as oil and coal. Several of this very small minority are in influential positions. For example, in early 2017, US President Trump, who does not accept that global warming is occurring, indicated he would pull the USA out of the Paris Climate Accord. However, the effect of the USA withdrawing from the Paris Climate Accord will not actually happen until 2020, because of the way the treaty was written.

Although there is a small minority who do not accept that global warming is occurring, there is general acceptance amongst almost all scientists that there have been already, and will continue to be, major impacts of the warming of the atmosphere. In summary the major impacts of global warming are:

- Disruption of traditional agriculture, particularly that dependent on seasonal rains and temperature changes (so nomadic subsistence farming is badly hit).
- Increased vulnerability of coastal areas and small islands to rising sea levels caused by melting ice caps.
- More unusual, exceptional weather events (storms snow, droughts).
- Increased vulnerability of all agricultural ecosystems and hence food production.
- Coral reefs bleached as oceans become more acid because of chemicals in water (usually referred to as acid rain).
- Diseases like malaria (vector borne diseases) will become more widespread as breeding areas increase, spread north and south from equatorial regions.
- Increased stress of vulnerable plant and animal species.

(Holden, 2016).

## Tourism and climate change

There is no certainty in relation to climate change and tourism. This is in itself an issue in attempts to counter any impacts, but also in terms of planning for the future. Without a clear idea of what will happen if, and when, climate changes, it will be very difficult to plan for this unknown future.

Much tourism depends on a stable climate because of its seasonal nature. So, for example, the Mediterranean area is very important for tourism in Europe because of its relatively stable and consistent climate from May to September. This climate region has dry, warm to very warm sunny weather in general throughout this period. As a result of this the region has had 'sun, sea and sand' holidays for a long time. Along the Mediterranean coasts of Spain, France, Italy, Croatia, Greece and Turkey, for example, very large numbers of tourists spend several weeks each year, tens of thousands of people are employed and hundreds of millions of euros and other currencies are involved in the tourism industry. Climate change may result in this Mediterranean area turning to desert and/or possibly experiencing violent storms and flash floods and more forest fires. The change in climate is likely to have serious consequences for tourism in the Mediterranean region.

Likewise, warming of the earth's atmosphere is causing ice caps and glaciers to melt. In important winter sports areas such as Switzerland and Austria, skiing and other snow based activities will almost certainly completely disappear, or be confined to just a few areas at high altitude.

In the early part of the 21st century the World Tourism Organizations (WTO) summarised the impacts of climate change on tourism. These were as follows:

- Rises in sea level will affect low-lying coasts and small islands
- Rising temperatures will change rainfall and other precipitation patterns
- Water supply problems will be exacerbated
- Climate change will increase the magnitude, frequency and risk of extreme events, such as storms and sea surges. (WTO, 2003)

It is possible to be more specific about likely effects of sea level rises as they are one particularly important aspect of climate change affecting tourism. The rise in sea level will probably lead to more beach and coastal erosion, more flooding, the loss of some coastal ecosystems and the complete submergence of some low lying islands (Holden, 2016). Rising temperatures will have the effect of making areas currently lacking large amounts of rainfall, and hence relatively dry, even drier. The temperature rise may also lead to movement of the climate zones (see Figure 4.5) which will possibly alter the amount and location of rainfall. Places that currently have snow in winter such as the lower slopes of the Alps are likely to have more rain and less snow and, as indicated in relation to Switzerland and Austria, ski tourism will no longer be feasible. One effect of less rainfall in some locations will be an unreliable water supply, which will affect both locals and tourists. In other locations there may be far more rainfall and this will probably be linked to high winds, violent storms and possibly extra high sea levels when there is a combination of high tides with wind from directions that will cause a sea surge and flooding of low lying beaches and coastal tourism destinations.

## ■ Tourism's contribution to climate change

Not only is tourism affected by climate change now and into the future, but it also has impacts as an activity on climate change. Tourism contributes to climate change through emissions of a number of GHGs, in particular carbon dioxide. In addition tourism contributes nitrous oxide, methane, hydrofluorocarbons, perfluorocarbons and carbon hexafluoride (Gossling *et al.*, 2013).

Most carbon dioxide emissions are associated with air transport. According to data produced jointly by the WTO and the United Nations Environment Programme, in 2015, aviation contributed as much as 41% of tourism's carbon footprint, car transport contributed 34% and accommodation 19%. The remainder of tourism's emissions included about 2% from cruise ships. In total in 2015, tourism contributed at least 5% of all $CO_2$ from human sources and the activity accounted for approximately 8% of all global warming (UNWTO/IUCN, 2016).

A key issue for the future is that although it may be possible to reduce the impacts of global warming generally, tourism is forecast to continue to expand over the next 15 to 20 years. So how will it be possible to limit the damaging effects of tourism in terms of climate change? As of 2013, no credible plan had been offered to reduce tourism's contribution according to Gossling *et al.* (2013), but they suggest that what is required is a combination of technological investment, management strategies and changes in consumer behaviour.

Making any attempt to reduce the effects of climate change far less likely to succeed has been the recent decision by the US government under Donald Trump to withdraw from the Paris climate accord of 2015. Although all other countries have remained 'on board' and are sticking to their targets, and some including China and India have actually exceeded theirs since 2015, the USA was viewed as a key player in this agreement. The loss of the country could be very significant for future attempts to offset the effects of climate change.

The following case study summarises documents produced by major climate scientists and international organisations and presents details on the effects of climate change on tourism, tourism's contribution to climate change and also suggestions on what can be done in relation to tourism to offset these likely changes.

## Case study: Climate change and tourism

### The effects of climate change on tourism

As a sector, tourism is highly exposed to the direct physical effects of climate change, such as sea-level rise and rising temperatures. It is also threatened by indirect impacts, such as changing availability of water and the spread of some diseases. Some positive impacts are likely, such as the attractiveness to tourists of new geographical areas and opportunities for so-called 'last chance' tourism. Coastal tourism is the largest component of the global tourism industry, with more than 60% of Europeans opting for beach holidays, and the segment accounting for more than 80% of US tourism revenues. It is particularly at risk from the effects of climate change on the world's oceans.

### Rising sea levels

These will have profound and multiple impacts on coastal tourism. Sea level rise will erode and submerge some tourism infrastructure and attractions, such as beaches. For example, nearly a third of Caribbean resorts are less than 1 m above the high water mark. Sea-level rise of 1 m would damage 49–60% of the region's tourist resort properties, lead to the loss or damage of 21 airports, and inundate land around 35 ports. The cost of rebuilding tourist resorts in the region by 2050 is estimated at US$10 billion to 23.3 billion. Higher sea levels and greater storm surges will also quicken the erosion of beaches, sand dunes and cliffs. Degraded beaches reduce the desirability of destinations, as studies of Martinique, Barbados and Bonaire have shown. Beach erosion could reduce the prices that operators can charge for accommodation.

### Rising temperatures and ocean acidification

These are affecting marine habitats and organisms. Coral reefs in particular are under threat. Reefs and the marine life they shelter are important tourist attractions: they contribute US$11.5 billion annually to global tourism revenues. More than 100 countries benefit from the recreational value of their reefs. Ocean acidification decreases the availability of calcium carbonate for reef-building corals, leading to the degradation of reefs. Reefs are also sensitive to high temperatures, leading to 'bleaching' episodes in which high proportions of the coral die. Dive tourists, particularly more experienced divers, can be sensitive to coral bleaching. Awareness of bleaching among dive tourists is mixed, however, and the economic impacts uncertain: while fewer than half of diving-related tourists surveyed in 1998 were concerned about the widespread coral bleaching that took place that year, other studies have recorded reduced tourist satisfaction as a result of dead coral. A scenario of at least 2°C of global warming by 2050–2100 would see reef structures degrade "with serious consequences" for tourism in Australia, the Caribbean and other Small Island States. By mid-century, coral dominated reef systems (those with more than 30% coral cover) are very likely to disappear in some regions.

## Rising temperatures

These could have a variety of effects on the sector:

☐ Variable snowfall, retreating glaciers and milder winters have reduced visitor numbers in winter sports areas in Europe and North America. Warming would reduce the number of resorts that are 'snow reliable', especially those at low altitude, as well as shortening the skiing season.

☐ Rising temperatures are seeing species shift towards the poles and to higher elevations where possible. This could have serious impacts on eco-tourism, such as safari operators, with nature reserves increasingly isolated geographically. In sub-Saharan Africa, up to 40% of species in national parks are likely to become endangered by 2080, assuming that they are unable to migrate. Most wine-producing regions would become less suitable for vine growing, with implications for wine tourism.

☐ Higher temperatures could lead to more, and more intense, forest fires in parts of the world. In southern Europe, for example, fire seasons may lengthen, and there may be an increase in the number of high fire danger days. However, increased humidity in northern Europe is projected to make forest fires less frequent. In North America, severe droughts have themselves contributed to forest die-back, and wildfires have increased in frequency and duration. Pest infestation has also led to wide-scale forest die-back.

☐ Tourists have a clear preference for the type of climate currently found in southern France, northern Italy and northern Spain – rising temperatures could drive tourists away from southern Mediterranean resorts. However, studies have shown that beach tourists are deterred not by high temperatures, but by rain.

☐ Climate change could lead to a reduction in the redistribution of wealth from rich to poor countries that tourism currently provides. The flow of tourists from cold, rich countries to warm, poorer ones could slow, as more tourists holiday nearer to home.

☐ There is a risk that climate impacts could make some resorts, hotels or facilities unusable, rendering them 'stranded assets' and bringing financial losses to investors and operators.

## Tourism's impacts on climate change

It is difficult to separate out tourism's emissions from other activities, but it is generally considered to contribute approximately 5% of all emissions that affect global climate change, as it is in parts an energy-intensive industry. Its customers often travel long distances, using highly polluting forms of transport. In developing countries, tourists tend to have a larger carbon footprint on average than the local population.

Given the significance of its climate impact, tourism will come under significant pressure to reduce its GHG emissions if governments enact policies to curb climate change in line with the 2°C target. These pressures will become all the more acute given the sector's projected growth. Under a business-as-usual scenario, the sector's emissions were forecast to grow by 130% between 2005 and 2035; the emissions from air travel and accommodation are projected to triple. Studies show that for some countries, such as the UK, unrestricted growth of tourism would, by 2050, see the sector consume the entire 'carbon budget' available under a 2°C scenario.

Pressures on the sector to reduce emissions are likely to trigger more efficient behaviour, and therefore some cost savings. However, by and large, reducing emissions will impose additional costs. While the built environment accounts for around 20% of the sector's climate impact, transport makes up 75%.

## Mitigating the effects of climate change

### The built environment

There is large potential for energy savings in both new and existing buildings. The technologies needed are well understood, allowing for the construction or retrofitting of buildings to very low – or even zero-energy standards. These investments typically pay back well within the building lifetime. 'Deep' retrofits of existing buildings can deliver energy savings of 50–90%. Mitigation options for buildings comprise four strategies:

☐ Building-integrated renewable energy systems, such as solar power;

☐ Energy efficient lighting, heating, cooling and other appliances;

☐ System efficiency, e.g through building codes and standards and urban planning;

☐ Behavioural and lifestyle changes.

☐ None of the strategies are unique to the tourism sector, but all can be applied to help reduce its emissions.

### Transport

Reduction in emissions from the tourism sector will depend to a large degree on improvements in efficiency made within the transport sector. Here, progress is being made across a number of fronts:

☐ **More efficient vehicles:** Internal combustion engines and jet turbines are becoming increasingly efficient. Expectations are for 40–70% improvements in the fuel efficiency of light-duty vehicles by 2035. New aircraft typically offer a 20–30% improvement in fuel efficiency over existing models, driven by improved engine performance, weight reductions, and design. Further gains of 40–50% between 2030 and 2050 are possible, compared with levels of the early 21st century.

☐ **Alternative fuels:** Airlines are experimenting with replacing kerosene with biofuels, which offer direct GHG emission reductions of 30–90% compared to fossil fuels. Shifting to electric or hydrogen-fuelled vehicles promises to dramatically reduce emissions from road vehicles used by tourists while at, or travelling to, their destinations.

☐ **Operational improvements:** Aviation $CO_2$ emissions can be reduced through more direct routes, flying at optimum altitudes and speeds, and reducing time spent waiting to land.

☐ **Modal shifts:** Further reductions can be delivered by shifting from road and aviation to high-speed rail, especially where electricity grids have been decarbonised.

## Life style changes necessary

Although emissions reductions from improvements in fuel efficiency and technological fixes are likely to occur, these will probably be offset by growth in tourism. Strong policy measures are likely to be necessary, especially to change passenger transport behaviour. Changes in lifestyle are therefore likely to be an important component of any effort to drive emissions reductions from tourism. Such changes might include, for example, a reduction in the demand for long-haul tourism in favour of holidaying more locally, using the concept of the 'staycation'. Air transport accounts for approximately 40% of the tourism sector's emissions, but only 17% of the total tourism trips taken. Cruises tend also to have high associated emissions in comparison to their percentage of all tourism trips. This means that reducing demand in a few, small sub-sectors of tourism (such as long-haul flying and cruise ship) could have a significant effect on emissions.

Source: Adapted from: *Climate: Everyone's Business, Key Findings from the Intergovernmental Panel on Climate Change, Fifth Assessment Report*, European Climate Foundation and the University of Cambridge's Judge Business School and the Institute for Sustainability Leadership (2005) and Sustainable Development of Tourism, WTO/OECD (2012), Madrid.

One of the world's major tourist attractions, which receives upwards of ten million annual visitors, could be a major casualty of global warming. Most of the older buildings in the Italian city of Venice are built on wooden pilings that have kept them out of the waters that surrounds them, for several centuries except during periods of very high tides. However, for the past 50 years the water level has been rising and global warming will exacerbate this problem. Before it was fully realised that global warming would make conditions in Venice very difficult for locals and tourist alike, a plan was created to attempt to alleviate this flooding. The plan, known in its abbreviated form as MOSE, involves a total of 78 metal barriers that are intended to stop flood water getting into the area around the city of Venice. The original plan was put forward in the late 1980s, but work did not begin until 2003, once funding from the EU and other sources had been secured. However the estimated cost of the project is almost €6 billion, and unfortunately the project has been beset by allegations of corruption, including the involvement of the Mayor of Venice (Windsor, 2015) causing significant delays in implementation. The original completion date was 2011, this was put back to 2014, then 2015 and it is now not likely to be finished before 2018 at the earliest and possibly 2020 (Windsor, 2015). The following case study discusses in greater detail the issues surrounding tourism in Venice and rising sea levels.

## Case Study: Venice, tourism and climate change

The Grand Canal in Venice, Photo by Wolfang Moroder

Venice is one of the World Heritage sites most at threat from sea-level rise, with major implications for its burgeoning tourism industry. The city's extraordinary assemblage of Byzantine, Gothic, Renaissance and Baroque architecture is under immediate threat from rising sea levels. Founded in the 5th century, Venice was built on the islands and marshes of the Venetian Lagoon as a trading post and refuge from attack. The villages and settlements expanded, and between the 9th and 15th centuries Venice was an immensely powerful and rich trading state.

Today, the city stands on 118 islands with connected canals and 338 bridges. Venice is now one of the world's most popular and iconic tourist destinations, hosting nearly 10 million overnight visits in 2013 (Città di Venizia, 2014) and at least twice as many day visitors. But tourism itself is becoming a major concern as the dramatic increase in visitor numbers and, in particular, the number of single day trips, has radically changed the visitor dynamic in Venice in recent years. Cruise ship disembarkations rose by a factor of nine between 1990 and 2011, from 200,000 to 1.8 million (Cocks, 2013).

The Venice Port Authority has indicated that the income and employment generated by cruise tourism is indispensable to the city – cruise ship passengers are said to spend up to €150 million in Venice each year (Comitato Cruise Venice) – and has promoted dredging in the lagoon to enable ships to enter the port without sailing through the town. Alternative proposals have also been made, including allowing the ships to dock on the mainland shore inside the lagoon, or building a floating dock in the sea outside one of the lagoon's entrances.

Today, in the face of such rapid tourism growth alongside rising sea levels driven by climate change and worsened by local land subsidence, Venice is struggling to maintain both the fabric of its buildings and the character of the city. As tourist numbers have continued to grow, the resident population has dropped dramatically – from 120,000 to 55,000 over the past 30 years – with people leaving as a result of high consumer prices, congestion, and a lack of affordable places to live (Ross, 2015).

Because of its low lying position, Venice can be subject to major storm damage. The worst flood in recent memory was in November 1966, when a massive storm system hit Italy, causing catastrophic damage to art and cultural heritage in Florence in the west and Venice in the east (Malguzzi *et al.*, 2006). Venice and its inhabitants have for centuries struggled with the water and the maintenance of the lagoon, and have had to find ways to live with the high tides and storms, but the 1966 event provoked major discussion about how to protect Venice from future catastrophic floods. After decades of debate and planning, a series of 79 flood gates distributed across the three entrances that connect the Venetian Lagoon to the Adriatic Sea – the MOSE project – is due to be completed in 2018 or later. These gates will rise whenever a tidal flood of 110 cms or more is predicted (Windsor, 2015; Tosi *et al.*, 2013), holding back the waters of the Adriatic until conditions improve. The total cost of these defences will be above €5.4 billion, and maybe more.

Flooding at especially high tides, or as a result of storm surges, has always been an issue for Venice. But now, with sea levels rising, the problem is much more severe. For decades the problem of sea-level rise has been exacerbated by land subsidence caused by water extraction – a practice that was ended in the 1970s to prevent Venice from sinking further. Venice has seen water levels rise by nearly 30cms in relation to the measuring point established in 1897 beside the Punta della Dogana, an art museum in Venice's old customs building, the Dogana da Mar. Of this, about 12cms is due to land subsidence and the rest to climate-driven sea-level rise (UNESCO, 2011; Carbognin *et al.*, 2010). The ever more frequent flooding events experienced by the city since 1950 will be controllable when the mobile barriers between the lagoon and the sea come into operation, at least until sea levels eventually overwhelm them, too (UNESCO, 2011). The water level in the lagoon, however, will continue to rise, eating away at the substance of the buildings as damp spreads up the brickwork. The barriers will be ineffective against this phenomenon, except by being closed for longer and longer periods, with significant water pollution implications for the lagoon (UNESCO, 2011).

Hundreds of buildings and monuments in Venice have already been damaged by rising seas. The city's buildings were originally constructed by driving wooden posts deep into the mud of the lagoon, with dense, water-resistant Istrian stone foundations laid on these pilings and the fabric of the house built on top using brick, plaster and marble. A projecting stone moulding that separates the stone from the brick prevented waves from splashing upwards and wetting, but Venice's waters have risen by some 30cms since the end of the 19th century, damaging the brickwork (Camuffo *et al.*, 2014). The water level is now often above the stone bases at high tide and the damp then rises by capillary action. Damage is caused by salts in the bricks or stone dissolving and then recrystallizing – San Polo Church, for example, has been severely affected (Camuffo, 2001). The situation has been made worse by the dredging of deep-water channels for shipping, allowing more sea water to enter the lagoon and increasing the salinity of the water (Camuffo, 2001; Penning-Rowsell, 2000). Where the waters have risen above the stone foundations, damp is rising to higher levels where it decays the iron tie-rods that stabilize buildings and hold their walls together, deteriorating the marble and, in St. Mark's Basilica, damaging the small tiles (tesserae) of the 1,000-year-old mosaics, 6m above the floor (Cocks, 2013).

Statues and monuments, too, are being damaged; for example, the marble statues of the cenotaph built by the 18th century Venetian sculptor Antonio Canova in the Santa Maria Glorioso dei Frari Basilica, are rapidly deteriorating as a result of water entering the building and being drawn up into the marble by capillary action, eventually emerging on the surface of the statues, causing areas of flaking and blistering. The statues are now wet more often than they are dry, and restoration will require waterproofing the room, dismantling the monument, removing the salts from the stone, sealing the bases of the statues and then reassembling the whole (Camuffo et al., 2014).

Venice is now under assault from rapidly growing tourist numbers as well as worsening climate driven water damage to the very buildings, and architectural and monumental heritage that draw visitors in the first place. Ironically, tourism is responsible for thousands of Venetian jobs and tens of millions of euros in revenue to the city and its businesses, but the effects of climate must be addressed if the historic centre is to survive at all, and tourism must be better controlled if Venice is to remain a thriving and diverse community. The ever more frequent flooding events experienced by Venice in the last 60 years will be controllable when mobile barriers between the lagoon and the sea come into operation, it is hoped by 2018.

*Source*: Adapted from 'World Heritage in a Changing Climate' (2016) UNESCO/UNEP/ Union of Concerned Scientists, Paris.

# Summary

Climate change is a major global issue. Tourism is being affected by and will continue to be affected by global warming, but tourism also contributes to climate change. One of the most important effects that climate change will have on tourism in the future is rising sea levels, meaning many coastal locations which are currently tourism destinations are likely to be flooded. Changes in climate zones are likely to occur and this will possibly result in areas currently very important for tourism no longer being that significant. However, climate change is also likely to lead to opportunities for new tourism destinations to emerge. However tourism is also adding to climate change in particular via travel and accommodation. Tourism, along with many other economic activities, will need to reduce its carbon footprint in future to assist in attempts to slow down the rate of climate change.

## Student activities

1   What do you understand by the phrase, used in this chapter: 'global warming is a natural process'?

2   Why has global warming speeded up in the last 250 years?

3   What is the link between the albedo effect and global warming?

4   Working in small groups (3/4 students) consider an important tourism destination that you know well and discuss how tourism here will be affected by global warming.

5   How does tourism contribute to global warming?

6   Why is Venice particularly susceptible to global warming?

7   What can be done to offset the problems that Venice is currently experiencing in relation to global warming?

# References

Camuffo, D. (2001). Canaletto's paintings open a new window on the relative sea-level rise in Venice. *Journal of Cultural Heritage* 4, 277–281.

Camuffo, D., Bertolin, C. and Schenal, P. (2014). Climate change, sea level rise and impact on monuments in Venice. In Rogerio-Candelara, M.A. (ed.) *Science Technology and Cultural Heritage*. London: Taylor and Francis Group.

Carbognin, L., Teatini, P., Tomasin, A. and Tosi, L. (2010). Global change and relative sea level rise at Venice: What impact in terms of flooding. *Climate Dynamics* **35**, 1039–1047.

Città di Venizia (2014). *The Annual Tourism Survey presented yesterday in Venice*: Figures help the City decide how to manage flows efficiently. http://www.comune.venezia.it/flex/, accessed 5 January 2016.

CO2Now (2015) Atmospheric CO2 for July 2015, *CO2Now.org*, accessed August, 2015.

Cocks, A. (2013) The coming death of Venice? *The New York Review of Books* **60**(11), June 20.

Comitato Cruise Venice (undated) . FAQ. Online: http://www. cruisevenice.org/faq.html, accessed 5 January 2016.

Collins (2004) *Dictionary of Geography*, Glasgow: Harper Collins.

European Commission (2016) https:// *ec.europa.eu/climate/policies/international/ negotiations/ paris. en.*

European Climate Foundation and the University of Cambridge's Judge Business School and the Institute for Sustainability Leadership (2005) *Climate: Everyone's Business, Key Findings from the Intergovernmental Panel on Climate Change, Fifth Assessment Report,* Cambridge, UK.

Guardian Scientist, (2011) *The Guardian* May 12, London (accessed 3 July 2017)

Goldenberg, S. (2014) 2014 Confirmed as hottest year on record, *The Guardian*, November, 26.

Gossling, S., Hall, C.M. and Scott, D. (2013) Challenges of tourism in a low carbon economy, WIRES Climate Change, DOI: 10.1002/wcc.245

Holden, A (2016) *Environment and Tourism*, London: Routledge.

Malguzzi, P., Grossi, G., Buzzi,  A., Ranzi, R. and Buizza, R. (2006). The 1966 'century' flood in Italy: A meteorological and hydrological visitation. *Journal of Geophysical Research* **111**, D24.

Penning-Rowsell, E. (2000). Has Venice crossed the rubicon? *Geography* **85**, 233–240.

Riebeek, H (2005) Paleoclimatology: The Ice Core Record, *Earth Observatory* December 19, accessed 3 July 2017.

Ross, W., (2015). The death of Venice: Corrupt officials, mass tourism and soaring property prices have stifled life in the city. *The Independent*, 14 May.

Tosi, L., Teatini, P. and Strozzi, T. (2013). *Natural versus anthropogenic subsidence of Venice. Scientific Reports* **3**, 2710. And doi:10.1038/srep02710. UKDEFRA. 2012.

UNESCO (2011). *The Future of Venice and its Lagoon in the Context of Global Change: Workshop Reports 1 and 2.* UNESCO Venice Office, Venice, Italy.

UNESCO/UNEP/Union of Concerned Scientists, (2016) *World Heritage in a Changing Climate,* Paris.

Windsor, A. (2015). Inside Venice's bid to hold back the tide. *The Guardian*, 16 June 2015.

WTO (2012), *Sustainable Development of Tourism*, Madrid: World Tourism Organization/ OECD, .

Wright, L., Kemp, S. and Williams, I. (2011). 'Carbon footprinting': towards a universally accepted definition. *Carbon Management.* **2** (1), 61–72.

**11**

# 12 Crises and Disasters

## Introduction

As indicated at the beginning of this section, some factors are likely to contribute to the continued growth of tourism, whilst others will potentially lead to a halt in growth, or even a downturn in tourism numbers. Crises and disasters are very likely to have an immediate effect on tourist numbers, will almost certainly lead to a change in image of a tourism destination and may even significantly affect tourism, in the longer term, leading to major changes in specific locations, larger regions or even at the global level.

## Key perspectives

In addition to the effects of global warming discussed in Chapter 11, there are a number of other events, and factors that can cause serious impacts on tourism. These can be classified as crises or disasters. Some of these are natural, whilst others involve some form of human agent that contributes to the issue. Some happen very quickly whilst others are more gradual. The effects of some are localized, whilst others can have global impacts. It may be possible for areas affected to recover quickly from these events, or it may take much longer depending on the cause of the crisis or disaster.

Despite the fact that the type of events referred to above can have every serious impacts on tourism, they have until relatively recently been little researched. Faulkner (2001), in attempting to create an agenda for this type of research, tried to distinguish between disasters and crises. He indicated that it is generally accepted that crises tend to be associated with ongoing change that an organisation has failed to respond to and therefore not adapted, while a disaster is the result of a sudden event (or events) that an organisation has failed to respond to at all.

There is still a lack of agreement on the meanings of crisis and disaster, but as Evans and Elphick (2005) suggested, perhaps the most useful typology of such events focuses on their gestation period. Evans and Elphick (2005) draw on the work of Seymour and Moore (2000) who distinguish between 'cobra' events (sudden and unexpected) and 'python' events (where the build-up is slower, but the grip gets worse over time). Booth (1993) uses a similar analysis of crises, but produced three types: gradual threat, periodic threat and sudden threat.

Of particular importance in relation to crises and disasters in tourism and the effects they may have, is the very nature of tourism itself and in particular, what motivates tourists to be involved in certain types of activity. As we saw in Chapter 2, there are a range of motivations for tourism which can be summarised under the headings 'push' and 'pull' (see Iso-Aloha, 1980; Ryan, 1991). Other than certain types of high risk adventure tourism (e.g. white water rafting, kite surfing and bungee jumping), the great majority of tourists are motivated by a desire for enjoyment, but in a safe environment. The safety, security and well-being of tourists is therefore of paramount importance to the tourism industry and providers of tourism experiences (Page and O'Connell, 2009).

On an individual level, if a holiday 'goes wrong', then the industry may face some form of legal action and be required to compensate the customer. The individual concerned may also use word-of-mouth communication to dissuade potential tourists from using the specific industry provider. This can become very serious for the industry if a large number of individuals have been affected by a major issue. Media interest in a 'tourism problem' can also affect the image of the industry. Subsequently, the industry may need to change its behaviour in relation to the events that led to the crisis or disaster and embark on new marketing. At the destination level, there can be a significant issue for the image of the location and consequently tourist numbers may decline, requiring some form of response from tourism planners and managers in the destination, as well as the likelihood of a revised marketing strategy. A decline in tourist numbers may well result in the loss of jobs and livelihoods for local residents in tourist areas, which will also need to be addressed by politicians, planners and managers in affected destinations.

## Natural events, crises and disasters

There are a number and variety of natural events that can greatly influence tourism. For example, the eruption of a dormant volcano on the Caribbean island of Montserrat in 1997 severely disrupted the tourism economy, not only because of the perception created that the island was a dangerous place to visit, but because the eruption covered some of the island's tourism resources in lava and ash, preventing the use of these for tourism activity (Mason, 2016).

Storms, floods and tsunamis are other natural events that can cause major disruptions to tourism activities. Although it is generally known, with some degree of accuracy, when such events might occur and even where, the specifics of the force of individual events, precisely when and exactly where they will occur is still not possible to accurately predict. So, in the example of the major tsunami that hit Southeast Asia and particularly Indonesia, Thailand, India and Sri Lanka on Boxing Day 2004, this was not predicted and its impact was far more significant than any other such event in the recent history of tourism (Holden, 2016). The tsunami resulted from a major undersea earthquake along the coast of Indonesia. There was no warning of when the tsunami was about to occur and there was also a failure to give advanced warning to many of the affected countries around the Indian Ocean as the tsunami approached.

Page and O'Connell (2009) indicate the effects of the Southeast Asian Tsunami and subdivide the impacts under four major headings: Environment, Economic, Social and Political. Under each heading they have at least six and as many as twelve major impacts, the total being 30 significant effects. As an indication of the seriousness of the impacts of the tsunami, for example, under the heading 'Environment' they refer to destruction of the coastal tourism resources and additionally destruction of the tourism infrastructure and resort area. In relation to economic impacts, Page and O'Connell (2009) refer to interruptions to the tourism industry, damage to uninsured property, loss of entrepreneurs' skills and loss of a general labour force. Major political effects include the humanitarian aid cost and the international media images, as well as a re-evaluation by politicians and planners of the role of tourism in the future. Loss of communities, kinship and families, pressure on housing, a general loss of control of residents over their future and a fear that there could be a repeat of the tsunami, were major social costs (Page and O'Connell, 2009:577).

In addition to the physical and psychological effects on the local population engulfed by the Southeast Asian tsunami, Holden (2016) considered the economic impacts of the tsunami on two specific countries, the Maldives and Sri Lanka. Holden indicates that there were over 30,000 deaths in Sri Lanka and 860,000 people were displaced. The cost to Sri Lanka was estimated as at least $250 million and 27,000 tourism jobs were lost. In the Maldives, where at least 33% of the GDP came from tourism, the direct damage to the tourism infrastructure was $100 million. On a personal level, in both countries many people had no shelter, no jobs or businesses to operate, no tourists to serve and no immediate source of income (Holden, 2016).

# Semi-natural crises and disasters

Although many crises and disasters in tourism have natural causes, there are some that have an element of natural factors, plus human dimensions as well. As we have seen in Chapter 11, climate change is one such example. However, diseases are another example with a combination of natural and human aspects, and in certain circumstances can have significant impacts on the dynamics of tourism.

Epidemic diseases, in particular, have had a devastating influence on the tourism industry. This has frequently been exacerbated by sensationalist press coverage (Behrens and Grabowski, 1995). During the early part of 2003, the outbreak of Severe Acute Respiratory Syndrome (SARS) had very major impacts on the movement of tourists. A key reason was that the spread of SARS was closely linked with international tourists visiting affected areas, returning home and passing on the disease. Various locations, including China and Vietnam, but also the developed countries of Canada and the UK had outbreaks of SARS and the World Health Organization (WHO) issued health warnings in an attempt to prevent tourist visits. Even when declared at an end in July 2003, there were isolated cases, such as that in Singapore in September 2003, and in China in January and again in April, 2004.

This case study considers the cause of SARS and its effects on global tourism.

## Case study: SARS

### An overview of the SARS outbreak

The first reported case of SARS was in Guangdong Province, China in November 2002. By the end of 2002 there were 300 cases reported in the area and in early January 2003 the disease was accidently taken by a shrimp farmer to the city of Guangzhou. It spread quickly through three hospitals in the city infecting medical staff, including a respiratory specialist, Dr Liu, who, before he was diagnosed, took the virus to Hong Kong. Dr Liu stayed at the Metropole Hotel in Hong Kong and infected (probably through sneezing in a lift) a number of tourists from several parts of the world. A few days later, hospitals in Hong Kong, Vietnam and Singapore began reporting cases. Several days after this, the disease began spreading around the world along international air travel routes.

After the disease moved out of its origin region of southern China, the new 'hot zones' of SARS were Hong Kong, Singapore, Hanoi and Toronto. The first official report of SARS (actually reported as an outbreak of atypical pneumonia) was made to the World Health Organization (WHO) on February 11th 2003. However, it was not until late February 2003 that the disease was first identified, by a Dr Urbani, an WHO epidemiologist working in Vietnam. It was a disease found in animals that had 'jumped species' from chickens to humans, it was believed. (However, more recently the main culprit has been regarded as the civet cat). In early April 2003, as the disease was spreading so rapidly, the WHO warned that SARS could become a global epidemic. By the end of April, more than 4,500 cases had been reported in 25 countries and there had been 300 deaths. At this time, it appeared that the number of cases had peaked and by then Vietnam had become the first country to stop local transmission of SARS. Despite a minor resurgence of the disease in Toronto in June, by early July 2003, only China was reporting new cases with Beijing and some other regions still infected.

By late July 2003, there had been over 7,000 cases of SARS. These had been reported in 32 countries and had killed at least 800 people, with 348 confirmed cases in China, 298 in Hong Kong, 84 in Taiwan, 32 in Singapore and 38 in Canada.

### The impacts of SARS on global tourism

The most immediate impact of SARS was on those who had the disease, as well as the families of sufferers and the hospital staff dealing with SARS victims. Nevertheless, by mid-2003, there was little doubt that SARS also had had major impacts on tourism industry sectors as well as on specific tourism destinations. These effects were not evenly spread, either by sector, or geographically, but contributed to a major downturn in tourism in a number of places during the first half of 2003.

The air travel industry sector was the most immediately affected and badly hit. In Guangdong, where the first SARS cases were reported, more than half of inbound international tour groups had been cancelled by early May 2003. Nearby Hong Kong was also badly affected and by April 26th 2003, it was estimated Dragonair and Cathay Pacific had lost two thirds of their traffic. At approximately the same date (April, 28th, 2003) it was suggested that Cathay Pacific had to cancel 40-50% of flights. It was confirmed that the operator, Travelsphere, was bringing 1000 clients back from China, and that the Federation of Tour Operators had suspended trips to affected areas. The China National Tourism Administration reported that approximately 130,000 overseas travellers had called off their proposed visits to Beijing, Shanghai and Guangdong during May 2003 and this had led to a loss of US$1.3billion in Beijing alone.

Other related sectors to the airline industry also reported major downturns in tourism activity. Hotel occupancy in Beijing during April 2003 fell by 23% compared with the same periods in 2002, with many four and five star hotels reporting less than 10% normal occupancy. The hotel industry in Hong Kong was also affected badly. In late April 2003, hotel occupancy in Hong Kong was below 10%, a drop of around 80%.

In late April 2003, Toronto was the major location in the developed world affected by SARS. Here, there were direct effects on tourism with restaurant turnover in Toronto's Chinatown severely hit, but in addition many downtown areas where people normally gathered, e.g. cinemas and theatres (where it was perceived SARS could be passed on) were almost deserted. Although the effects were felt beyond the tourism industry, SARS also contributed to revised perceptual images of destinations, that directly affected the industry. Hence, Toronto normally viewed as an extremely safe destination, became a 'dangerous' place to visit and 'off limits'.

This downturn in tourism was frequently translated into economic costs to regions, countries and the global economy, and into revision of economic forecasts, with for example, Hong Kong's forecast 3% growth in 2003 being reduced to 0.5%. In early May 2003, the Asian Development Bank was reported to have estimated the cost of SARS to China, Hong Kong, South Korea and Taiwan to be around US$20 billion, while the cost to China alone was estimated to be US$4.2 billion.

Although China was the epicentre of the SARS outbreak, other neighbouring countries were also significantly affected. At the end of April 2003, Thailand, with 8 confirmed SARS cases and no deaths, was reported to have lost 70% of its business, and Singapore, with 192 cases, 74% of business. Although this drop in visitation to these areas may reflect tourists changing their travel plans rather than abandoning them totally, it is clear that some potential travellers stayed at home. For example, there was a reported drop of Japanese overseas travel in the traditional May holiday, "Golden Week", of almost 50%.

## The media and SARS

A major aspect of the SARS outbreak, particularly in terms of its impact on global tourism, was the attention given to it by the media. However, it was not just that SARS was reported copiously by the media, but that it was reported in often sensationalist and alarmist tones. This contributed to the overall 'SARS effect'. It is generally accepted that the media has a central role in the influencing of public opinion. This is mainly the result of the amount of attention given by the media to the issue. The media also plays a major role in influencing consumers' images of destinations and informing them whether or not a place is safe and secure.

The alarmist tones of the media and the near panic generated can be seen in relation to reports about regions and countries only marginally affected by SARS. Hence, Thailand with only eight reported cases and no deaths by the end of May was put into the same category as Hong Kong that had several reported deaths at this time. In a similar vein, the media painted an almost identically gloomy picture for both the Chongqing and Kunming regions of China, despite the fact that the latter had no confirmed SARS cases. This provides some evidence for claims that the global media was much less interested in providing accurate information and more concerned with selling copies of their publication through sensationalist (but inaccurate) stories.

A very unusual feature of the SARS outbreak was the unprecedented WHO global health alert, given on March 15th 2003. This offered health advice to potential travellers and also helped raise awareness amongst doctors and medical services of the seriousness of the outbreak. In terms of global tourism it appears that potential and actual tourists were pleased to gain new information on the safety of destinations. However, the WHO found itself in somewhat of a dilemma here – it wanted to use the global media to publicise its message about SARS and travel, but could not write word-for-word the article or web site commentary and hence could not control the tone or precise nature of any media communication. Therefore, it appears that the way the WHO health alert was reported by the world's media is also likely to have contributed to a feeling of panic amongst travellers. For example, many Canadians were outraged when in April 2003 the WHO advised people officially not to visit Toronto, putting it on the same footing as Beijing. The reaction of the mayor of Toronto to being included in the WHO travel warning was to appear on national television denouncing this WHO decision. The reaction of the authorities in Toronto to being included in the WHO health alert, as a location 'off-limits' to international travellers as a result of SARS, is further confirmation of this state of alarm at least in part generated by media commentary

## SARS, tourism and crises

The reaction to SARS by the affected destinations, the WHO and international media provide strong evidence that this was a major crisis that affected the global tourism industry. Until relatively recently tourism and crises have received little interest from researchers. However, they actually appear to be relatively common yet remain little researched. Traditionally, stereotypical big crises, such as floods, large explosions, fires and natural disasters have been viewed as not having significant impacts on tourism, but the industry is perceived as more likely to involve small scale crime, human resource crises and bad management issues. Tourism is also a very broad and difficult to define industry, covering various sectors including accommodation, food, hospitality, attractions, transport and travel agencies. The links between the parts of the industry are not always overt or strong. Hence, the multi-faceted nature of tourism means that it has not generally been prepared to cope with major international crises.

However, there is little doubt that tourism is particularly vulnerable to crises. A major reason is that in tourism, 'perception is reality'. Hence, crisis such as the 'Foot and Mouth' outbreak in the UK in 2001, the aftermath to the bloodless coup in Fiji in 1987 and attitudes to visiting Hong Kong after the Tiananmen Square massacre in Beijing, were far more about perception of the destinations than actual real events on the ground, and were at least as devastating to tourism as a real physical disaster would have been.

Source: Adapted from Mason *et al.*, 2007

As indicated earlier in this chapter, Faulkner (2001) tried to distinguish between crises and disasters, but he also added that in reality there may be little difference, in terms of the features each exhibits and from the perspective of those suffering the consequences. Fink (1986) attempted to distil the main ingredients of disasters and crises and produced a number of key features. These are summarised below:

- A triggering event that is so big that it challenges existing structures and routines
- They are characterised by fluid dynamic situations
- There is an element of surprise, with a high threat and short decision time
- For at least part of the event, a feeling of inability to cope
- A decisive turning point which may have both positive and negative dimensions, meaning, that however well managed, there may yet be irreversible changes

In relation to the SARS outbreak, it would appear that it is possible to apply Fink's (1986) suggestions on the main ingredients of crises and disasters. The 'triggering event' could be considered to be the transmission of the disease by the medical specialist in the Metropole Hotel, Hong Kong. For a few weeks after this, events were very fluid as the disease spread around the world from developing to developed countries, with accompanying reactions from the world's media, as well as governments and international organisations. The surprise elements can be considered to be both the reaction of the WHO in issuing a global health warning and, that subsequently, a number of developed world cities were put on the same footing as developing world cities such as Beijing. During the initial stages, before SARS was identified and spread around the world very quickly, there was certainly a feeling of inability to cope. A decisive turning point could be regarded as occurring when the disease was finally stopped in Vietnam.

SARS would also seem to fit the criteria of a 'big crisis' (Fink, 1986), which traditionally the tourism industry has not been prepared for (Santana, 2003). Additionally, it would appear that the SARS crisis fits Seymour and Moore's (2000) 'cobra' typology and Booth's (1993) 'sudden threat' classification (see earlier in this chapter). As has been discussed above, SARS really did have significant impact on specific tourism destinations, but the media also played a key role. In relation to some destinations, this led to the exaggeration of the dangers of SARS (McKercher, 2003). Hence, the perception of destinations as being 'unsafe' and 'off-limits' was often more important than the reality on the ground. The reaction to the WHO declaration by the authorities in Toronto is a very good example of this, and provides further evidence of the arguments of Wahab (1996) and Wall (1996) that perception *is* reality in tourism.

# Tourism and terrorism

In relation to what has been discussed so far in this chapter, it is possible to summarise that in the early part of the 21st century, many tourism destinations have suffered from usually localized problems, affecting visitor numbers, including the effects of natural phenomenon such as volcanic eruptions, storms and flooding, but that these events are not particularly unusual in terms of the history of global tourism development. Although it can be stated that SARS was a new disease, the process by which tourists accidently helped transport the disease around the world was not new. In some ways this is not dissimilar to the spread of AIDS, which involved a similar tourism-linked form of spreading of the disease, although the precise process and mechanism of transmission (through sexual contact in the case of AIDS) was different.

However, the events of 11 September 2001 in the United States, and other related terrorist attacks since, appear more unusual and may have long-term effects on the global tourism industry. The terrorist attacks have been seen as different, as they are viewed as part of a global, not local threat. In terms of tourism, in the United States particularly, the terrorist attacks have had a significant impact on potential and real travellers. The impacts of the events of 11 September, 2001 continued well after the event. In terms of consequences for the tourism industry, for example, the bankruptcy of the large carrier, American Airlines in 2002, was linked closely to the drop in passenger numbers following the terrorist attack.

Although the terrorist attacks of 11 September 2001 had effects on tourism at a global scale, in the immediate aftermath of the attacks they were seen as having only indirect effects. However, in October 2002 this perspective changed radically when tourists became the major target of terrorists (Mason, 2008). On the Indonesian island of Bali, two night-clubs, containing mainly international tourists were targeted by terrorists who were linked by the media to the groups

12

that had perpetrated the attacks in the United States in September 2001. Almost three years later, in 2005, bombings occurred again on Bali.

The first bombings in Bali were in October 2002 and 183 people were killed and over 300 injured. The largest group of dead and injured came from Australia, but British, Americans, New Zealanders, Germans and French were among the casualties, as well as local Indonesians. Those blamed for this terrorism were a cell linked to the terrorist group Al-Qaeda. Bali was regarded as a 'soft' terrorist target, as it is a Hindu island in a predominantly Muslim country and was very dependent on tourism (Weiping, 2010)). The island's relaxed attitudes to sex and dress codes, as well as general expectations of tourist behaviour, compared to many other parts of Indonesia, had encouraged foreign tourists, including young Western backpackers, to visit. It was probably the relatively unrestrained nature of life on an island surrounded by a country with generally stricter Islamic beliefs, coupled with the presence of large numbers of foreign visitors that made Bali a 'suitable', and relatively easy, target for militant Muslim terrorists (Mason, 2016).

The media response to this event was very similar to that for the outbreak of SARS, with much immediate reaction and concern, some sensationalist reporting, human dimension stories, and then a fairly rapid decline in interest. However, it was also very much a global media response as the victims came from Europe, the UK, the USA and Australia and New Zealand. The effect on the tourism industry was immediate. Only two days after the bombings, several tour operators from the UK,USA and Australia were flying clients out of the island. A large number of Western tourists in Bali were on round-the-world tickets and many of them left earlier than expected (Weiping, 2010).

Three years later there was another terrorism attack in Bali in almost the same location, but with two bombs in places popular with international tourists. On this occasion the bombs were detonated by suicide bombers who also died in the incidents. The suspects were part of an active terrorist network, linked to Al-Qaeda, and had allegedly carried out the 2002 bombings. International media reaction to the 2005 bombings was swift and condemned the bombers and expressed much sympathy with the victims and their families. However, many countries also issued travel warnings against visiting Bali. By November 2005, the Indonesian authorities had made a number of arrests, and a key suspect for the 2002 bombings, who was also probably involved in planning the 2005 bombings, had been killed in a shot-out with police (Weiping, 2010).

However, the reaction of tourists on Bali was not the same as in the aftermath of the 2002 bombings. Relatively few people left the island, although a large number cancelled or postponed their visit. The reasons for the cancellation were the continued travel warnings issued by the Australian government, the televised confessions of the suicide bombers and the ongoing hunt for terrorists in Indonesia (Mason, 2016). Hence, during the Christmas/New Year Period of 2005/2006, hotel occupancy in Indonesia as whole fell by 40%. By late November 2006, the Bali based airline Air Paradise International had closed its service completely and laid off 350 employees. The Indonesian airline Garuda reduced its flights between Australian cities and Indonesia/Bali from 32 to 25 services and between Japan and Indonesia/ Bali from 22 to 16 flights per week by mid-2006. A year on from the 2005 bombings, the effects were as bad if not slightly worse in terms of international tourist numbers reaching Bali. However, amongst the Balinese there seemed to be far more resolve than in 2002. Local people were angry and blamed non-locals for the bombings and were more intent on trying to kick-start their ailing tourism industry and welcome back tourists than previously (Mason, 2008).

Following the Bali bombings, research was conducted into the image of Bali amongst UK tourists and their reaction to the bombings (Weiping, 2010). This research revealed that tourism numbers were almost back to the pre-2005 level by 2008. It also indicated that tourists who had actually visited Bali in the aftermath of the bombings were less likely to be concerned about security issues than other tourists who had not visited Bali at all. The effect of the media on the perception of the UK tourists who had not actually visited the island was suggested as the main reason for this finding (Weiping, 2010).

In the last 20 years or so, there have been several other terrorist attacks in other parts of the world. Egypt is one country that has experienced several such attacks and here tourists have frequently been a target of terrorists. In 1997, 62 tourists were massacred at the major tourism destination of Luxor, by a terrorist group allegedly with links to Al-Qaeda. In 2004, a terrorist bombing in the Sinai Peninsula led to the death of 34 tourists, with 172 being injured. The Egyptian government claimed the terrorists were from Palestine. In 2005, at the Red Sea resort of Sharm-el-Sheik, a series of terrorist bomb attacks resulted in 88 deaths and over 200 injured. In 2006, in the Gulf of Aqaba/Sinai Peninsula resort, at Dahab, 23 tourists were killed and in December 2015, a Russian passenger plane returning from Sharm-el-Sheikh was blown up (Mason, 2016).

In June 2015, in the Tunisian resort town of Sousse, 39 people, mostly for-eigners, were killed and 36 injured in an attack on a beach. The victims of the beach attack by gunmen who arrived by boat, were Tunisians, British, Germans, Belgians, French and Irish, and ISIS claimed responsibility. This followed an attack in March, 2015 carried out by militants which killed 22 people, mainly foreign tourists, in a museum in the capital Tunis.

However it is not only developing world countries that have suffered terror-ism events; a number of European countries have also been targeted. A Christmas market in Berlin was hit by a terrorist attack in 2016, and a main street, Las Ramblas, a favourite tourist location in Barcelona, was the scene of a vehicle hit and run incident in August 2017, in which 14 people died and over 100 were injured. ISIS claimed responsibility for this. In the UK, London was targeted in 2005, and then again in 2017, and in that year attacks also took place in Manchester. Although the UK events were largely carried out by Muslim fundamentalists (the most recent ones by those sympathising with ISIS (or DAISH)), they have usually involved locals from the UK and not foreign terrorists. Also in 2017, in the UK, there was what appeared to be a reaction to the alleged ISIS inspired terrorism, with an attack on a group of Muslims outside a mosque in north London

France has also experienced a number of terrorism events since 2015, with these taking place in Paris and Nice. In Nice, in 2016, tourists were amongst the total of 86 victims killed and nearly 500 injured, by a truck driver who deliberately drove into a crowd celebrating Bastille Day (July 14th). In Paris, in January 2015, a number of journalists working for the satirical magazine *Charlie Hebdo* which had printed cartoons of the prophet Mohammed were shot dead and in November 2015, cafes, a music venue and football stadium all in Paris, were targets in which over 130 people were killed. Although tourists were not the main target of the November 13th attacks in Paris, the terrorism events there have had a significant impacts on the image of Paris and the number of tourists visiting in the aftermath of these attacks are the subject of the following case study.

## Case study: The impacts of terrorism in Paris

Paris is one of the most popular city destinations in the world, and for the majority of the time in the period from 1990 to 2015 was the major urban destination in Europe, and has been the most important tourism destination in France for many years. This state of affairs changed following the terrorist attack in the city of November 13th 2015. These attacks, the work of ISIS, resulted in 130 people being killed and many more injured. The attacks took place inside and outside Paris cafes, a music concert hall, the Bataclan, and at the 'Stade de France' stadium during a major international football match. The terrorists initially escaped but were caught and killed a few days later, some in Brussels. Tourists were not the target of the terrorists in this attack, but the image of Paris as a romantic place for tourists, and of pleasure-seeking locals was significantly affected.

At the time of the ISIS November 13th terrorist attacks, the city and France as whole had barely recovered following the terrorist attack at the *Charlie Hebdo* magazine offices in Paris which killed 11 people in January 2015. Things were made worse, when in the summer of 2016, a driver ploughed a truck into crowds of people celebrating Bastille Day (July 14th) in the French Riviera city of Nice in 2016, killing at least 86 people, some of whom were international tourists.

Paris welcomes over 16 million visitors a year and is one of the world's top tourist destinations. However, in 2016, there were a million fewer visitors between January and June compared with the same period in 2015. The drop is estimated to have cost about €750m (£644m) in lost revenue. One senior official described it as 'an industrial disaster'.

France relies heavily on tourism, which generates more than 7% of its annual GDP. About half a million people in the Ile-de-France region, which includes Paris, have jobs linked to tourism, making it the biggest employer in the area. The Paris Region Tourism Board said, in August 2016, that even the staging of the European football championships in the summer of 2016, failed to arrest the decline.

The Ile-de-France figures also show:

- ☐ A 46.2% decline in Japanese visitors compared with the same period in 2015
- ☐ A 35% decline in Russian visitors
- ☐ A 19.6% decline in Chinese visitors
- ☐ A 5.7% decline in visitors from the US

"It's time to realise that the tourism sector is going through an industrial disaster," the Paris Region Tourist Board head said in a statement. "This is no longer the time for communication campaigns, but to set up a relief plan", he said as he called for major investment to protect jobs in the tourism sector and government and trades union action to address the problem.

Also in August 2016, a souvenir shop owner near the Arc de Triomphe, who did not want to be named, said: "It's due to terrorism, nobody mentions it but everyone watches the news. We've sold fewer postcards and souvenirs this summer." A rickshaw driver, who also withheld their name, said: "There are definitely fewer tourists. I look around and I can see the decrease. It's due to the terror attacks – the November attacks, but definitely the Nice attack in July. People stopped coming after that. It's also the economy, tourists, European tourists have less money to spend."

The general manager of the Hotel Napoleon, said he had seen a drop in business, especially from American and Japanese customers. He said Paris was now seen as 'less safe' after major terror attacks in the city. The Ile-de-France Regional President indicated that the decline in the number of tourists had worrying economic implications and that recent attacks were the main reason for it. But she said, Paris must also work out why tourists were spending less time in the city compared with London and "improve the quality of our offer".

Source: BBC News, August 2016

# Summary

A number of natural causes of crises and disasters have affected tourism in the past 20 years or so. These include volcanic eruptions, earthquakes and tsunamis. A key issue with these natural crises is that although where they may occur can be predicted, precisely when and how severe they will be is extremely difficult to predict. Diseases can also cause major problems on a global scale and in the case of SARS actually be spread by international tourist movement.

In the recent history of tourism, terrorism has become a very significant activity. In some parts of the world, including Bali and Egypt, tourists have been the direct target of terrorists, but even where this is not the case, as in the November 2015 attacks in Paris, the image of a destination where the attacks have taken place, can be significantly affected and there is likely to be a resulting decline in tourism numbers.

## Student activities

1  Historically speaking, crises and disasters have been researched relatively little in relation to tourism. Why do you think this is so?

2  Why was the Southeast Asian tsunami of December 26th 2004 so damaging to tourism?

3  How was tourism affected by the disease SARS and how did tourism contribute to SARS?

4  In small groups (3/4 students) discuss the reasons why international tourists have been targeted by terrorists.

5  Although tourists were not the target of terrorists in Paris in November, 2015, tourism was affected. Explain what the effects have been and why these have occurred.

# References

BBC News (2016) Paris tourism hit by terrorist militants, strikes and floods, August 23rd BBC http://www.bbc.co.uk/news/world-europe-37164217, accessed January 2017

Behrens, R. H. and Grabowski, P., (1995), Travellers' Health and the Economy of Developing Nations, *The Lancet*, **364**, December, p 1562

Booth, S.A. (1993) *Crisis Management Strategy: Competition and Change in Modern Enterprises*, London: Routledge

Evans, N. and Elphick, S. (2005) Models of crisis management: an evaluation of their value for strategic planning in the international travel industry, *International Journal of Tourism Research*, **7**(3), 135-150

Faulkner, B. (2001). Towards a framework for tourism disaster management. *Tourism Management*, **22**, 135–47.

Fink, S. (1986). *Crisis Management*. New York: American Association of Management.

Holden, A. (2016) *Environment and Tourism*, 3rd ed., London: Routledge

Iso-Aloha, S. (1980). *The Social-Psychology of Leisure and Recreation*. Iowa: Brown

McKercher, B. (2003), Trinet email message, 28/04/2003

Mason, P., Grabowski, P. and Wei, D. (2007) SARS, tourism and the media, *International Journal of Tourism Research*, **7**(1) 11-21.

Mason, P. (2008) *Tourism Impacts, Planning and Management*, 2nd ed., Oxford: Butterworth-Heinemann

Mason, P. (2016) *Tourism Impacts, Planning and Management*,  3rd ed., London: Routledge

Page, S. and O'Connell, J. (2009) *Tourism: a modern synthesis*, 3rd ed., Andover: South Western Cengage Learning

Ryan, C. (1991). *Recreational Tourism*. London: Routledge.

Santana, G. (2003) Crisis management and tourism: behind the rhetoric, *Journal of Travel and Tourism Marketing*, **15** (4) 299-321

Seymour, M. and Moore, S. (2000*), Effective Crisis Management: Worldwide Principles and Practice,* Cassell: London.

Wahab, S (1996). Tourism and terrorism: synthesis of the problem with emphasis on Egypt. In A. Pizam and Y. Mansfeld, eds. *Tourism, Crime and International Security Issues*, New York: John Wiley, pp. 175-86.

Wall, G. (1996) Terrorism and tourism: An overview and an Irish example, in A. Pizam and Y. Mansfeld, eds.,*Tourism, Crime and International Security Issues*,  pp. 143-158. New York: Wiley.

Weiping, L. (2010) Unpublished PhD thesis, Bedfordshire University, Luton.

**12**

# 13 Protected Areas

## Introduction

There are a significant number of protected areas in the world today, but their creation has occurred only relatively recently. The designation of protected areas can be linked back to the Romantic Movement in England and continental Europe (Mason, 2016). A related movement in the USA also contributed significantly to the establishment of protected areas there. As indicated in Chapter 3, until the latter part of the 18th century, large areas of the natural landscape were not looked upon as having much potential for human use. So mountain regions, such as the Alps, were viewed as a barrier to communication and transport, and similarly uplands and mountain areas in the UK were viewed as offering little scope for economic use, except possibly sheep farming.

This chapter indicates that the first protected areas were established in the USA, provides a case study of the very first national park, Yellowstone Park, and discusses the issues that can arise when the designation as a park acts as form of marketing and leads to increasing numbers of visitors with the related impacts. The chapter also discusses changing concepts of the term 'wilderness', the implications of this and provides a case study of the largest and most remote wilderness on earth, Antarctica.

## Protected areas

Although for hundreds of years in Europe, wild areas such as mountains and high moorlands were viewed as undesirable places for almost any form of human activity, towards the end of the 1700s, and partly in response to the Industrial Revolution which used large areas of land in towns and generally created an unattractive human/urban landscape, as well as putting pressure on land adjacent to cities, 'natural' landscapes including mountain ranges were being viewed for the probably first time as attractive and the word 'beauty' was being attached to them (Holden, 2013). This was the results of a number of influential writers (for example, Wordsworth and Coleridge in Britain, and Catlin in the USA) who extolled the beauty of such areas as the English Lake District and Yosemite in the USA. For example, Wordsworth's famous poem, 'I wandered lonely as a cloud' with the lines 'I wandered lonely as a cloud that floats on high o'er vales and hills, when all at once I spied a crowd, a host of golden daffodils' was about Ullswater, a remote lake hemmed in by steep mountains, in the English Lake District.

Within a relatively few years of this change in view on natural and wild areas, there were the first attempts to protect them. By the early 21st century, protecting such landscapes was a common approach in many countries. Hence today, there are many protected areas that have been set up by governments around the world for a number of related reasons. According to Holden (2013) there are several different types, differentiated partly by what they allow and how strict the regulations and laws concerning them are. These are shown in Table 13.1.

In Table 13.1, based on Holden (2016), eight types of protected area are indicated. Those with the most restrictive in terms of use are shown at the top, and then there is a descending order of restrictions on use.

**Table 13.1:** Types of protected areas

- ☐ Scientific reserve/ strict nature reserve
- ☐ National parks
- ☐ Natural monuments/landmarks
- ☐ Managed nature reserve/wildlife sanctuary
- ☐ Protected landscapes
- ☐ Resource reserve
- ☐ Naturally biotic areas/anthropological reserve
- ☐ Multiple use management area/managed resources

In relation to Table 13.1, in the *scientific reserve/strict nature reserve*, the main aim is to protect the ecological balance for scientific research and also to provide opportunities for environmental education. Commercial activities in such areas would be seriously restricted. *National parks*, which have been set up to protect landscape and scenic values, have similar aims to *scientific reserves*, but have a wider remit as they also include recreational use, whilst *natural monuments/landmarks* have the aim of protecting nationally significant natural features, defined in terms of their especially significant characteristics, or their uniqueness.

A *managed nature reserve/wildlife sanctuary* will involve human intervention to manage some aspects of the landscape or ecosystem. This could involve, for example, the culling of a specific predator to enable a rare/endangered species to survive. *Protected landscapes*, as shown in Table 13.1, are important natural or semi-natural areas where it is recognised that there is a harmonious relationship between humans and the landscape. The emphasis here, however, is on economic viability, as much as landscape protection, and the economic activity in the area is protected.

13

*Resource reserves* and *naturally biotic areas/anthropological reserves* are in some ways similar to each other, as they are set up in an attempt to protect or sustain resources or areas for future use, by prohibiting certain development activities that threaten them, but to permit ways of life for societies living in harmony with the environment, to continue, without interruption, by modern technology or damaging human activities. *Multiple use management area/managed resources* allow a range of activities to take place, but these should be planned and managed for the sustainable use of, for example, wildlife, forests, timber, water, pasture land and outdoor activities.

Tourism is prohibited in some of these designated areas, allowed in others and is likely to be promoted in a number of them (Mason, 2016). Hence in *scientific reserves*, tourism will usually be prohibited. Tourism will usually be allowed in *national parks* and in many such parks, will be actively promoted (Holden, 2016). This situation will also be the case in relation to *natural monuments/landmark* areas. In *managed nature reserves/wildlife sanctuaries*, tourism may be allowed but not if it is likely to cause disruption or damage to the area. In relation to *protected landscape* designated areas, tourism will often be promoted, but as the emphasis is on ensuring economic viability, tourism must be seen to not come in conflict with other economic activities. Tourism may also be important in *resource reserves* and *biotic reserves*, as well as *multiple use management areas*.

The very first area in the world that was put forward for protected status was Yosemite National Park in the USA. This was in 1864, but it took some time for the status to be confirmed and it was not established until 1872. However, it had the two key aims that remain very important today in such areas, of conserving the landscape and environment, but also allowing visitors to enjoy this landscape. As Holden (2013:276) argues this causes: "dilemmas of how to best deal with the interaction of tourism and conservation in protected areas. "

Holden (2013) considers that national parks are landscapes that have special status. Many of these have been created in relation to national laws, so they may differ from country to country. However, the International Union of Conservation of Nature (IUCN) definition is as follows:

> *A clearly defined geographical space, recognised, dedicated and managed, through legal or other effective means, to achieve the long terms conservation of nature, with associated ecosystem services and cultural values (IUCN, 2011).*

Although Yosemite National Park was the first to be put forward for special protected status, it was another US area that can claim to be the very first national park in the world. This is Yellowstone Park, which is located in the state of Wyoming. It has distinct geological features, including geysers, the most famous of which is Old Faithful. It also has wildlife that has traditionally attracted large numbers of tourists, in particular bears. Wolves and wolverine are also animal species that can be seen in Yellowstone Park. Hence it is a combination of unusual geological landscape features, coupled with wildlife that led to the designation as a national park.

As Holden (2016) argues, it was no coincidence that Yellowstone and Yosemite National Parks were set up in the second half of the 19th century, as this was a time in US history of increasing urbanisation. This movement to develop cities meant more pressure on the rural areas of the US, as is clear in the aims of Yellowstone Park, which included the intention to provide places for urban dwellers to enjoy recreational spaces beyond the city (Holden, 2016). Hall and Lew (1998) claim that the drive to establish national parks in the US was also related to a desire that Americans should be reminded of the pioneering mentality of those (modern immigrants) who initially 'created' the country. The intention here was that people should stay, at least metaphorically, in close contact with nature, despite increasingly living in cities. The promotion of the desire to visit wild areas, or wilderness in the USA, was partly the result of the American John Muir, who believed, in a similar way to the English Romantics, that visiting mountains and nature was good for one's soul (Eagles *et al.*, 2002).

MacCannell (1992) believes there was a very different and a less positive reason for the creation of national parks in the US in the late 19th century. He argued that there was a feeling of guilt at the destruction of nature across the whole of the USA, and that the setting up of the parks was an attempt to show that human society could also value the landscape for its intrinsic and aesthetic qualities, rather than regarding it as simply a resource to be exploited, with little regard for the long term consequences.

Given the time at which the two parks of Yellowstone and Yosemite were created, it is perhaps not surprising that the interests of the indigenous peoples were largely ignored and preference was given to the perceived desires of settlers who had arrived from Europe from the mid-1800s (Holden, 2016). However, in a similar vein to MacCannell's views on the concern of some at the destruction of nature, as early as the 1830s, the American poet Catlin was expressing guilt at the destruction of aboriginal cultures and arguing that national parks should be set up in areas where this destruction was occurring, to preserve these cultures.

By the 1980s, national parks had become very important recreation and tourist attractions in many countries. In these areas, it was perceived that visitors could get close to nature and observe flora and fauna that was frequently unusual and often endangered and likely to be unique. The geology and human geography of the landscape of many national parks was frequently aesthetically pleasing and perceived as 'natural', or at least semi-natural, as national parks in many countries, including the UK, have at least part of their landscapes that are farmed or forested – in other words they have significant human activity where commercial land use is prevalent.

However, a major issue in the early part of the 21st century, is that the very designation of a landscape as a 'protected area' can lead to increased interest from tourists, and an even greater desire to visit. Hence, the marketing of such areas, whether overtly or implicitly, could be summarised as: 'Come and see the last remaining..., before it disappears!' Therefore, within this marketing concept are,

**13**

potentially, the seeds of destruction for the object of the visitors' attention, in that the invitation to visit will lead to tourists, in their desire to see whatever it is that is fast disappearing, damaging even more quickly what they have to come to see!

The following case study, which focuses on the Yellowstone National Park, considers the attractions of the park and the impacts of increasing numbers of visitors on the landscape and wildlife.

## Case Study: Tourism in Yellowstone National Park

In the early 1990s, a U.S. senator from Wyoming, set out on a summer drive with friends in Yellowstone National Park. It wasn't long before they were in a traffic jam that extended for miles. The cause: a road construction project and countless "wildlife jams."

The notion that gave birth to America's first national park in 1872, "a public park or pleasuring-ground for the benefit and enjoyment of the people," was an important concept then and remains so today. Today it involves the idea of loading up the car, before making a pilgrimage to commune, peacefully, in nature. But what the senator experienced was closer to the reality, and embodies one of the biggest problems in Yellowstone today: wilderness contained, nature under management, wild animals obliged to abide by human rules. The senator sought a way to solve the problem. He received $300,000 in federal funds so that the National Park Service could study the feasibility of erecting monorails in America's first national park. He called for the potential use of "air trains, magnetic levitation transportation" and other "environmentally cautious" ways to move people smoothly and safely through Yellowstone Park. "We should look at how Disney World moves vast numbers of people, the senator argued in 1991. "One thing Disney has been able to do that national parks haven't is separate Americans from their cars and make them enjoy it."

The senator's vision of an alternative to motor tourism won praise from the leaders of several conservation organisations. But Park Service planners declared the price tag—between $15 and $25 million a mile for a monorail—too high. In 1990, the cost for repairs of each crumbling mile of Yellowstone's 380-mile, two-lane highway system was one million dollars. With the benefit of hindsight, the monorail may have been a bargain! Today, a quarter century later, traffic problems have only worsened during the height of the summer holiday season, and Yellowstone's roads are once again crumbling. The estimated cost for required maintenance of Yellowstone structures and roads in 2016 was a massive $633 million. For Yellowstone's neighbour to the south, Grand Teton National Park, the cost was over $200 million.

Travellers from near and far have come to both parks in record numbers, last year – over four million – and the same was expected in 2017. Here's the good news: Government and independent economists have placed the combined value of nature-based tourism in Yellowstone and Grand Teton at close to one billion dollars, annually. The main attraction has always been bears, although as wildlife numbers declined through the first half of the 20th century, geothermal features, such as Old Faithful geyser became the main draw.

Old Faithful erupting, Yellowstone National Park (http://www.freeimages.com/photo/old-faithful-geyser-1402701)

Since the 1990s, with the re-introduction of wolves and a rebounding population of grizzly bears, Yellowstone and Grand Teton as destinations for American wildlife safaris have once again become highly sought after. One study showed that visitors coming from outside the Greater Yellowstone region spent $35.5 million annually, specifically to see wolves. Another recent study showed that visitors to Yellowstone would be willing to pay an additional $41 on top of the $25 vehicle entrance fee to see roadside bears. In fact, hypothetically, if tourists had no chance of glimpsing bears along the roadside, annual visitation proceeds could drop by $10 million.

Some economists have suggested that the total value of nature-related commerce across the entire Greater Yellowstone area may actually be two or even three times greater than that generated in just the Parks. This rise in outdoor recreation has occurred at the same time that logging, mining, and livestock production have waned. Property at the base of major downhill ski resorts has yielded billions of dollars in sales. Another attraction of the Yellowstone Park is elk shooting, In the entire state of Wyoming which extends beyond Yellowstone, revenue from elk licenses reached $10 million, and guides, hotels, and restaurants yielded millions more, in 2015.

The negative consequences are that 'too much love' has its downsides. "Last year's visitation tested the capacity of Yellowstone National Park," said one Park superintendent. "We are looking at ways to re-prioritize in order to protect resources, provide additional

13

ranger programs, and keep facilities clean." The superintendent indicated that the day might be approaching when the number of people allowed into Yellowstone at any one time will need to be limited, a tactic he was aware that would meet with stiff resistance.

The surge in new forms of recreation is bringing with it a whole set of other impacts on wildlife: skiers fly down backcountry slopes where rare wolverines live; hikers, mountain bikers, and boating enthusiasts frighten animals away from their habitats. Tourism also means that animal migration routes are blocked and this can cause accidents. In Jackson Hole, where wildlife must navigate across landscapes criss-crossed with roads, at least 377 animals (including moose, elk, deer, and bears) were killed on highways in 2015, prompting calls for special wildlife crossings, such as bridges over roads or tunnels beneath them.

The northwest corner of Greater Yellowstone, which contains the headwaters of three famous trout-fishing streams—the Madison, Yellowstone, and Gallatin—has attracted so many anglers that quotas on numbers of fishermen have been considered for certain stretches of the streams. Catch-and-release regulations, meaning anglers must put back the trout they catch, already exist on those rivers.

Tourism dollars represent a mighty engine for the regional economy, but so does people's desire to play, work, and live close to protected public lands. One study found that for every 100,000 acres of protected public land in Greater Yellowstone and other non-major metropolitan areas in the West, there has been a corresponding rise of $4,360 in per capita income.

In western rural counties with more than 30% of land safeguarded as national parks, federal wilderness, or national forests, job creation increased collectively by 345% over the past 40 years, compared with an increase in employment of 83% in similar counties with little or no protected federal land.

"The thing we need to figure out," the Park Superintendent indicated when addressing the problems that arise when nature is threatened even as it drives economic growth, "is how to deal with an unprecedented wave of newcomers, without turning Greater Yellowstone into the places people fled from—and want to leave behind."

Source : Adapted from Wilkinson (2016), National Geographic.

The case study of Yellowstone National Park clearly indicates the dilemma raised by Holden (2016), discussed at the beginning of this chapter, of trying to balance the need for conservation of protected areas with the aim of allowing recreationists and tourist to visit, and as suggested in the paragraph preceding the case study, the possibility that too many tourists may damage and disrupt the very thing they wish to see.

# Wilderness

In addition to the types of protected area referred to by Holden (2016), there is another very special landscape that in many countries has protected status, and that is *wilderness*. Once regarded of little value to humans, wilderness is now viewed by individuals and recognised by large numbers of countries as a key resource for tourism and recreation. This section discusses the history of the concept of wilderness, before a consideration of major issues in relation to the current use of wilderness for tourism experiences.

The modern concept of wilderness is closely linked to European perspectives dating back at least 1,000 years. In the past, European culture (which subsequently contributed significantly to American culture) held that wild nature or what can be termed 'wilderness' was an alien landscape, which was feared and had to be tamed (Holden, 2013). As Hall and Page (2014) state, the 18th century European concept of wilderness, is a very good example of what can be termed 'the other'. For the majority of Europeans at this time, wilderness was regarded as unlike the controlled rural landscapes, where farming and forestry were major activities or, the recently human created urban landscapes, and hence regarded as an alien landscape.

Nevertheless, wilderness is a difficult concept to define. This is partly because it has not been a static concept, having changed over several hundred years (Hall and Page, 2014). It is also as Nash (1967) indicated, the case that wilderness is not so much a place, as a quality that produces a feeling in an individual about a place. Whilst agreeing that it is difficult to define, Saarinen (2013; 145), nevertheless suggests that the term wilderness "conjures up meanings and images referring to wild, remote, rough, free and untrammelled natural areas".

The attitude to wilderness prevalent up to around 1800 in much of Europe and also in the emerging USA was based very much on Northern European Judaeo-Christian concepts, derived largely from religious sources, particularly the Bible (Hall and Page, 2014). The main idea of wilderness in this Judaeo-Christian context, was that it was a 'place' where those who had committed some form of sin were sent to pay the penalty for their misdemeanour. This could be for a period of weeks, months or even years and the wilderness was usually viewed as a hostile environment, with the possibility or even likelihood of savage animals, disease, drought or floods – in other words it was a very unpleasant environment where no one would willingly choose to go. For those who were compelled to go into the wilderness, in Biblical stories, it was a place to test one's abilities (e.g. resist, or even fight the devil) and through this testing to get closer to God.

However, there was an alternative to this view of wilderness in Europe, in the ideas of St. Francis of Assisi and several other medieval thinkers, who believed that wildlife was placed on earth not for human use, but for God's use. This was a revolutionary idea when first suggested, and removed the emphasis on people in an anthropocentric world that most supporters of Christianity and Judaism

**13**

believed in. Eventually this revolutionary idea underpinned the ideas of the English and American 18th and 19th century Romantic movements where nature, not man, was placed centre stage (Hall and Page, 2014).

Unlike Christianity and Judaism, eastern religions and philosophical ideas did not regard nature as something hostile that needed to be tamed. Instead, religions such as Shinto and Taoism venerated the wild and 'fostered love of nature not hatred' (Nash, 1982:21). As early as the fourth century AD, people in China were finding an aesthetic appeal in mountain areas, almost 1,500 years before a similar belief in Europe and North America began to take hold. This view of wilderness, without fear of the wild, meant there was a potential for recreation in such areas.

The varied perceptions of wilderness in different parts of the world indicates that the concept has important cultural dimensions. Until only about 200years ago, as noted above, 'wild nature' was largely feared in many European countries, which largely precluded use for recreation purposes. This perception of nature was also held by many of the European settlers who migrated to North America, Australia and New Zealand. This view was partly reflected in the rationale for the establishment of the first national parks in the USA. However, the pioneering spirit that was important in the settling of the USA also featured in the attitudes to the establishment of national parks there. This view was that nature was awe-inspiring, need not invoke fear in observers, but could still be tamed.

Not only has there been significant geographical variations in the concept of wilderness, but even a brief reflection on the current attitudes to wilderness, suggests how much the concept has changed over time. In European culture, by the middle of the 19th century, once feared mountain and moorland areas were becoming chosen locations for the wealthy to take their holidays. Many of the visitors were international tourists and they were involved in sporting activities such as skiing, as well as rock climbing and hiking. By the late 19th century, as more and more people travelled to mountain areas for tourism activities, there was the first real concern about the impacts that visitors would have on the landscape and this contributed to a drive towards protection and conservation and hence the establishment of protected areas, particularly national parks.

It is in the USA, particularly, that attitudes to wilderness reveal the complexity of the evolution of the concept. In particular, they indicate how links to changing views in other western societies influenced US views, how the history of settlement of the USA influenced developing concepts of wilderness there, and then, in turn, how this led to these ideas influencing other countries views on wilderness. Also very importantly, consideration of US attitudes to wilderness, reveals how these new concepts provided greater scope for recreation and tourism opportunities. This evolution of the US concept of wilderness is discussed below.

Early European settlers in the USA saw wilderness in Biblical terms, as uninhabitable and of little use. It was not until the late 18th century that there was the beginnings of a positive response to, and admiration of, American nature. Part of the appreciation of nature was a reaction against the old European colonial masters (Britain, France and Spain, in particular) and a desire to extol the virtues of a landscape 'pure' in terms of it being free from the control of any European power (Hall and Page, 2014). It was the American Romantic movement that was particularly important in asserting the importance of American wildlands. A combination of artistic, literary and political perceptions of the need for contact by US citizens with wild lands, provided a stimulus to positive attitudes to wilderness. Over time, societies were established that had as their chief aim to preserve wilderness and individuals influential in political and cultural circles promoted concepts of landscape protection.

However, in the USA, it was the extremely 'wild lands' that tended to be preserved, as the pioneering spirit of American settlers meant that it was only the areas that were viewed as having little or no commercial potential for e.g. farming or forestry, that were designated as wilderness. This meant that high mountains, with steep valleys and also desert areas became the first wilderness areas that were protected. However such areas, although having no apparent commercial use at the time, usually had major aesthetic qualities which were soon to be exploited for recreation and tourism usage. In this way, these wild areas began to have commercial value, and the realisation of the potential, or actual commercial value of such areas in terms of tourism, was a further spur to protecting them.

Similar trends to those in the US development of the concept of wilderness can also be discerned in Canada, Australia and New Zealand, although the national parks in each of these countries tended not to have the same status and perceived importance in the minds of inhabitants as those in the USA (Hall and Page, 2014). It is also important to note that in northern European countries, in particular Norway, Finland and Sweden there was a similar Romantic movement in the 18th and 18th century to that in the UK and later the USA, and wilderness was perceived as of high value, which contributed to its use then and increasingly later for tourism purposes.

Despite the evolving concept and growing importance of wilderness, it was not until the mid-1960s that a legislative framework defining the nature and purpose of wilderness, and how it was to be protected, was established in the USA. The definitions of wilderness in the US 1964 Wilderness Act are set out below as they embody key components of such an area that still remain important today and also give an indication of the significance of wilderness for recreation and tourism. The Act indicates that such areas:

- generally appear to be affected by the force of nature, with the evidence of human activity generally unnoticeable
- have outstanding opportunities for solitude or for 'primitive' forms of recreation
- are large enough spatially (the figure in the Act is at least 5000 acres) to make preservation possible
- may also contain features of ecological, and/or geological, and/or scientific, and/or educational and/or scenic and/or historical value.

**13**

By the early part of the 21st century there were over 100,000 protected areas around the globe (IUCN, 2003). The most important protected area in terms of numbers of such areas was managed nature reserve areas with over 27,000 of these, followed by national monuments of which there were over 19,000. There were nearly 4,000 national parks and 1,300 wilderness areas at this time and national parks accounted for 4.4 million square kilometres, amounting to almost 24% of all protected areas, whilst wilderness areas covered over 1 million square kilometres which was just over 5% of all protected areas (IUCN, 2003).

Arguably the most important wilderness left on earth is Antarctica. Its remoteness in relation to other inhabited regions and its inhospitable climate have resulted in it being the only continent that does not have a long history of human settlement and hence resource exploitation. The continent was only 'discovered' at the end of the 19th century and there have only ever been a few hundred people resident there in the last hundred or so years, and most of these are scientists. The combination of its remoteness, extreme climate which has produced a unique environment, combined with fact that around the edges of the continent there is a large number and range of wildlife species means that in the last 50 years there has been a small, but growing, tourism industry (Mason and Legg, 1999).

The following case study considers Antarctica as a tourist attraction and the importance of this wilderness area in its potential to inform and educate visitors about not just its unique environment, but also how it may develop more heightened and general awareness and concern for environmental issues on earth.

## Case study: Tourism in the Antarctic Wilderness

Antarctica is probably the last terrestrial tourism frontier. It is a remote, unique wilderness environment. The land-based ecosystems on the continent are limited because of the almost permanent snow cover which accompanies the very low temperatures. Unlikely as it may seem, Antarctica is one of the driest places on earth as it has very little rainfall – its precipitation is mainly in the form of snow. However, the continent is a huge island, and the marine ecosystems are rich in wildlife. So, it is the very edge of this continent, around its coastline, that is relatively rich in biodiversity. The periphery of Antarctica is the breeding ground for seabirds and a number of species of penguins. Killer whales are also found, as well as seals and walruses. The interior landscape is mountainous with active volcanoes, but also ice sheets and glaciers. At the edge of the continent, glaciers fall into the sea, creating huge icebergs. It is only the very edge of the continent that loses its snow cover during the brief Antarctic summer, which last for only a few weeks, whilst the interior remains permanently snow covered, and underneath this is a very deep ice sheet.

The continent is unique by global human standards in terms of never having any permanent inhabitants, and substantial human contact with the continent has only occurred since the early 20th Century. Its remoteness and inhospitable climate limited attempts to travel to it until only just over 100 ago. This means that its geography throughout much of history was almost unknown. Its short period of contact with humans has given it a unique political status – it is the only continent that is one political entity, but does not belong to one nation. It is administered by a very unusual process using what is known as the Antarctic Treaty System (ATS). This unique form of government involves representatives from countries that have an interest in Antarctica, which includes the USA, the UK, France, Germany and Russia, but also China, Malaysia and India. These countries, which over the past 100 years have had major political differences and in some cases fought wars against each other 'back home', work together to administer the ATS and disputes over, for example, fishing are resolved through the ATS.

The unusual status means that Antarctica is frequently viewed as a barometer of human use of the global environment, and activities here are often compared with what goes on elsewhere on the planet. This reflection on activities here and comparison with the other parts of earth is often expressed in the following manner: 'if we cannot get it right in Antarctica, there is little chance of success anywhere else on earth'!

In an attempt to prevent conflict and exploitation, it is the only continent devoted primarily to scientific activity and it is a neutral de-militarised zone. Scientists from many countries work together investigating, for example, glacial activity, ancient climate records stored in the ice, geology and marine biology. The scientists live on the continent for weeks, months, or in some case years, but there are still very few permanent inhabitants. Most commercial activity on the continent is banned, particularly mining and oil extraction. However, tourism has the very unusual status of being not only allowed, but actually promoted.

Why would tourists come to, what at first glance appears to be, a very inhospitable place for visitors? The landscape is an important attraction, particularly when it is accompanied by the significant amount and variety of wildlife in the margins of Antarctica. There are also a small number of heritage attractions in the form of the huts of the early explorers such as Scott, Shackleton and Mawson. Unusually, scientists and the work that they do are a very significant attraction for tourists. This is partly because the work in which many scientists are engaged, has global importance, particularly that to do with climate change. As science is the major activity of Antarctica and the scientists are funded by taxpayers from the countries of many of the visitors, it also provides an opportunity for these people to see how their taxes are being spent! Some tourists want to see what they regard as a unique environment (perhaps before it is irrevocably changed?). Some may also come to experience the 'otherness' of place and what some regard as the last remaining true wilderness on earth.

The tourist season is short, taking place during the short Antarctic summer from November to February. Tourism is also very concentrated in the coastal margins and particularly the area known as the Antarctic Peninsula, where many of the huts of the explorers are located. This area receives about 90% of all visitors, with the South Pole itself

13

also being significant for tourist visits. Almost all of the tourists arrive by cruise ship – they come from several countries, particularly Chile, Australia and New Zealand and the ships anchor offshore from the landmass. Visitor numbers appeared to have peaked at just over 30,000 per year in 2008, but have fluctuated since and have been generally lower than this at about 25,000 per year.

The reaction of tourists to their experience of Antarctica was investigated by Maher (2011). Maher was particularly interested in whether the experience was such that visitors were so affected that they became 'ambassadors for Antarctica'. What he meant by this was that tourists would be so impressed and even overawed by the Antarctic environment that they would have three reactions:

☐ They would believe that Antarctica is a unique environment, and tell their friends/family about Antarctica's attractions.

☐ They would tell their friends and family about the need to conserve the continent.

☐ They would become much more aware, generally about the importance of 'natural environments' and the need for their conservation.

Maher suggested that there are three phases of a tourist's experience:

1 Travel to the site – this is the anticipation phase.

2 The on-site experience – which Maher considered was likely to be an 'extraordinary experience' for the visitors because of what Antarctica has to offer.

3 The travel back from Antarctica – which involves memory and recollection. This process involves the on-site experience interacting with the pre-visit (anticipation) and post-visit (recollection/memory). Maher considered that this third stage (memory and recollection) would be most likely to contribute to the possible 'ambassador' role.

Maher examined the different phases of the experience, but concentrated on the 'anticipation' and the 'recollection/memory phase'. He used a sample of both 'ordinary' tourists to Antarctica, but also included 'VIPs to Antarctica' who comprised scientists, politicians, writers, artists and photographers, who are able to travel to the continent as a result of grants from countries such as New Zealand and Australia. Maher used questionnaire surveys, interviews and personal narratives. In total there were 87 respondents in phase 1 of the field research (as indicated above as phase 1 of the 'experience') and 75 of these in phase 2 of the field research (phase 3 of 'experience' above).

In relation to the potential role as ambassadors for Antarctica, all the respondents indicated that they had shared the experience after the visit with friends and family; some respondents also shared this with other groups; and all respondents regarded this as a very important activity. Respondents suggested that they had done this sharing mainly via informal discussion. However, some had also given formal speeches about their experiences. Respondents suggested that the motivations for sharing their experience was to make Antarctica 'come alive', 'bring it closer to the listeners' and 'whet their appetite'.

In terms of what they had learned during the visit, respondents indicated that they had found out more about the impacts of humans on Antarctica, the vulnerability of Antarctica, dealing with litter/pollution, and specific wildlife information.

Most of Maher's research questions were indirectly concerned with the role of ambassador for the Antarctic, and these did not make overt references to this role. However, Maher also asked a direct question about the role and just over 80% of respondents indicated that they felt they had become ambassadors for the continent as a result of their experience. However, Maher also injected a note of caution in relation to his results, when he stated that they should be interpreted carefully, as Antarctic tour operators would naturally be pleased to regard tourists as 'ambassadors', as this would be a very good marketing device for them.

(Based on Mason and Legg, 1999 and Maher, 2011)

## Summary

Protected areas have been established for a number of reasons in many countries around the world. A major motivating factor behind their establishment has been the desire to protect landscape and flora and fauna that have important aesthetic and scientific dimensions, but are threatened by potentially damaging human activity. Some protected areas allow tourism, but others do not.

One of the major types of protected area is the national park. Most parks have as an aim to protect the landscape, but also the intention to allow recreation and tourism activities. However, a significant issue is that these two activities do not always sit well together, and tourism can damage the very thing that tourists have come to visit.

Wilderness as a special kind of protected area is still found in certain areas on earth, but is threatened by human activity. Nevertheless in the case of the Antarctic wilderness, there is evidence that those who have visited not only believe strongly in the need to protect the entire continent, but have developed increased awareness and concern for environmental conservation in general.

## Student activities

1   Holden (2016) indicates that a key issue is how to best deal with the interaction of tourism and conservation in protected areas. What do you understand by this issue and how can it be resolved?

2   What factors contributed to the introduction of national parks in the USA in the 19th century?

3   In relation to the case study of Yellowstone Park, what are the major problems here and what can be done about these?

4 In small groups (3/4 students) discuss why wilderness is a difficult concept to define.

5 Why is wilderness important in relation to tourism today?

6 What attracts tourists to Antarctica?

7 Why could tourists become 'ambassadors for Antarctica'?

# References

Eagles, P., McCool, S. and Haynes, C (2002) *Sustainable Tourism in Protected Areas: Guidelines for Planning and Management*, Cambridge: IUCN

Hall, C.M. and Lew, A (2009) *Understanding and Managing Tourism Impacts: An Integrated Approach*, London: Routledge

Hall, C.M. and Page, S. (2014) *The Geography of Tourism and Recreation*, 4th ed., London: Routledge

Holden, A (2013) Protected areas and tourism, in Holden, A. and Fennel, D. (eds) *Routledge Handbook of Tourism and the Environment*, pp 276-284, London: Routledge

Holden, A (2016) *Environment and Tourism*, 3rd ed., London: Routledge

IUCN (2003) *Guidelines for Protected Area Management Categories*, Gland, Switzerland

IUCN (2011) *IUCN Protected Areas Category System* www.iucn.org accessed May 5 2017

McCannell, D. (1992) *Empty Meeting Grounds, The Tourist Papers*, London: Routledge

Maher, P (2011) Antarctic human dimensions: Ambassadors for the experience, in Maher, P., Stewart, E. and Luck, M. (eds) *Polar Tourism: Human, Environmental and Governance Dimensions*, New York: Cognizant Communications, 121-141.

Mason, P. (2016) *Tourism Impacts, Planning and Management*,3rd ed., London, Routledge

Mason, P. and Legg, S. (1999). Antarctic tourism: activities, impacts, management issues and a proposed research agenda. *Pacific Tourism Review*, **3**, 71–84.

Nash, R (1967) *Wilderness and the American Mind*, Newhaven CT: Yale University Press

Nash, R. (1982) *Wilderness and the American Mind* (3rd ed) Newhaven CT: Yale University Press

Saarinen, J. (2013) Tourism into the wild: the limits of tourism in wilderness, in Holden, A. and Fennel, D. (eds) *Routledge Handbook of Tourism and the Environment*, pp 145-154, London: Routledge

Wilkinson, T. (2016) Booming tourism becomes a stress test for Yellowstone, *National Geographic Magazine*, May 2016

# Tourism Management, Sustainability and the Future of Tourism

The final chapter of the previous section indicated that an important tourism issue is the need to protect some areas in order to conserve them for future tourism use. Protecting environments involves the process of management. The section that follows discusses the nature of management. In Chapter 14, the processes of management are linked to planning and policy and the specific focus is on the nature of planning and management in tourism and leisure. Chapter 15 is concerned with sustainable development and in particular sustainable tourism. It considers the changing meanings of sustainability and sustainable tourism over the last 30 years or so and discusses how planning and management have been used in attempts to bring about sustainable tourism. The final chapter of the book discusses the future of tourism, considering factors that may lead to the continued increase in tourist numbers, as well as those that my inhibit or even stop this growth, and in addition presents a number of possible future tourism scenarios for analysis.

LIVERPOOL JOHN MOORES UNIVERSITY
LEARNING SERVICES

# 14 Tourism Planning and Management

## Introduction

The first chapter in the final section of the book considers planning and management issues in relation to the geography of tourism. This chapter initially discusses the nature of planning and management in general terms. It then focuses on tourism planning and management, and considers the relationship between tourism planning, policy and management. It ends with a discussion of destination planning and management.

## Urban planning

The physical planning of the layout of urban areas dates back over 2,000 years to the Greek era (Gunn, 1988), but modern Western-style planning is linked to town planning in the United Kingdom which originated about 200 years ago (Gunn, 1988; Williams, 1998) and emerged when the population became increasingly urbanized. Planning was to a great extent a response to the perceived 'evils' of urban living. These evils consisted of poor quality housing, which was overcrowded, poor drainage and sanitation, as well as inadequate roads. All of these factors contributed to appalling living conditions for many people. Those involved in planning for utopian cities to replace the rapidly built unplanned creations of 18th century Britain, however, were still concerned primarily with the physical appearance of cities.

In the early 20th century, almost all urban planning in Britain was linked to a number of central government planning acts, and from the 1930s onwards, there was additionally a focus on rural areas with a succession of Town and Country Planning Acts (Mason, 2013a). In federal countries such as the USA, Canada and Australia, it has been the governments of individual states which have usually created specific laws and regulations restricting the places where particular activities can take place, and in New Zealand the planning system which affects land use activities, including tourism, is set within the Resource Management Act of 1991 (Mason 2013a).

In many European countries, particularly France and Spain, land use planning is officially centralized, although local and regional authorities in France have a good deal of power, whilst in Spain regional authorities such as in Andalusia and, in particular, Catalonia also have a large amount of power. In Germany, the history of planning has some similarities to the British situation with much concern about urban planning, but also in other ways not dissimilar to the USA, as the individual federal states have much power in relation to planning.

If early attempts at planning were to create order in response to social and environmental degradation, this is still an important rationale for planning today. As Williams (1998) suggested, without planning there is the risk that an activity will be unregulated, formless or haphazard, and likely to lead to a range of negative economic, social and environmental impacts, and as Gunn (1988) argued, the absence of planning may result in serious malfunctions and inefficiencies.

In 18th and 19th century Europe, much planning was reactive in relation to, for example the problems of housing and overcrowding, but by the late 20th century it was far more proactive and future oriented (Gunn, 1988) and remains so today. Although modern planning originated largely in Europe and North America, some form of official planning now takes place almost everywhere, in both developed and developing countries.

# The nature of planning

Planning is a difficult term to define, mainly because it is used in a variety of contexts. For example, it can be used in connection with individuals, groups, organisations and governments. It can be used in relation to different geographical settings, such as urban and rural, as well as being applied at different scales from local, through regional up to national. A plan can mean little more than partially thought-through ideas that are barely articulated, or a carefully considered document.

Hall (1992: 1) suggested that part of the problem with the concept of planning is that "although people realise that planning has a more general meaning, they tend to remember the idea of the plan as a physical representation or design." This focus on the plan as a physical design has probably contributed to the failure to recognize the processes that have led to the creation of the actual physical plan. However, if planning is considered to be mainly a process, rather than conceiving of it as a product, there is the danger that it is thought of as being rather vague and abstract (Gunn, 1988). Nevertheless, it is the process part of planning that is particularly important. McCabe *et al.* (2000:235) emphasise that planning is a process when they suggested:

> *A plan ... enables us to identify where we are going and how to get there – in other words it should clarify the path that is to be taken and the outcomes, or end results. It also draws attention to the stages on the way and ... helps to set and establish priorities that can assist in the scheduling of activities.*

According to Williams (1998), planning is, (or should be), a process:

- for anticipating and ordering change: that is forward looking:
- that seeks optimal solutions:
- designed to increase and ideally maximize possible development benefits
- and that will produce predictable outcomes.

In discussing the processes involved in planning, Williams (1998) suggests that the aim of modern planning, is to seek optimal solutions to perceived problems, and it is designed to increase and, hopefully, maximize development benefits, which will produce predictable outcomes. Williams (1998:126) claimed planning 'is an ordered sequence of operations and actions that are designed to realise one single goal or a set of interrelated goals'.

One of the key elements of the process of planning is decision-making (Veal, 1994; Hall, 2000). As Veal (1994:3) stated: 'planning can be seen as the process of deciding'. Hall (2000:7) suggested that this process is not straightforward, as it involves 'bargaining, negotiation, compromise, coercion, values, choice and politics'. Hall (2000) also stated that decision-making is part of a continuum that follows directly from planning and this, in turn, is followed by action. Gunn (1988) believed that action was a very important part of planning and employed the ideas of Lang (1985) to differentiate between conventional planning and strategic planning. Lang (1985) suggested that conventional planning has only vague goals, is reactive rather than proactive, periodic rather than consistent, separates the planning from the implementation stage, and fails to consider the values of those individuals and organisations involved. Strategic planning, however, according to Lang is action-oriented, focused, ongoing, pro-active, and does consider the values of those involved.

Wilkinson (1997) supports the notion that a plan is very much about process and indicates the important geographical dimension when suggesting that a plan provides the rationale for and details of how implementation will take place within a country or region, and sets this within a wider economic and social context. He also indicated that planning involves not only the formulation of plans and their implementation, but also their monitoring and review.

A key element of both the rationale for, and the process of, planning is that it is future-orientated. As Chadwick (1971:24) suggested 'planning is a process, a process of human thought and action based upon that thought – in point of fact, forethought, thought for the future, nothing more or less than this is planning'.

# Planning and policy

In general parlance, planning and policy are closely related terms. Wilkinson (1997) linked the two terms when stating planning is a course of action, while policy is the implementation of the planned course of action. Policy is very often created by, and emanates from, public bodies or organisations. Creating public policy is a major concern of government activity and public policy can be summarized as what governments decide to do or not to do (Dye, 1992).

However, it is important to note that planning is not just a process conducted by governments. Private sector organisations in tourism, which could include hotels and tour operators, prepare careful plans and usually have a number of policies through which they operationalize these plans. Hence, planning covers private as well as government and public enterprise (Elliot, 1997).

Public policy, by definition is in the public domain, and often provokes detailed and possibly heated discussions. However, the policies of individual private organisations are often protected because of commercial concerns and may not be so easily discerned. In relation to public policy, it is important to recognize that it is not created in a vacuum, but is greatly influenced by the social, economic and environmental context in which it is created. Therefore, it is important to be aware that policy results from political structures, value systems, institutional frameworks, the distribution of power and the decision-making process (Hall and Jenkins, 1995).

## Values and planning

The section above on policy and planning suggested that values are important in planning. Healey (1997:29) indicated that public policy and planning are 'social processes through which ways of thinking, ways of valuing and ways of acting are actively constructed by participants'. Hall (2000) argued that is important to be aware of the standpoint or value position of those involved in decision making in planning.

Although planning in leisure and tourism is discussed in more detail in the next section of this chapter, it is important to note at this point that planning for recreation and tourism relies heavily on values, and that community values are particularly important. Therefore, it is essential, that a recreation or tourism policy should reflect the values of stakeholders and interested parties (Gunn, 1988; Veal, 1994).

Returning from the specifics of leisure and tourism planning to general factors, if planning is accepted as being a process that is intended to represent the views of all stakeholders and interested parties in the decision making process, then it should be realized and acknowledged that there will not automatically be unanimity and homogeneity in values and views. However, Wilkinson (1997) claimed that much thinking and writing about planning tends to assume that it is a simple, almost value-free, scientific process and criticized the conventional definitions of the planning process where:

> emphasis (is) on a straightforward approach that accepts the…possibility of comprehensive rationality. Such a process assumes several factors: consensus on objectives, lack of uncertainty, known alternatives, a high degree of centralised control, and ample time and money to prepare a plan (Wilkinson, 1997:24).

14

Wilkinson argued such factors rarely exist in any planning context, and this includes the setting of tourism planning. Cullingsworth (1997) has similar views to Wilkinson and is particularly concerned about the idea that planning is believed to be a rational process and argued:

> Rational planning is a theoretical idea. Actual planning is a practical exercise of political choice that involves beliefs and values. It is a laborious process in which many public and private agencies are concerned. These comprise a wide range of conflicting interests. Planning is a means by which attempts are made to resolve these conflicts (Cullingsworth, 1997:5)

Hall (1992) argued very strongly that planning is not a tidy process as posited by theorists of the activity and stated that a key problem is trying to predict the future when there are conflicts of values. As he claimed: 'The systems view of planning is therefore a condition to which planners aim, but will never be the reality' (Hall, 1992:256).

This discussion of planning being about views and values, and partly about conflict resolution, indicates that it should be seen as very much as part of a wider political process. As Jenkins (1997:25) stated: 'a plan is a document that has been the focus of political debate and is available to the public'.

The relationship between planning and policy in relation to differing values and the wider political context is discussed in the next section which focuses on recreation leisure and tourism planning.

# Planning and policy in leisure, recreation and tourism

## ■ Leisure planning

Tourism planning, when involving public authorities, usually fits within the wider context of leisure planning; the planning framework for tourism therefore falls within leisure. This is because tourism is a recreational activity that takes place in leisure time and is viewed as such by most public policy bodies (Veal, 1994; Hall and Page, 2014). Traditionally in many developed countries, there has been a split between outdoor recreation and tourism provision. Outdoor recreation has been provided by the public sector, whilst tourism tends to be provided by the private sector (Hall and Jenkins, 1995). However, from the mid-1980s, this distinction began to disappear in many Western countries (Hall and Page, 1999). In the second decade of the 21st century, in relation to tourism provision, there is much overlap between the public and private sectors in many countries, despite the fact that this tends to create complications in terms of responsibilities for planning.

The planning process adopted in the leisure field tends to display the same characteristics as those found in planning more generally, and discussed in the previous section, and it is often disjointed and reactive. It is complicated by the fact that it frequently involves a variety of land-owners, public bodies and private providers, as well as different user groups (Glyptis, 1994; Williams, 1998), meaning that the process is complex and at times difficult to operationalize. Within the British context, Veal (1994) identified three phases of leisure planning between the 1960s and the mid-1990s. The first of these was the 'demand phase' (1960–1972), which was in response to a rapidly growing population base. The 'need phase', which occurred according to Veal between 1973 and 1985, saw a focus on the needs of particular groups. The 'enterprise phase' (from 1985 to the mid-1990s) saw the rise of private providers, with the government seeking to distance itself from leisure provision. This approach of allowing more private providers has continued to occur since the 1990s, but also there has been specialist provision, for example for the disabled, and this has some parallels with the stage between 1960 and 1972.

Spink (1994) introduced the concept of leisure action spaces, which range from the home, through the local neighbourhood and the region, to national and international levels. Focusing on the United Kingdom, Spink (1994) argued that, although leisure can take place in many geographical locations, most leisure/recreation activities take place within urban areas, including the urban fringes such as country parks, green-belt areas, footpaths and bridleways. However, by definition, those people involved in leisure/recreation activities in their home area will be residents of the area, those who have travelled into an area will be classified as tourists (see Mason, 1995; Cooper *et al.*, 1998). Therefore, planning for tourism is likely to be targeted at different groups and involve different processes (Mason, 1995). Therefore, tourism planning can be regarded as different from leisure planning in certain respects and the nature of tourism planning is discussed below.

## ■ Tourism planning

In the early 1980s, there were two major aims of tourism planning – to satisfy the needs of visitors and to improve conditions for local residents in areas receiving tourists. These two key aims of tourism planning were summarized by Mathieson and Wall (1982:186) in the following way: 'to ensure that opportunities are available for tourists to gain enjoyable and satisfying experiences and at the same time to provide a means for improving the way of life for residents and of destination areas'.

In the late 1990s, Williams (1998) was more specific and suggested that tourism planning had a number of key objectives. These are, he suggested, as follows:

- ■ The creation of a mechanism for the structured provision of tourist facilities over quite large geographic areas.

- ■ The coordination of the fragmented nature of tourism (particularly in relation to accommodation, transport, marketing and human resources).

- ■ Certain interventions to conserve resources and maximize benefits to the local community in an attempt to achieve sustainability (usually through a tourism development or management plan).

■ The redistribution of tourism benefits (the development of new tourism sites or the economic realignment of places that tourists have begun to leave).

Planning can also be an attempt to match supply and demand for tourism services/activities, Williams (1998) suggested, and he considered that planning gives tourism a political significance and hence provides legitimacy to an activity which has not always been accorded this status. Williams also claimed that a major problem of tourism planning is that it encompasses many activities, and although it may address physical, economic, environmental and business concerns, it does not necessarily blend these together well. Coccossis and Parpairis (1996) concur with this view and argued one of the activities relating to tourism planning, that of environmental conservation, was seen as being a threat to economic and social development for most of the period up until the mid-1990s, and continues to be viewed in this way by some sections of the tourism industry (Mason, 2013). Hence, planning for recreation and tourism has not necessarily been a straightforward process (Gunn, 1988; Veal, 1994; Coccossis and Parpairis, 1996; Williams, 1998).

Another important issue in tourism planning, providing further evidence that it is not a straightforward process, is that it can involve attempts to resolve conflict between different user groups (Moore, 1994; Hendricks, 1995; Ramthun, 1995; Watson, 1995). Reference to conflict is confirmation that tourism planning, like other types of planning, is a political process. Hall (2000) supported this view when he argued that tourism policy is what governments decide to do or not do about tourism.

Fennell (1999) argued that tourism planning requires a policy, which states the aims and objectives to be implemented in the planning process. Fennell further stated that implementation is usually done by governments. However, Lickorish (1991) claimed that governments have often viewed the responsibility of tourism policy as being with the private sector. Williams (1998) and Hall and Jenkins (1995) also discussed this problem, and indicated that tourism planning increasingly involves both public and private sector bodies.

As with policy in generic terms, tourism policy involves a number of ideas and statements that can be implemented via a tourism plan (Wilkinson, 1997). However, Hirschmann (1976) suggested that tourism policy is different from many other policies created by government and that one of the reasons it is different, is that, unlike agricultural reform or industrial policies which are frequently forced on government, tourism policy is usually chosen. It is also different from policies like industrial policy because there tends to be little conflict, or little perceived conflict (Hirschmann, 1976). However, an industrial policy involving restructuring frequently leads to job losses, environmental change and attempts to relocate industry. This will usually contribute to at least controversy, and possibly conflict between workers and managers. This is not the way tourism policy has been perceived, as unlike industrial policy, tourism policy is not linked to major problem solving, such as the economic and social changes associated with, for example, the closure of a coal mine or steel works.

Tourism policy may, in fact, be viewed as 'simple' by those whose job it is to create and implement it (Wilkinson, 1997). However, as Cooper *et al.* (2005) suggested, the process of tourism planning is not simple, although it may well follow a systematic approach. Cooper *et al.* (2005) indicated that tourism planning in many developed countries, and some developing countries, follows a number of stages, which are fairly consistent, and these are shown in Figure 14.1.

**Stage 1 Recognizing the need for a tourism plan/strategy**
*What is the issue/problem being addressed by the plan?*

**Stage 2 Setting objectives/goals for a specific planning strategy**
*Why do we need (this type of) tourism development?*

**Stage 3 Survey of existing data**
*What do we already know from our sources of information?*

**Stage 4 Implementation of new surveys**
*What new information do we need and how shall we obtain it?*

**Stage 5 Analysis of secondary and primary data**
*What have we learned from our research?*

**Stage 6 Initial policy and plan creation**

**Stage 7 Recommendations of the plan**

**Stage 8 Implementation of the plan**

**Stage 9 Monitoring, evaluation and re-formulation.**

**Figure 14.1:** The process of planning in tourism showing stages and related questions

Cooper *et al.* also stressed that, in addition to following the nine stages indicated in Figure 14.1, to ensure that the planning process is successful, the nature of the team of planners is very important. The team will need a good deal of expertise and experience, and should contain physical planners, economists, market planners, social scientists, environmental scientists, engineers, draughtsmen and legal experts (Cooper *et al.*, 2005).

Figure 14.1 can be viewed as a summary of what the stages of tourism planning are likely to be in general terms, but the following case study provides suggestions on how a tourism plan should be put into action, and also shows the main processes involved, who should participate, the time frame and the anticipated outcomes. This example, which is from the body (VisitEngland) that acts as the main tourism marketing organisation to promote England within Britain, also provides the rationale for the use of the plan.

14

## Case Study: VisitEngland 'Principles for Developing Destination Management Plans'

### Rationale for Developing Destination Management Plans (DMPs)

Two sets of reasons for developing a DMP should be considered in deciding whether to embark on the process and in seeking to convince others.

1  The importance of actually having a plan:

☐ Addressing fragmentation: The visitor economy involves a whole set of experiences delivered by many organisations in the public, private and voluntary sectors. It is essential that they work together and in doing so achieve a better use and management of resources.

☐ Recognising, strengthening and coordinating different functions: Supporting the visitor economy is not just about promotion but must cover a whole range of activities aimed at strengthening the quality of the visitor experience and the performance of businesses.

☐ Managing and monitoring impacts: Tourism has a range of impacts on society and the environment and is inherently an activity that benefits from management.

☐ Prioritising and allocating resources: A key benefit of having a plan is to identify what the real needs and priorities are so that financial and human resources can be used most effectively.

☐ Winning more support and resources: Well researched, argued and presented action plans can strengthen the case for funding and help to identify projects for support.

2  The importance of the visitor economy and its wider linkages: This second set of reasons concerns the overall importance of the visitor economy to most destinations and its implications for the quality of life of residents and for the wider local economy:

☐ By strengthening the visitor economy, services enjoyed by local people, such as restaurants, attractions, arts and entertainment will benefit.

☐ Looked at the other way, actions directly aimed at making somewhere a better place to live and work will also make it a more appealing place to visit.

☐ Strengthening and promoting the image and awareness of a destination and the services available can be highly important in attracting new business and investment across all sectors.

☐ Tourism has demonstrated its ability to stimulate growth in jobs and is a relatively accessible sector in which to start a new business

☐ The health of tourism related businesses can be very important to other parts of the local economy who supply them, such as food producers, maintenance services etc.

In summary, a DMP can play a very important role in identifying how the full range of local authority policies and services (in planning, transport, environmental management, leisure and recreation, culture and the arts) can support the visitor economy on the one hand and be supported by it on the other. By showing these links it prevents tourism being treated in a silo, rather than as a core contributor to economic development.

**Table 14.1:** The stages of a DMP

| Stage | Time in months | Key stakeholder engagement | Wider consultation | Outputs |
|---|---|---|---|---|
| Getting started | | Initial meeting | Announcement | N/a |
| Gathering evidence | 2-6 | Assistance and participation | Extensive consultation | Summary results |
| Establishing strategy | 1-2 | Stakeholder workshop | Information as required | Strategic directions |
| Developing action plan | 1-4 | Agreement on tasks and responsibilities | Information as required | Draft destination management plan (DMP) |
| Implementing plan | 1-2 | Approval of DMP | Consultation on draft plan | Final DMP launched |
| Monitoring, evaluating and reporting | N/a | Report every quarter | Regular communication | Annual report |

(source: VisitEngland, 2013)

Although the case study is located in England, it reveals many similarities with the generic planning approach discussed by Cooper *et al.* (2005), particularly in terms of the nature and sequencing of the planning stages and the actual processes occurring within each stage. The focus of the VisitEngland planning principles is on destinations and much early tourism planning was very site specific and linked to the supply side – the destination end – of tourism activity (Gunn, 1988) and it often remains as the major focus of much tourism planning today (Mason, 2016). This geographical focus on the destination helps to explain the rationale often provided for much tourism planning. This rationale has been frequently linked to negative consequences of tourism in destinations and as Williams (1998) argued, unplanned tourist destinations are those associated with negative impacts.

A major section of this chapter to follow is devoted to a more detailed discussion of destination management, but immediately prior to this is consideration of the relationship between planning and management, which is followed by a focus on tourism management.

**14**

# Planning and management

As with the term *planning*, *management* also has a number of different definitions. Gilbert *et al.* (1995:8) defined the activity in the following way:

> *Management is a goal-oriented process that involves the allocation of resources and the coordination of the talents and efforts of a group of people.*

Gilbert *et al.* (1995) also note a major link between planning and management, when they stated one of the key activities involved in managing is planning. They suggested that managing is the first part of a process that also involves organizing, empowering and controlling. They further elaborated their ideas on managing by suggesting that it is in reality a cyclical process, with a link back from controlling to planning. They also argued that each of activities in any given situation may be ongoing simultaneously and therefore is not an entirely discrete process.

Doswell (1997) has similar views to Gilbert *et al* and indicated the functions of management are as follows: planning, organising, giving direction, providing coordination and monitoring. He expanded on each factor indicating that planning is about what one is trying to achieve, organisation is concerned with mobilizing and deploying resources, giving direction relates to the provision of leadership and maintenance of a sense of purpose, while coordination is the provision of a unifying force, and monitoring is a control function achieved through the reporting and analysis of results.

Hall and Page (2014) also recognized this link between planning and management. They suggested that the proactive approach of planning should be intertwined with the, frequently reactive, reality of management. If management is perceived as a goal-oriented process, then it is necessary to have some measure of its effectiveness in relation to these goals (Gilbert *et al.*, 1995). The performance of management is therefore part of the management process; it should be assessed and is, in effect, a measure of the quality of management.

# Tourism management

Tourism management is largely concerned with ways to manage the resources for tourism, the interaction of tourists with physical resources and their interaction with residents of tourist areas (Mason, 1995). This focus of tourism management is concerned primarily with tourism impacts in resorts areas or destinations. It is in such areas that the supply side of tourism (physical resources, built environment and resident population) interacts with the demand side (tourists, travel agents, tour operators, transport operators, tourist boards and tourism developers).

A clear indication of the link between planning and management can be found in Doswell's (1997) claim that tourism management is what tourism planners are, or should be, engaged in. However, as Doswell indicated, tourism planning and tourism management are often treated as separate activities and this, he claimed, is due to planning being linked to physical planners. In this case, planning is not seen as an ongoing process of management, but a one-off activity which precedes the construction of whatever was planned (Doswell, 1997).

A particularly useful definition of tourism management is that produced by Middleton and Hawkins (1994):

> 'Strategies and action programmes using and coordinating available techniques to control and influence tourism supply and visitor demand in order to achieve defined policy goals'

(Middleton, cited in Middleton and Hawkins, 1998:84).

Middleton and Hawkins (1998) indicated that there are five variables that tourism management is attempting to control and influence. These five variables are: location, timing, access, products and education. Middleton and Hawkins suggested in relation to *location* that there may be too few, or too many visitors and tourist businesses in a particular destination. In relation to *timing*, they indicated there may be too many or too few visitors, at particular places at particular times of the day, week or month. They indicated that *access* relates to the relative ease or difficulty and associated cost of reaching chosen places. They suggested that there could be too many or too few *products* in a particular location and perhaps a lack of infrastructure to support certain products. *Education* is concerned with the awareness of the cumulative behaviour of visitors and tourism businesses, and awareness of residents' wishes for the destination.

Middleton and Hawkins (1998: 85) provided a good summary of tourism management in practice when they stated:

> 'Tourism management focuses on ways and means to influence visitors' choices of location, access, timing and product provision, and to develop local understanding and knowledge'.

The reality of 'influencing visitors' choices' means ways to persuade tourists and tourism businesses to voluntarily change their naturally occurring behaviour where 'naturally occurring behaviour ' is what people do when exercising their instincts and choices in a free society (Middleton and Hawkins, 1998). Changing this behaviour may require selective inducements, or by obliging people and businesses to change through the imposition of regulations, controls, taxes or penalties of various types (Mason and Mowforth, 1996; Middleton and Hawkins, 1998).

In most countries, controlling visitor numbers at destinations is beyond the influence of either public sector bodies, such as tourist boards, or private sector organisations. In some cases, control can be exerted by such methods as high entrance charges  and/or limited car parking spaces. However in the majority of destinations, such measures are not employed. Instead, what Middleton and Hawkins (1998:85), term 'selective influences and control' are used. These are designed to achieve stated and quantified objectives at destinations. They are:

- Making judgments on carrying capacity;
- Selecting and targeting particular market segments or groups;

**14**

- Identifying partner organisations in planning and marketing for tourism;
- Developing a variety of management techniques for visitor segments and products;
- Systematically monitoring results and making any required changes.

These selective influences and controls are shown in Figure 14.2. The left-hand column shows examples of mainly public sector resource constraints, while the right-hand column shows controls as market forces, which are primarily associated with the private sector.

| Resource constraints (supply-orientation) mainly public sector | Market forces (demand-orientation) mainly commercial sector |
|---|---|
| Regulation of land use | Knowledge of visitor profiles, behaviour, needs and trends |
| Regulation of buildings | |
| Regulation of environmental impacts | Design of visitor products (quality and satisfaction) |
| Provision of infrastructure | Capacity (products marketed) |
| Control by licensing | Distribution of products/access for customers |
| Provision of information | Provision of information |
| Fiscal controls and incentives | Price |

**Figure 14.2:** Resource constraints and market forces – tourism management controls and influences at destinations (based on Pearce, 1989; Middleton, 1994)

In the early 1990s, the English Tourist Board produced an influential report on the relationship between tourism and the environment (ETB, 1991). The report included a triangle, shown in Figure 14.3, which can be considered to be at the heart of all approaches to tourism management.

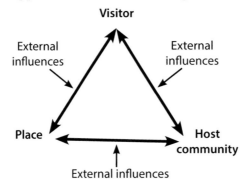

**Fig. 14.3:** The ETB/DoE Triangle

This triangle indicates that the three major components to be taken into consideration in tourism management are: the visitor, the host community and the environment. These three factors are inter-related and significantly impact upon each other. Although the triangle is relatively simplistic, it does 'neatly encapsulate the three main focal points for management decisions' (Middleton and Hawkins, 1998: 86).

However, the situation is somewhat more complex than this, as there are more than just visitors and residents interacting with the environment. In addition, there are 'other key players' (Mason, 2016) including elected representatives and appointed officials, as well as tourism-related businesses that need to be taken into account. The elected representatives and appointed officials are responsible to residents for the goals and management of a destination. Businesses involved include accommodation providers, cafes, restaurants and hotels as well as transport providers and visitor attractions. Residents are usually not homogenous, but will be made up of different interests groups and visitors will possibly comprise a number of different market segments. Swarbrooke (1999) produced a very similar set of stakeholders in tourism management to that suggested by Mason, (2016). In addition to the 'players' provided by Mason (2016), he also included the voluntary sector, particularly pressure groups and professional bodies, as well as the media.

Much of this discussion concerning tourism management has implied a major separation between the public and the private sector. However, there is significant evidence of the importance of partnerships in tourism management (Bramwell and Lane, 2000). Such partnership may involve the voluntary sector as well as links between private organisations and public bodies (Mason *et al.*, 2000). Partnerships are likely to be significant in future attempts at tourism management (Bramwell and Lane, 2000) particularly as the private sector is likely to have the best information about demand and also influential marketing techniques, while the public sector should be most aware of acceptable levels of tourism impacts and be able to apply sanctions in relation to agreed resource capacities.

# Destination planning and management

A good deal of this book has been an investigation of the nature of, and processes operating in relation to, tourism destinations. Chapter 5 was devoted to a focus on the nature of destinations and was concerned particularly with the image of destinations and how image can change over time. There have been a number of references to destinations and planning and management in earlier sections of this chapter, and this section of the chapter focuses on destination planning and management in greater detail.

We have noted earlier in this chapter the links between planning, policy and management in generic terms. Looking at the case study based on VisitEngland early in this chapter provides support for the argument that the processes of planning and management in tourism are also strongly linked, and, in particular, this is the case in the context of destinations, as the publication that forms the basis of the case study is titled: 'Principles of Developing Destination Management Plans'.

Ritchie and Crouch (2003) discuss the nature and specific details of the processes of destination planning and management, but initially indicate, when focusing on the specific factors affecting planning and management, that the tasks of *developing a tourism policy* and then *implementing policy* may appear to be part

14

of the same process, but are not. As Ritchie and Crouch (2003) state, although there is an overlap between first, the policy and planning processes and second, the processes of management of a destination, particularly when both processes focus on maintaining tourism in the destination and making the destination more competitive, they are in fact different activities.

Ritche and Crouch (2003) indicate that *policy and planning development* is an intellectual process that uses information to create macro-level decision-making, in order to develop the type of destination that is viewed as desirable. It will involve monitoring how well the destination is performing in relation to criteria established in the planning and policy formulation, and also in comparison with other destinations. It is intended that the policy, planning and development process will provide the framework to implement the vision for the destination and enable the day-to-day management of the destination.

However, *destination management* is much more of a micro-level process. During this process, all industry stakeholders and many destination residents carry out organisational activities, on a day-to-day basis, in an attempt to achieve a macro-level vision contained within the destination policy and planning strategy (Ritchie and Crouch, 2003).

## ■ Destination management organisations

As Ritchie and Crouch (2003) indicate, the implementation of the tourism policy is usually the responsibility of a Destination management organisation (DMO). There are a number of key activities involved in the destination management process, in which a DMO will be involved. These processes are not separate but interdependent. Nevertheless, in an attempt to understand the processes, they are listed below and this is followed by a brief discussion of each.

- Organisation
- Marketing
- Providing quality of service experience
- Gathering information/conducting research
- Human resource development
- Finance
- Visitor management
- Resource stewardship
- Crisis management

The first point is a pre-requisite for achieving the other processes in the list, as before any others can occur, some form of organisation is essential, as this will ensure that there is the leadership and coordination necessary to carry out these processes. The structure of a particular organisation, which is in effect the DMO, is usually linked closely to the different level or scale at which it operates. Hence, at national level the DMO will almost always be a government department with a tourism brief – usually a national tourism office. At the state or province level, the organisation may also be a government office or possibly a joint public/private partnership. At the city or urban area level, there may be a city tourism department or the tourism role may be combined with another role, such as leisure or recreation. It is also possible, as evident in the examples of Birmingham and Barcelona in Chapter 5, that chambers of commerce, (private sector business representatives) may have a significant role. It may be the case, particularly where events are a key element of a destination, that a convention bureau has a major role in the DMO.

With regard to the other DMO processes listed above, it is frequently marketing that is regarded as the key one (see Morgan *et al*, 2010). Indeed for many authors marketing is the most important role of a DMO, and in fact so significant, that the 'M' in DMO has often been understood to stand for marketing and not management. The marketing role has traditionally been seen as one of promotion and selling (Ritchie and Crouch, 2003). A key element of the marketing activity is identifying the various visitor segments who come to the destination and the DMO's role will be to match the differing visitor segments to the potential visitor experience. In relation to the marketing aspect of the DMO, another key activity will be to gain an understanding of the level of awareness of the destination, as this is likely to be very important for the long term sustainability of a destination.

Obtaining an understanding of the level of awareness of a destination amongst actual visitors and potential visitors can lead to a better understanding of the image of the destination, and image is important in relation to the various visitor segments. Hence, if those involved in the DMO know the level of awareness of the destination and understand its image amongst visitors, then it will be possible to plan promotional activity to attempt to sustain current visitor numbers and hopefully bring more visitors to the destination. Those working in the DMO also want to establish the destination's image in the mind of potential visitors and in this way, they are attempting to create a brand. The process of creating a brand is very important for the DMO as it is intended that visitors will link the brand with their experience in the destination and return to the same destination in the future. The DMO will also hope that visitors, satisfied with their experience, will inform their friends and family about the destination. This is referred to as 'word-of-mouth advertising' and is often considered the best form of advertising in tourism (see Morgan *et al*, 2010).

The DMO also has the role to ensure that the visitor experience involves enjoyable encounters and interaction with those actually working in the tourism industry. Visitors desire a pleasurable experience, where they also feel comfortable and secure and they want to be able to feel they have interacted well with service providers and to take away good memories of this encounter (Ritchie and Couch, 2003). In an attempt to ensure that visitors have an enjoyable experience in a destination, a part of which is the interaction with tourism industry staff, then another major role of the DMO will be to ensure staff working in tourism

14

are well prepared for this work. This means the DMO will be involved in training and certification programmes, although this may not be direct involvement, but will be at least ensuring that tourism staff are suitably qualified and experienced.

A DMO should be actively involved in research and in particular gathering information about, for example, the nature of visitors and specifically their demographics, the visitor experience of the destination and visitor level of satisfaction with this (Ritchie and Crouch, 2003). The information gathered will provide feedback on the current situation in the destination and should help in further marketing activity.

DMOs also have a role in relation to the financial aspects of a destination, as a DMO may have the possibility of gaining access to finance in a way that separate businesses will find very difficult to obtain. DMOs may be able to gain venture capital (Ritchie and Crouch, 2003), but if this is not possible, then a DMO should be in a position to offer financial advice. The DMO may also be able to act in an advisory role and provide information to the financial community on the role and importance of tourism.

A key role that has assumed much more importance for a DMO recently is a stewardship role of taking care of the tourism resource base. This role is important as there has been growing concern, as discussed in other chapters of this book, about negative impacts on tourism resources in destinations and consequently calls for more sustainable forms of tourism. Related both to the stewardship role and that of providing a good service experience, a significant role of the DMO is visitor management. This role will try to ensure that visitors have minimum negative impacts on the local environment, also attempt to make sure visitors have the best possible experiences in their interaction with service providers and local residents, and contribute financially to the destination economy.

As indicated in Chapter 12, there are now so many examples of destinations being unexpectedly hit by human-induced problems such as diseases or war, or natural disasters, including tsunamis and volcanic eruptions, that a DMO must also be involved in crisis management. Crisis management is essential as a destination without a contingency plan may not survive even a small short-lived crisis.

The different roles of a DMO have been presented and discussed above. In the discussion, emphasis has been placed in particular on the significance of the marketing role and how DMOs try to create a destination image and establish a brand. The examples in Chapter 5, concerned with Birmingham and Barcelona, focused on cities that were previously important for traditional industries, but have recently attempted to re-brand themselves and create an image that can be used to promote each city as a tourism destination. There are, however, around the world a number of geographical locations which have been devoted to attracting tourists for long periods and in some cases tourism is their main economic activity. Such locations have particular images that have been developed over relatively long periods. One such example is Brighton, which is located on the channel coast of England.

# ■  Tourism management in Brighton

Brighton is a 'traditional' British seaside tourist destination. It has attracted visitors for over 250 years and benefitted from being a destination relatively close to London. In the past, it attracted aristocracy and members of the British royal family. The future King George IV visited in the 1780s and subsequently built the Royal Pavilion. Brighton's popularity grew particularly rapidly in the mid-1800s, during the age of steam trains. The first trains arrived in 1841 and by 1860 Brighton was receiving 250,000 annual visitors, with most of them coming by train.

During British summer, Brighton has 'sun, sea and sand' providing swimming and sunbathing opportunities. From Victorian times (1839-1901), it developed traditional seaside facilities, including piers and a beach side promenade, as well as hotels, bed and breakfast accommodation, restaurants, cafes, bars, public houses and entertainment venues.

As early as 1900, Brighton was being described as outdated and unattractive. It suffered because of its location on the south coast of Britain during both World Wars, developed a reputation for crime in the 1930s, made famous by Graham Greene in his novel *Brighton Rock*, and was the scene of mob violence in the 1960s when 'mods' and 'rockers' clashed, which became the subject of the film *Quadraphenia*. By the 1970s, British tourists were more likely to go to Benidorm than Brighton, and it began to decline as a tourism destination. This continued until the mid-1990s.

In the early 21st century Brighton's fortunes began to improve. It became a city in 2000 (having had the status of a town before), and developed a trendy, cultural dimension, via an artists' quarter, with clubs, bars and restaurants. It has a three week annual festival beginning in May, and its theatres often premiere major London West End productions. It has developed a laid-back, bohemian atmosphere and has become important for gay tourism, being frequently voted the best gay destination in the UK. It is known by many as the 'city by the sea', or 'London by the sea'. Being only one hour from London by train and 30 minutes from Gatwick Airport, it has also developed significant international tourism. By 2012, it had a reputation for culture, good food, good shopping and a range of accommodation, including the traditional and contemporary. There were 8 million visitors, a combination of leisure tourists and conference attenders, to the city in 2012, and they spent over £400 million.

Despite the recent change in its fortunes, the City Council was aware of what had happened during the previous 250 years and as part of its tourism management plans did not want to see tourism decline in Brighton. In 2006/7 the Council began research in an attempt to re-brand Brighton so it could keep ahead of its competitors and create a recognised brand. Nine focus groups, held in 2006-7 and a questionnaire survey with just over 1000 visitors, were conducted. A major element of the research was asking respondents the Strengths (S), Weaknesses (W), Opportunities (O) and Threats (T) in relation to Brighton as a tourism destination. The main results of the SWOT analysis were as follows:

14

| Strengths | Weaknesses |
|---|---|
| Interesting architecture | Conflict between the night-time economy and the need to be perceived as safe by all visitors |
| A successful conference and business tourism market | |
| English language students and recent modern English Language training centres | Out-of-season supply (particularly hotels) exceeds demand |
| A young, tolerant and liberated culture | Poor weekend connectivity to London by train, due to engineering works |
| Proximity to the sea | Parking – lack of availability and expensive |
| **Opportunities** | **Threats** |
| Plenty of off-peak capacity | Neighbouring resorts along the coast who compete with Brighton |
| Greater use of heritage values in the city | |
| Attract more international visitors | Lack of skilled workforce |
| Perception (and reality) that Brighton is a 'green' city | Failing to address the lack of demand at certain times of the year |
| | Continued general economic uncertainty locally/globally. |

**Figure 14.4:** SWOT analysis of Brighton. (adapted from Mason, 2013b).

The SWOT analysis of Brighton reveals the City Council's use of research to gather information. This information obtained from the sample of visitors will have been used to reveal not just the views of visitors to tourism in Brighton, but will have also been useful in attempts to find ways to overcome perceived weaknesses and also respond to potential opportunities. Dealing with the perceived threats may also be a part of the strategy to enable Brighton to compete with other destinations as part of its overall destination management plan.

Brighton's use of the SWOT analysis responses is intended to create a better quality tourism destination. The term 'quality', when applied to a tourism destination, has become particularly important in the past 20 years or so, in the belief that a quality tourism destination will be more competitive and thus attract more visitors. However, although the term has been used frequently, there is no clear definition of what quality in relation to a destination actually means, but for some it is linked to service quality, whilst for others it is concerned with the range and nature of tourism facilities. According to the results of research involving tourists (Seakhoa-King, 2007), it would appear that it is a combination of elements of the service encounter and the destination facilities, including aspects such as affordability, variety of facilities, authenticity, cleanliness, security, comfort, friendliness of the host community and the nature of weather conditions, that help define a quality tourism destination.

In addition to destinations, such as Brighton, which are easy to recognize as tourism-focused, because they are concentrated geographical spaces, containing tourism facilities such as hotels, bars, entertainment complexes, themes parks or swimming pools, there are other places that attract tourists but do not have the same facilities and therefore may be far more difficult to immediately recognize as locations attracting significant numbers of tourists. The area of southern Warwickshire in England is such a location. It is famous for possibly the world's best known playwright, William Shakespeare, who was born there, but the area is less obvious as a major tourism destination. The following case study discusses destination management in 'Shakespeare's England'.

# Case study: Shakespeare's England Destination Management Plan 2015-2025

'Shakespeare's England' is centred on the town of Stratford–upon-Avon in Warwickshire, England, which is the birthplace of Shakespeare.  Stratford is in the county of Warwickshire and there are other places in the area that are important for tourism, in particular the spa town, Royal Leamington Spa and the county town of Warwick.

Tourism is one of the key drivers of economic growth to the South Warwickshire economy and surrounding areas. It generates a total business turnover to the area of £547 million annually and supported 9,588 jobs in 2011. Across the whole county in 2011, it generated a total business turnover of just under £1 billion to the local economy which supported 20,800 jobs and 3610 firms.

The Destination Management Plan (DMP) has the backing and support of key strategic partners across the region including: Royal Shakespeare Company, Shakespeare Birthplace Trust, Birmingham Airport, Bicester Village, Warwick Castle, English Heritage, Shakespeare's England DMO membership, Eden Hotel Group, Warwick District Council, Stratford-on-Avon District Council, Warwickshire County Council, Coventry and Warwickshire Local Enterprise Partnership (CWLEP).

The DMP has seven priorities

1   Evidence base and intelligence – understanding of the destination, current position and opportunities.

2   Destination (infrastructure) development – focus for key infrastructure development opportunities, the strategic direction and connectivity.

3   Market development – establish what markets provide the best opportunities to increase volume and value of visitors.

4   Communication and profile – communication of location and wider offer, pinpointing position in the UK and profile as a destination of international importance.

5   Product development – actions needed to develop products and offers to attract new markets and extend the dwell time/return propensity of existing visitors.

6   Welcome, information, experience – improve the welcome provided to visitors, the information they receive and the overall experience they have.

7   Skills, business development, education and careers – developing businesses, careers and people working in, and wishing to enter, the industry.

**14**

The major aim of the DMP is to have sustainable growth, which is better than the national average in England, but mindful of environmental impacts. The key approaches are:

☐ Value not volume: marketing campaigns encourage visitors to stay overnight, stay longer, spend more, and to return

☐ A distinctive offer: investing in a "sense of place"

☐ An inspiring message: backing a coherent identity which builds on acknowledged market strengths

☐ A strong partnership approach: which avoids duplication and clarifies roles

☐ Local ownership: initiatives have the widespread backing of business communities

☐ Quality experience: offering excellent, easily-accessible information and joining up services to make high-quality, memorable experiences.

## Stratford-on-Avon District

The Stratford-on-Avon Core District Strategy provides the strategic context for development decisions up to the year 2031. Around 4.9 million people, with spending of £336m, visit the District each year, with Stratford-upon-Avon, the Shakespeare Birthplace Trust and the Royal Shakespeare Company being of international significance. This provides significant economic benefits but also major challenges in managing the 3.5 million or so visitors that come to the town each year, while also retaining the character of the town and the quality of life for its residents. Tourism is one of the main sources of employment in the District with over 8,000 jobs supporting the industry.

The DMP recognises the following key issues in Stratford:

☐ It is critical that the location and nature of development does not compromise the valuable historic and natural assets of the District. Priority will be given to protecting and enhancing the wide range of historic and cultural assets that contribute to the character and identity of the District with any developments designed to maximize the benefits to local communities.

☐ Local distinctiveness – the need to protect the distinctive character of the market towns, villages and hamlets, including their settings, townscapes, streets, spaces and built form.

☐ Rural nature of area means lots of cars leading to congestion, e.g. in Stratford at peak times – affecting quality of experiences for residents and visitors.

☐ Important to support the growth and improvement of existing attractions and to encourage new attractions and disperse them throughout the District, in order to support the local economy and to provide the opportunity for local communities to enjoy the benefits that are derived.

☐ Stratford-on-Avon represents a huge opportunity as the gateway to discover not only the town but also the surrounding attractions in the rest of Stratford District (attract and disperse) and thereby maximise opportunities to increase the number of overnight stays, length of visitor stay and visitor spend.

☐ Tourism is crucial to the local economy and is facing significant challenges with ever increasing competition.

## SWOT Analysis

Prior to the creation of the DMP, a SWOT analysis was conducted. This was the result of various consultations and discussions with partners, businesses and individuals in Shakespeare's England region, and has been used to give direction and focus for the DMP.

### 1 Strengths

The following section provides an overview of the strengths of Shakespeare's England region which should be maximised and the opportunities it faces.

☐ Shakespeare's England is a world class destination – possibly the best in UK – with a very strong tourism offer. Shakespeare's England has a number of attributes which other tourism destinations do not have.

☐ The region has a central location in the country with some good infrastructure links; these include Birmingham Airport, good rail links to London and North and the proximity to Birmingham, Coventry and the Cotswolds.

☐ Transport to the area is good, as is location in terms of travel times. Good motorway and train links from key catchment areas. The airport is very close, and a great gateway to the region.

☐ The region benefits from a strong brand presence with domestic and international recognition, Shakespeare being a particular USP for overseas markets.

☐ Shakespeare's England is rich in art and culture, has a wealth of cultural and heritage attractions and experiences.

☐ There is a good standard of accommodation across the region from large branded 4-star to independents and self-catering, there are also facilities for walkers and niche markets.

☐ The supporting product (retail/eating out/local produce) is very strong with a variety of independent and specialist shops (e.g. saddlery), in Stratford, Warwick and Leamington Spa. There are a number of high quality restaurants and dining pubs.

☐ There is a strong retail offer, and huge variety of retail which touches all price points – lots of independent shops (from craft to independent boutiques).

☐ There are a number of new developments, such as JLR resort at Gaydon and Genting Casino at the NEC site. These provide the potential for new strategic partners, who will be looking to be part of the regional profile.

☐ The importance of great customer service and welcome is recognised by all partners as being fundamental to the destination. The quality of welcome across the region is of a good standard and provides the foundations on which to build exceptional customer service and welcome.

☐ The region benefits from attractive countryside towns and quintessentially English rural countryside, as well as its riverside location (River Avon) and canals.

14

- ☐ Rural activities and the rural product is strong, this includes water based activities, walking and cycling. This is supported by well-maintained canal towpaths, as well as canal side attractions and marinas, walking and cycle ways, supported by local pubs, which are located along the waterways.
- ☐ Great education and skills opportunities, linked to great employment opportunities across a wide spectrum in the region/sector.
- ☐ Shakespeare's England DMO benefits from a very strong board, with key partners actively involved and a distinct lack of organisational ego.
- ☐ The DMO is able to work with a range of partners, destinations and DMOs in the area – which is a strength for building the destination offer.

**2 Weaknesses**

- ☐ The destination is not communicating the current offer effectively enough. It is 'timid' from a national perspective.
- ☐ Shakespeare's England has all of the ingredients for a great visitor destination, the issue is bringing it all together in one offer and communicating that offer effectively.
- ☐ The overall visitor experience should be developed across the region. Shakespeare's England is a region of iconic attractions, however, the destination towns do not reflect that iconic status and should raise their games to mirror the reputation/gravitas of the attractions in their areas.
- ☐ It appears that there could often be complacency about the Shakespeare/RSC/Iconic attractions connection, and little appetite or perceived need to make improvements, just 'piggy backing' or depending on the success and profile which these icons bring.
- ☐ The ability to pinpoint where the region is in the UK and its make-up is an issue. Clarity is needed to give a geographical location and a description of what experiences there are, where they are and how easy they are to find. There is a need to better understand the 'place' which is labelled Shakespeare's England, give it a clearer sense of identity and a sense of place.
- ☐ There is a need to communicate the location better to unlock potential of visitors from London/South East (domestic) and also those who are in London (overseas) and exploring England.
- ☐ Transportation to, and across the region, is an issue. The link from the airport to the region needs strengthening; the airport is a great connection but it is an issue to connect the region with 'Birmingham' as the two products are so different. The airport provides a gateway, but the name Birmingham Airport does not connect to the product Shakespeare's England.
- ☐ In general, it is not easy to travel across the region. There are a number of very scenic public transport routes, but they are not easy to understand and therefore not easy to use. Need a really easy and joined up transport solution for visitors.

- ☐ There is no direct bus, coach or train service from Birmingham Airport to Stratford Upon Avon or Warwick.

- ☐ Parking is expensive and not joined up – each local area with own fees and no consistent purchase price for a visitor touring the area.

- ☐ There is a need to raise the profile of Shakespeare's England DMO in towns/areas outside of Stratford-on-Avon to ensure that all potential partners and businesses are clear about what the DMO delivers, and what else is on offer across the region.

- ☐ There is a perceived dominance of Shakespeare and Stratford in activity (Stratford seen as a 'bubble'); there needs to be more understanding from businesses in all towns about the fact that they are part of a region and what part they play, and with the local population in terms of economic impact and supply chain support (Visitors are sometimes perceived as a nuisance).

- ☐ Whilst the destination is home to cultural icons, there must be a better connection between culture and tourism, a clearer cultural identity to maximise the value of culture.

- ☐ Public realm, the look and feel of the towns (street scape), should be more consistent and viewed in a whole to develop a 'sense of place' wherever a visitor is within the region. For example, consistent welcome signage and finger posts. In addition, the movement of visitors from major attractions to the town centres must be improved with better pathways and signage.

- ☐ Overall welcome and destination understanding can be patchy – welcome must be improved at key touch points and the visitors should be able to access information in the easiest possible way.

- ☐ In terms of product, consultees commented that there is a perceived lack of quality hotels to again, mirror the world class attractions.

- ☐ There is also little 'night-time' economy in the towns, again, which is in conflict with the evening appeal presented by the theatre and other evening events or late openings of attractions. This also has impact as it does not attract the younger (18-30) market

### 3 Opportunities

- ☐ Due to the strong board of Shakespeare's England DMO, there is an opportunity for other 'key players' to make a connection with the region, via one focal point.

- ☐ There is an opportunity to appoint a senior and influential person to act as an ambassador or spokesperson for the visitor economy, armed with the facts about the importance of the visitor economy and what needs to be done, what the priorities are and how this can be funded/supported.

- ☐ There is an opportunity to build places within Shakespeare's England with national and international appeal – world class destinations, to complement the iconic attractions located within them.

14

- ☐ New developments (JLR resort at Gaydon and Genting Casino at the NEC site) in the area show there is a clear opportunity to sweat the 'world class' asset to attract similar world class, or high profile, organisations.

- ☐ Opportunities exist to make more use of 'Heart of England' in connection with Birmingham and Birmingham Airport (there is a question about whether the airport name should have a wider geographical recognition)

- ☐ Make closer links between Stratford upon Avon and Leamington Spa in terms of attracting and dispersing the younger (18-30) market.

**4 Threats**

- ☐ Currently this is a period of reduction in public funding and staffing which is likely to continue in the future.

- ☐ This is also a period of reduced private sector funding, which is likely to continue.

- ☐ The age range of visitors (where there are few younger people than old) threatens the future sustainability of tourism and there is need to appeal to all markets.

- ☐ Continued fragmentation of planning and management of tourism experiences

- ☐ There is a lack of consistency of tourism product and this needs to be overcome.

- ☐ The potential to develop a destination brand is limited in some parts of the region where individual attractions are more important than the brand of the region.

- ☐ The visitor experience needs to be improved to develop 'compelling destinations'.

- ☐ The advancements in digital technology in tourism is not being embraced.

(Source: Destination Management Plan, Shakespeare's England, March, 2015)

# Summary

This chapter has indicated that modern planning is intended to be a forward-looking, future-oriented activity, whilst in the past, much planning was a largely reactive process in response to perceived problems.

- ■ Tourism planning is concerned specifically with ideas on the future of tourism and is, or at least should be, a coherent process of ordering change with the intention of deriving maximum benefits, while minimizing negative effects.

- ■ Tourism policy is the implementation of a tourism plan.

- ■ Tourism management involves the day-to-day, ongoing overseeing and monitoring of the effects of a tourism plan and tourism policy.

The relationship between planning and management is relatively complex, with one of the key roles of managers in the process of management being planning. Hence, planning activities and management processes are likely to be taking place simultaneously in a given context. Tourism planning and tourism management take place in contexts where there are different individuals and groups, different value systems, varying and often conflicting interests and the processes of negotiation, coercion, compromise and choice all conspire to ensure that these activities are not necessarily rational or straightforward.

The chapter has also focused on planning and managing of tourism destinations, where there are a large number and range of impacts. Destination planning and policy in a destination are however not the same thing as destination management. Planning and policy are usually thoughtful, reflective, but pro-active macro-level processes, whilst management is a much more immediate, hands-on, day-to-day, micro-level, and probably re-active activity. The destination management process involves DMOs and these perform a range of activities, in which marketing and increasingly stewardship of tourism resources are very significant. The SWOT analysis conducted in relation to the case study, 'Shakespeare Country', indicates a range of factors that are involved in the planning and management of a tourism destination.

## Student activities

1 Why was planning a largely reactive process in the past?

2 What are the key a) similarities b) differences in relation to the concepts and processes of planning and management?

3 Why are both the public and private sectors involved in tourism planning?

4 Why did the City Council in the British coastal resort of Brighton believe it was important to conduct a SWOT analysis of tourism in the city?

5 In relation to the SWOT analysis of 'Shakespeare Country' for each of Strengths, Weaknesses, Opportunities and Threats, select what you believe are the three most important factors.

6 Working in small groups (3/4 students) consider a tourism destination you know well and conduct a SWOT analysis for it. Once you have conducted the analysis, compare your results with another group's. Discuss, with this other group, what you have learned from the process of conducting the SWOT analysis.

**14**

# References

Bramwell, B. and Lane, B. (2000). Introduction. In B. Bramwell and B. Lane, eds., *Tourism Collaboration and Partnerships: Policy Practice and Sustainability*, pp. 1–23. Clevedon: Channel View Publications.

Chadwick, G. (1971). *A Systems View of Planning*. Oxford: Pergamon.

228 Geography of Tourism

Coccossis, H. and Parpairis, A. (1996). Tourism and carrying capacity in coastal areas: Mykonos Greece. In G. K. Priestley, J. A. Edwards and H. Coccossis, eds., *Sustainable Tourism? European Experiences*, pp. 153–75. Wallingford, UK: CAB International.

Cooper, C., Fletcher, J., Gilbert, D. and Wanhill, S. (1998). *Tourism: Principles and Practice*. London: Longman.

Cooper, C., Fletcher, J., Gilbert, D., Fyall, A. and Wanhill, S. (2005). *Tourism: Principles and Practice* 3rd ed. London: Longman.

Cullingsworth, B. (1997). *Planning in the USA: Policies, Issues and Processes*. London: Routledge.

Doswell, R. (1997). *Tourism: How Effective Management Makes the Difference*. London: Butterworth-Heinemann.

Dye, T. (1992). *Understanding Public Policy*,7th ed. Englewood Cliffs: Prentice Hall.

Elliot, J. (1997). *Tourism Politics and Public Sector Management*. London: Routledge.

ETB (1991). *Tourism and the Environment: Maintaining the Balance*. London: English Tourism Board/ Ministry of the Environment.

Fennel, D. (1999) *Ecotourism: An introduction*, London, Routledge.

Gilbert, J., Jones, G., Vitalis, T., Walker, R. and Gilbertson, D. (1995). *Introduction to Management in New Zealand*. Sydney: Harcourt Brace.

Glyptis, S. (1994). *Countryside Recreation*. Harlow: Longman/ILAM.

Gunn, C. (1988). *Tourism Planning*, 2nd ed. New York: Taylor and Francis.

Hall, C. M. (2000). *Tourism Planning*. London: Prentice Hall.

Hall, C. M. and Jenkins, J. (1995). *Tourism and Public Policy*. London: Routledge.

Hall, C.M. and Page, S. (2014) *Geography of Recreation and Tourism* (4th ed.) London, Routledge.

Hall, P. (1992). *Urban and Regional Planning*, 3rd ed. Harmondsworth: Penguin.

Healey, P. (1997). *Collaborative Planning: Shaping Places in Fragmented Societies*. Basingstoke: Macmillan.

Hendricks, W. (1995). A resurgence in recreation conflict research: introduction to the special issue, *Leisure Sciences*, **17**, 157–8.

Hirschmann, A. (1976). Policy making and policy analysis in Latin America: a return journey. *Policy Sciences*, **6**, 385–402.

Lang, R. (1985). Planning for integrated development. Paper presented at *Conference on Integrated Development Beyond the City*, 14–16 June, Rural Tourism and Small Town Research and Studies Programme, Mount Allison University, Sackville, New Brunswick, Canada.

Lickorish, L. (1991). Roles of government and private sector. In L. Lickorish, ed., *Developing Tourism Destinations*, pp. 121–46. Harlow: Longman.

McCabe, V., Poole, B., Weeks, P. and Leiper, N. (2000). *The Business and Management of Conventions*. Melbourne: John Wiley and Sons.

Mason, P. (1995). *Tourism: Environment and Development Perspectives*. Godalming, UK: World Wide Fund for Nature.

Mason, P (2013a) Zoning, land use planning and tourism, in Holden A. and Fennel D. eds. *The Routledge Handbook of Tourism and the Environment*, pp.266-85, London: Routledge.

Mason, P (2013b) *The Future of the British Seaside Resort*, Presentation given at Scarborough Business School, Hull University, March 10.

Mason, P. (2016) *Tourism Impacts, Planning and Management*, (3rd ed.) London: Routledge.

Mason, P., Leberman, S. and Barnett, S. (2000). Walkway users: an urban based case study from New Zealand. *Conference Proceedings: Tourism 2000: Time for Celebration?* (M. Robinson, P. Long, and B. Bramwell, eds), pp. 207–20.

Mason, P. and Mowforth, M. (1996). Codes of conduct in tourism. *Progress in Tourism and Hospitality Research*, **2**, 151–67.

Mathieson, A. and Wall, G. (1982). *Tourism: Economic, Social and Environmental Impacts*. London: Longman.

Middleton, V. (1994). *Marketing in Travel and Tourism*. London: Routledge.

Middleton, V and Hawkins, R. (1998). *Sustainable Tourism: A Marketing Perspective*. Oxford: Butterworth-Heinemann.

Moore, R. (1994). *Conflicts on Multiple-use Trails: Synthesis of the Literature and State of the Practice*. Raleigh, NC: North Carolina University.

Morgan, N., Pritchard, A. and Pride, R. (2010) *Destination Branding*, Oxford: Butterworth Heinemann.

Pearce, D (1989). *Tourist Development*. London: Longman.

Ramthun, R. (1995). Factors in user group conflict between hikers and mountain bikers. *Leisure Sciences*, **17**, 159–70.

Ritchie, J. and Crouch, G. (2003) *The Competitive Destination:A Sustainable Tourism Perspective*, Wallingford: CABI.

Seakhoa-King, A (2007) *Conceptualising Quality in a Tourism Destination*, Unpublished PhD Thesis, Bedfordshire University, Luton.

Shakespeare's England (2015) *Shakespeare's Country Destination Management Plans*, Stratford-on-Avon, shakespeares-england.co.uk

Spink, J. (1994). *Leisure and the Environment*. Oxford: Butterworth-Heinemann.

Swarbrooke, J. (1999). *Sustainable Tourism Management*. Wallingford: CABI Publications.

Veal, A. (1994). *Leisure Policy and Planning*. Harlow, UK: Longman/ILAM.

VisitEngland (2013) *Principles for Developing Destination Management Plans*, London, VisitEngland.

Watson, A (1995). An analysis of recent progress in recreation conflict research and perception of future challenges and opportunities. *Leisure Sciences*, **17**, 235–8.

Wilkinson, P. (1997). *Tourism Planning on Islands*. New York: Cognizant Communications.

Williams, S. (1998). *Tourism Geography*. London: Routledge.

14

# 15 Tourism and Sustainability

## Introduction

Sustainability is a concept used with increasing frequency in relation to tourism. It is often linked to terms such as 'green' tourism or 'ecotourism' and may also be considered to be a form of 'alternative' tourism. However, despite being used for over 30 years, the term sustainability, has not been well defined, which does not stop it being used often. To a certain extent, it can be argued that sustainability is now an overused term and is open to abuse (Mason, 2016), particularly from sectors of the tourism industry, who use it as a marketing term in an attempt to indicate that their product is worthier than another's.

## Sustainable development

The modern usage of the term 'sustainability' would appear to date from the late 1980s and is associated strongly with the Brundtland Report of 1987 (Holden, 2000). In this report, the term *sustainable development* was used. The Brundtland Report focused on the environment, linked this with global development, and was largely concerned about resource use associated with what was seen as too rapid development and hence, considered unsustainable.

Five years after the Brundtland Report, at the Earth Summit, in Rio de Janeiro in 1992, the concerns that were expressed in the Brundtland Report were once again evident. The Earth Summit set out a programme for promoting sustainable development throughout the world. This was to be achieved using the main ideas contained in what became known as Agenda 21, and as Holden (2000:164) indicates, this is an: 'action plan laying out the basic principles required to progress towards sustainability'. Unlike much thinking about sustainable development up to the early 1990s, the particular approach of Agenda 21 is to involve local communities in a 'bottom-up', or grass roots, approach to their own development.

However, the concept of sustainable development was not fully defined in either the Brundtland Report or at the Earth Summit. This means that private organizations, governments, non-government organizations (NGOs) and academics may each have had then, and continue to have, very different views on the meaning of sustainable development and this is a very significant issue in relation to concerns about how to apply the concept in specific geographical contexts. Nevertheless, the Brundtland Report stressed that sustainable development is intended to be a dynamic concept, and does not mean preservation of the environment, but a process with the focus on conservation and not preservation.

Holden (2000) suggested that although there is a diverse range of views on sustainable development, they can be generally classified into two camps; there are 'techno-centric' views and 'eco-centric' views. The **techno-centric view** suggests that problems can be quantified and solved largely through the application of technology. The **eco-centric view** places great emphasis on 'quality of life' rather than measurements of economic growth that use terms such as 'standard of living' and other quantitative terms. The differing views of the spectrum of techno-centric and eco-centric ideas are shown in Figure 15.1. Here the eco-centric view is represented under the 'deep ecology' heading which follows from the ideas of Doyle and McEachern (1998). In the late 1990s, the techno-centric view was recognized by most commentators as being the dominant one globally (see Bartelmus, 1994), hence it is represented as such in Figure 15.1. However, it should be noted that Fig 15.1 shows a *spectrum of views* and there are many views lying between the extremes.

| Dominant world-view | Deep ecology |
|---|---|
| Strong belief in technology for progress and solutions | Favours low-scale technology that is self-reliant |
| Natural world is valued as a resource rather than possessing intrinsic value | Sense of wonder, reverence and moral obligation to the natural world |
| Believes in ample resource reserves | Recognizes the 'rights' of nature are independent of humans |
| Favours the objective and quantitative | Recognizes the subjective such as feelings and ethics |
| Centralization of power | Favours local communities and localized decision-making |
| Encourages consumerism | Encourages the use of appropriate technology |
| | Recognizes that the earth's resources are limited |

**Figure 15.1:** Differences in views of development between the 'dominant world-view' and 'deep ecology' (adapted from Bartelmus, 1994)

# Sustainable tourism

Given that there is a range of views on sustainable development, perhaps it is not surprising that there is also a number of different perspectives on sustainable tourism. The WTO (1998) attempted to define sustainable tourism and suggested that it is:

> *"tourism which leads to management of all resources in such a way that economic, social and aesthetic needs can be filled while maintaining cultural integrity, essential ecological processes, biological diversity and life support systems".*

15

The WTO definition indicates a number of important dimensions of sustainable tourism, including economic, social, cultural and ecological. However, it is important to be aware that at the time that the WTO created its definition of sustainable tourism, there were two major ways of viewing the world. These different views – a more appropriate word would be *paradigms* – had important underlying perspectives that contributed to the views being different. One paradigm suggested that economic factors were most important and should underpin thinking about sustainable tourism; the other had it that ecological factors were more important when defining the concept (Mason, 2016). These paradigms not only have important underlying differences, but the consequences of each is important in terms of what type of tourism is developed. The economic paradigm, which until very recently most people would accept as being the dominant view, and is very similar to the techno-centric view indicated in Figure 15.1, would suggest, for example, making a profit, job creation and income generation as key principles, whilst the ecological paradigm (similar to the eco-centric view in Figure 15.1) would include, for example, minimising habitat disturbance, promoting animal species conservation, and maintaining landscape aesthetics, as major principles.

The first part of the WTO definition also makes it clear that achieving sustainable tourism, whether it is based on a largely economic or a mainly ecological set of principles, requires management. In other words, sustainable tourism has to be worked at, and planned and managed appropriately to achieve what is required, and it is unlikely to occur without this human intervention.

One relatively early view on sustainable tourism, that has been in existence for at least a quarter of a century, is that of a sustainable tourism industry (Coccossis and Papairis, 1996). In this view of sustainable tourism, the development of tourism is one alternative amongst several options, and seen as more acceptable than other more environmentally damaging activities such as logging or mining (Holden, 2000). However, Hunter (1996) indicates that little allowance is made in this view for the cumulative impacts of tourism on the environment. Hunter (1996) suggested a number of other perspectives and contexts in which the environment is more or less central in concepts of sustainable tourism. He suggests that there is another position in which the environment is given more consideration than in the 'sustainable tourism industry perspective' of Coccosis and Papairis (1996). However, even in this position, the environment comes second to attempts to develop tourism, but Hunter (1996) stated this position may be defensible in communities that are heavily dependent on tourism and where any changes would lead to significant threats to the community.

Hunter suggested a third form of sustainable tourism that he termed 'environmentally-led tourism'. In this form, a high quality tourism experience is equated with a high quality environment, and there would be a strong link between the success of the tourism industry and environmental conservation. Unlike the former example of product-led tourism, here the environment is prioritized and forms of tourism are developed that are not damaging to it (Holden, 2008).

Hunter (1996) suggested a fourth scenario, which he termed 'neotenous' tourism, in which very little, or no, tourism is permitted. This could occur, for example in relation to particularly environmentally sensitive areas.

Underlying much of what has been stated above, but not made explicit, is that statements on sustainable tourism should be linked to value judgments. Hence, it is important to be aware that the interpretation of the term 'sustainable tourism' is very closely related to the political context in which the term is being applied. Butler and Hall (1998) argue that it is impossible to separate a particular concept of sustainable tourism from the value system and political context in which it is being used.

If, in early definitions of sustainable tourism, to counter the dominant economic focus of the times, the environment became central, during the early-mid 1990s, socio-cultural factors were also linked closely to the concept. By the last decade of the 20th century, sustainability was usually assumed to refer to the specifically environmental and cultural aspects of the visitor destination area. Today it is possible to suggest that it is artificial to consider only these aspects from the total of all elements that make up the tourism experience. Hence, 'tourism sustainability' has an economic and organizational dimension, as well as socio-cultural and environmental aspects, and as the WTO (1998) definition indicates, also has an important aesthetic dimension.

One of the early thinkers on tourism sustainability was Innskeep, and his views give an indication of how sustainable tourism was conceived in the early years of the last decade of the 20th century. Innskeep (1991) suggested that, in relation to practical applications of concepts of sustainable tourism, there are a number of assumptions that underpin these concepts, and these as indicated below:

- It is possible to define and achieve the type of tourism you want.
- It is possible to establish and sustain appropriate levels of visitor flow.
- It is possible to define and promote equity in development and to reconcile any conflicts arising between the different stakeholders involved, such as the tourist, the resident, the industry agent and the government, and that an appropriate balance of interests can be achieved between host and guest and between private interest and public good.
- It is possible to maintain sustainability over the long term.

Drawing on the work of Innskeep (1991), the key ingredients of sustainable tourism can be discerned, and are as follows:

- Non-depleting in its use of local resources.
- Non-intrusive in the way it fits with the local physical, social, cultural and economic environments.
- A user of natural resources that are minimally transposed or re-configured.
- Integrated with the local physical, social, cultural and economic environment rather than being shut-in on itself.

15

- More focused on the high-quality–high-yield end of the commercial product spectrum in contrast to the high-profit rapid turnover model.

- More centred on the qualitative aspects of individual experience than a quantitative 'been there, done that' model of many group-centred options.

- One in which the balance of market power lies with the host community and in which the resident has a recognized voice in the definition and management of the tourism product and its context.

- One in which the industry is managed by an appropriate blend of public sector good and enlightened private sector self-interest.

Up to and including the time that Innskeep was writing, sustainable tourism was largely considered to be an alternative to mass tourism. In other words, sustainable tourism could be regarded by the tourism industry, tourists and local residents in destinations, as another product within a range of different tourism products. If viewed in this way, it would be have been possible for the tourism industry to largely ignore sustainable tourism, as a minority-interest, specialist product, and cater for the majority of tourists with other products that did not need to offer sustainability credentials. However, the concept of sustainable tourism has been increasingly viewed, since Innskeep's ideas were put forward, as the way in which all forms of tourism should be considered – in other words every tourism activity, not just those offered to a small specialist group, should be sustainable (Mason, 2016).

At approximately the same time as Innskeep was producing his ideas on tourism and sustainability, the UK Department of Environment, working with English Tourist Board, (ETB/DoE) produced a report that developed some guiding principles for sustainable tourism. These are as follows:

- The environment has an intrinsic value that outweighs its value as a tourism asset. Hence, its enjoyment by future generations, and its long-term survival, must not be prejudiced by short-term considerations.

- Tourism should be recognized as a positive force with the potential to benefit the community and the place as well as the visitor.

- The relationship between tourism and the environment must be managed so that the environment is sustainable in the long term. Tourism must not be allowed to damage the resource, prejudice its future enjoyment or bring unacceptable impacts.

- Tourism activities and development should respect the scale, nature and character of the place in which they are sited.

- In any location, harmony must be sought between the needs of the visitor, place and the host community.

- In a dynamic world, some change is inevitable and change can often be beneficial. However, adaptation to change should not be at the expense of any of these principles.

- The tourism industry, local authorities and environmental agencies all have a duty to respect the above principles and to work together to achieve their practical realization in achieving sustainable tourism. (ETB, 1991).

In these guidelines there was particular emphasis on the need for a balance between the place, the visitor and the host community. Although Holden (2000) criticized the ETB/DoE Report as being somewhat simplistic in that implies tourists are one homogenous group, nevertheless the report does emphasize the important role of the local community in sustainable tourism.

By the middle of the first decade of the 21st century, sustainable tourism had been in existence and practically applied for long enough to discern three 'traditions' (Saarinen, 2006). The first, the 'resource-based' tradition, according to Saarinen, links tourism with conservation and focuses on restricting or trying to prevent the damaging effects of tourism on the environment and in this way tourism is generally not regarded as making positive contributions to environmental conservation. The second is termed the 'activity-based' tradition (Saarinen, 2006) and it suggests that tourism can actually make a significant contribution to sustainability. In this tradition, it is the demand from tourists to experience the environment that leads to the rationale for and attempts to conserve, for example, certain landscapes and heritage attractions that tourists want to visit. Perhaps, not surprisingly, this is the tradition particularly supported by the tourism industry (Holden, 2008). The third tradition suggested by Saarinen (2006) is the 'community-based' one, and in this, the local community or host population has a vital role in bringing about sustainability. Holden (2008) also considers these three traditions and distinguishes between them by indicating that the first (resource-based) may frequently uses 'real' measurements of sustainability, (such as those acquired from Environmental Impacts Assessments), whilst the second and third traditions usually involve social constructs of sustainability. In the second and third traditions, judgements are frequently made about 'acceptable levels of trade-off between economic and social gains against natural resource losses' (Holden 2008: 165).

The ETB/DoE (1991) report guidelines, discussed above, can be seen to fit in the resource-based tradition highlighted by Saarinen, and they clearly indicate the central importance of the environment. The ETB/DoE guidelines also refer to the local community's role in sustainable tourism, and increasingly it is being argued that the local community should not just be involved in attempts to make tourism more sustainable, but should have control over tourism development. This involvement of the local community should bring about greater democracy in tourism decision making, it is suggested (see Mason, 2016). However, even with tourism decision-making under local control, there is no guarantee that sustainable forms of development will be selected. Indeed, Holden (2000) reported two examples in which local communities in Scotland and South Africa, respectively, supported development that was damaging to the environment. The rationale for the choice of the particular development in each case was the perceived economic and social benefits and the environmental impacts were viewed as less important

15

by the local communities. It appears therefore, that these two examples fit more closely with the 'activity-based' and 'community-based' tourism sustainability traditions, than the 'resource-based' one (see Saarinen, 2006).

The ETB/DoE guidelines are an example of the involvement of the government of one country in tourism planning for sustainability. International organizations have also produced advice and guidelines for policy makers who are attempting to achieve sustainable tourism. The UN Environment Programme, working in conjunction with the World Tourism Organization, produced a major document *Making Tourism More Sustainable: a Guide for Policy Makers* in 2005 (UNEP/WTO, 2005). This is particularly important because, not only does it provide advice on the process of developing a sustainable tourism strategy, but also gives advice on the instruments that governments can use to help bring about sustainable tourism.

The instruments are presented in Figure 15.2. There are five main types, and within each are a number of sub-categories leading to a total of thirteen instruments, although they are interlinked. UNEP/WTO (2005) indicate that *Measuring Instruments* should be used to determine the current levels of tourism and their impacts. The processes involved here include benchmarking and identifying the limits of tourism. The *Command and Control Instruments* are largely regulatory and involve various forms of legislation, regulation and licensing. The *Economic Instruments* involve the use of taxes and charges to influence the behaviour of tourists, whilst the *Voluntary Instruments* include codes of conduct and guidelines as well as voluntary certification. The *Supporting Instruments* involve infrastructure provision and management, capacity building, (which includes increasing the knowledge, confidence and skills of stakeholders), and also marketing initiatives.

*(1) Measuring instruments.*
    (a) Sustainable indicators and monitoring: benchmarking
    (b) Identifying the limits of tourism: carrying capacity, limits of acceptable change
*(2) Command and control instruments*
    (a) Legislation, regulation and licensing
    (b) Land use planning and development control
*(3) Economic instruments*
    (a) Taxes and charges
    (b) Financial incentives and agreements
*(4) Voluntary instruments*
    (a) Guidelines and codes of conduct
    (b) Auditing and reporting
    (c) Voluntary certification
    (d) Voluntary contributions
*(5) Supporting instruments*
    (a) Infrastructure provision and management
    (b) Capacity building
    (c) Marketing and information services

**Figure 15.2:** Instruments for More Sustainable Tourism (adapted from UNEP/WTO, 2005)

# The Tourism Area Life Cycle

One of the key theories in relation to tourism planning, which has important implications for attempts to ensure sustainable tourism, was created by the geographer, Butler, who built on the ideas of earlier authors to create what he termed the Tourism Area Life Cycle (TALC) or Destination Life Cycle. Butler (1980) made use of earlier researchers' ideas, in particular those of Cohen, Plog, Doxey and Christaller, to create his TALC theory. In Chapter 2, there was discussion of the ideas of the sociologist Cohen (1972), who put tourists into four different groups, based on the their activity and behavior, and those of Plog (1972) who considered the psychological make-up of tourists and created a spectrum in which at one end were psycho-centrics and at the other, allo-centrics. As indicated in Chapter 8, Doxey (1975) considered the reaction of local residents to increasing numbers of visitors over time, when creating his Irridex. Christaller (1963) a geographer, was one of the first researchers to investigate the location of tourism. He considered the way that parts of urban areas, in particular Paris, had developed a strong tourism focus over time and also investigated the mechanisms of future change. Christaller's ideas can be summarized as follows:

- Destinations develop and change over time
- The tourist experience (the product) changes over time
- There are different types of visitor at different times
- The impacts of tourism change over time
- The involvement of locals in destinations changes over time
- New cycles involving new destinations will occur

Butler's model appeared in 1980 and he not only acknowledged that his ideas were linked to these earlier researchers, but he also indicated that they were based on the marketing concept of the 'product life cycle'. The product life cycle is a theory in which sales of a new product are seen to grow slowly, initially, and then experience a period of rapid growth, before stabilizing and continuing at this level for a period of time, before subsequently declining. When applied to tourism destinations, Butler's model suggests that resorts develop and change over time and there are a number of separate, but linked stages: exploration, involvement, development and consolidation. During these stages, a tourism industry develops and the destination has an increasing number of tourists. After the consolidation stage there are a number of possibilities, Butler's theory indicates. The resort/destination could 'stagnate', without any increase or decrease in numbers; it could 'decline' or it could 'rejuvenate'.

Figure 15.3 shows the relationship between destination development and time, indicating each stage, while Figure 15.4 provides more detail on the processes occurring during each stage of Butler's model. Of particular importance in relation to sustainable tourism, is that the theory predicts there is a strong likelihood that a destination will decline after it reaches the consolidation and stagnation

**15**

stages. To ensure that the destination has a sustainable future, Butler argues it is essential that there is planning and management to achieve rejuvenation, rather than allow decline to set in.

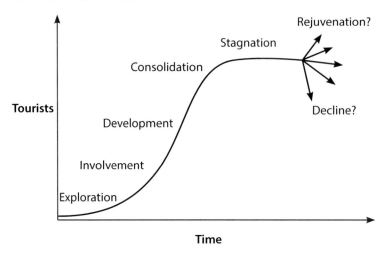

**Figure 15.3:** Butler's TALC theory

| Stage | Characteristic |
|---|---|
| **Exploration** | A few adventurous tourists, visiting sites with no public facilities |
| | Visitors attracted to the resort by a natural physical feature |
| | Specific visitor type of a select nature |
| **Involvement** | Limited interaction between local residents and the developing tourism industry leads to the provision of basic services |
| | Increased advertising induces a definable pattern of seasonal variation |
| | Definite market area begins to emerge |
| **Development** | Development of additional tourist facilities and increased promotional efforts |
| | Greater control of the tourist trade by outsiders |
| | Number of tourists at peak periods far outweighs the size of the resident population, inducing rising antagonism by the latter towards the former |
| **Consolidation** | Tourism has become a major part of the local economy, but growth rates have begun to level off |
| | A well-delineated business district has taken shape |
| | Some of the older deteriorating facilities are perceived as second rate |
| | Local efforts are made to extend the tourist season |
| **Stagnation** | Peak numbers of tourists and capacity levels are reached |
| | The resort has a well-established image, but it is no longer in fashion |
| | The accommodation stock is gradually eroded and property turnover rates are high |
| **Post-stagnation** | Five possibilities, reflecting a range of options that may be followed, depending partly on the success of local management decisions. At either extremes are rejuvenation and decline |

**Figure 15.4:** Stages of resort development and associated features in Butler's theory

Almost 20 years after the first publication of his theory Butler (1998) reconsidered his original ideas and he indicated a number of key points that he suggested confirmed its validity, which were as follows:

- The key concept is *dynamism* and hence resorts do change over time.
- There is a common *process* of development of tourist destinations.
- There are *limits to growth*. If the demand for visits exceeds the capacity of the destination, then the visitor experience will be diminished and visitors will subsequently decline.
- There are *triggers* – factors that bring about change in a destination.
- *Management* is a key factor, and may be necessary, in particular, to avoid the decline stage of the model.
- *Long-term viewpoint*. There is the need for a long-term view and resorts need to look ahead for 50 years, not 5 years, to avoid some of the pitfalls suggested by the theory.
- *Spatial component*. There is likely to be a spatial shift of tourism activity as the destination declines (i.e. tourists go elsewhere).
- *Universal applicability*. The model applies to all destinations.

In the period since Butler first developed his model, there have been many attempts to apply the theory, including that by Zhong *et al.* (2007) in the relatively unusual setting of a national park in China. In this context there was almost no tourism before the late 1950s, but Zhong *et al.* indicated that they believed that the area had passed through the first four stages of Butler's theory reaching the Consolidation Stage by 2000, and they provided a significant amount of evidence to support this. In a rather different context, Bernerman and Petit (2007) applied Butler's theory to the development of festivals and events in the Rhone-Alpes area of France. They indicated that the theory was not only useful in indicating the stage at which a particular festival in the area was, but it was also potentially helpful in predicting what might happen regarding the festival in the short and long term.

Not only have there have been attempts to apply the theory, but also new theories, based on Butler's original ideas have been developed. Of particular significance is Weaver's (2000) ideas in which he argued that Butler's model is just one interpretation of resort development and given the point in time that it was developed, does not take into consideration attempts at alternatives to mass tourism and the development of sustainable tourism that have occurred since 1980. It is also the case that resorts have been able to learn from the events that have occurred in destinations that have existed for a relatively long time such as Brighton and Blackpool in the UK, and to use the knowledge gained, in attempts to prevent the 'inevitable' decline predicted in the final stage of Butler's theory from actually occurring.

15

# Ideal types of sustainable tourism

Although, as stated above there is a lack of agreement on precisely what constitutes sustainable tourism, it is becoming increasingly possible to discern what can be termed *ideal types* of sustainable tourism. These types can be represented by the extremes, which are at opposite ends of a spectrum (Weaver, 2006). At one end is 'minimalist sustainable tourism' and at the other 'comprehensive sustainable tourism' (Weaver, 2006). These ideal types are shown in Figure 15.5.

| Minimalist sustainable tourism | Comprehensive sustainable tourism |
|---|---|
| Environmental, socio-cultural or economic impacts | Environmental, socio-cultural and economic impacts |
| Site specific or local focus | Regional or global focus |
| Short-term effects of actions | Long-term effects of actions |
| Tourism sector only | Tourism in the context of other sectors |
| Direct impacts only | Direct, indirect and induced impacts |
| Inter-generational equity | Intergenerational and intra-generational equity |
| Status quo sustainability | Enhancement sustainability |
| ↓ | ↓ |

Weak or strong sustainability approach, depending on context
Financial sustainability

**Figure 15.5:** Minimalist and comprehensive tourism ideal types (adapted from Weaver, 2006)

- **Minimalist sustainable tourism** is concerned largely with environmental, socio-cultural and economic impacts of tourism. It is generally site or product specific, focuses on the short term, tries largely to maintain the status quo and does not link tourism to wider societal issues.

- **Comprehensive sustainable tourism** involves a holistic approach, setting economic, environmental and socio-cultural impacts of tourism within a wider societal and global context. Therefore, it is not just concerned with tourism but other major economic and social activities. Comprehensive sustainable tourism also involves a long-term approach in an attempt to achieve inter-generational equity, which was one of the key principles embodied in the Brundtland Report of 1987. Unlike minimalist sustainable tourism, it is not necessarily destination or product specific, but starts from the premise that the environment is already degraded and that some areas are economically impoverished, and is therefore focused on enhancing what remains (Weaver, 2006).

As Weaver indicated, it is important to recognize that these are *ideal* types and this means that real examples can be compared with them.

This reference to comprehensive sustainable tourism and holistic perspectives indicates that discussion on sustainable tourism in this chapter, so far, has concentrated largely on the impacts of tourism itself, and how tourism can become more sustainable in terms of, for example, the environment or local communities. However, this ignores the fact that tourism like many other human activities is affected by events beyond the control of those directly involved in it, such as tourists, host communities and members of the tourism industry. In other words, tourism is subject to important external forces, both natural and man-made. For example, we have seen in Chapter 11 that climate change is being caused partly by tourism, but the chapter also indicates that tourism is affected by climate change, in particular by rising sea levels. Also we saw in Chapter 12 other factors that can affect tourism, such as natural disasters and diseases, and this can contribute to major problems for tourism such as crises and disasters.

A particularly significant example of where tourism both affects and is affected by the environment is the Great Barrier Reef of Australia. The reef is a combination of flora and fauna found close to the surface of a tropical sea, stretching from north to south for hundreds of miles, to the east of the Australian coast. The fact that this visitor attraction is in, and under, the sea causes significant problems for its management and attempts to create sustainable tourism, in an area where other commercial and non-commercial activities are also important, as is highlighted in the following case study.

## Case study: Sustainability issues on the Great Barrier Reef

The Great Barrier Reef is one of the largest coral reefs in the world with over 600 islands, 300 cay islands and almost 300 submerged reefs. There are more than 15,000 species of fish, 4,000 mollusc species and 400 sponges, as well as over 350 different types of coral. Until the mid-20th century, because of its location off the eastern shore of Australia, it remained relatively undeveloped for tourism. From 1975 onwards, tourism developed rapidly. The number of traditional charter boats grew dramatically after this date and in the mid-1980s high speed catamarans were introduced. Between 1982 and 1992 visitor numbers increased 35 fold and visitors were visiting four times as many sites. By 1989 there were almost one million visitors, by 1996 this has reached two million and by 2004 over 2.5 million and a significant proportion by this date were international visitors. The main activities in this period were snorkeling and scuba diving, as well as site-seeing from semi-submersibles and glass bottomed boats.

By the late 1990s, there was evidence of significant environmental impacts, including physical destruction of reefs by anchors, moorings, snorkeling, diving and divers' feet, as well as localized water pollution from sewage and fuel. There were also changes in fish behaviour, largely as a result of boat operator's crews feeding fish to entertain tourists. Additionally there was the taking of souvenirs – visitors removing pieces of coral as well as fish specimens.

In 1975, the Great Barrier Reef Marine Park was established, largely in an attempt to provide a framework for dealing with the effects of increasing numbers of tourists. The main strategy within the Park management system is in an attempt to create sustainable activities including tourism was zoning. Three main categories of zoning were established:

15

☐ A General Use zone (approximately 80% of the Park in the late 1990s) where almost all activities are permitted providing they are ecologically sustainable

☐ National Park zones that allow only activities that do not remove living species

☐ Preservation zones which permit only scientific research.

Tourism was permitted in the first of these two zones, but not in the Preservation Zone. Nevertheless permits were required for both the first and second zones. Factors considered in relation to the granting of permits at the time were the size, extent and location of usage, access conditions, likely effects on the environment in general and ecosystems in particular, and likely effects on resources and their conservation. A number of educational strategies including pictorial symbols, guides and codes of conduct were aimed at tourists and these were backed up with local controls and prohibitions depending on particular circumstances.

In 2004 the zones were revised and new zones introduced. Seven major zones were:

☐ General Use zone

☐ Habitat Protection zone

☐ Conservation Park zone

☐ Buffer zone

☐ Scientific Research zone

☐ Marine National Park zone

☐ Preservation zone

In this new scheme, the General Use Zone had the widest range of permitted activities, while the Preservation Zone was the most restricted in terms of usage. The permit system was maintained after 2004 as well as the targeting of visitors with a variety of educational strategies. Combined, these are still the approaches being used today, to encourage responsible behaviour amongst tourists and conserve the marine environment in an attempt to create sustainable tourism.

Despite these management efforts, the Great Barrier Reef is under threat of being placed on the UNESCO 'List of World Heritage Sites in Danger', having lost half of its coral between 1985 and 2015. Tourism is only one activity causing damage to the reef, as climate change is leading to bleaching of the coral as sea temperatures rise and the water becomes more acid. This is being accompanied by more frequent tropical cyclones. Agricultural run-off in the form of farm fertilisers has also increased in the past 25 years and there is increasing sewage from urban areas on Australia's mainland. If the Great Barrier Reef is put on the UNESCO 'List of World Heritage Sites in Danger' then scientific research programmes will be threatened and there will be inevitably a decline in tourism demand.

(Adapted from Mason, 2013 and Holden, 2016)

The case study of the Great Barrier Reef focuses largely on environmental factors in relation to attempts to bring about sustainable tourism. However as indicated in the WTO definition above, sustainable tourism also includes socio-economic factors and stresses the importance of the involvement of the local community. The following case study, which is concerned with a long-running music festival in England indicates impacts on, and the role of, a local community, as well as considering other socio-economic aspects in relation to sustainability.

## Case study: Fairport Cropredy Convention – a sustainable music festival?

Cropredy is a small English village, in the Oxfordshire Cotswolds, north of the town of Banbury, with only 700 inhabitants. Since 1979 it has been the location of a relatively large annual music festival, with around 20,000 attenders, meaning a ratio of visitors to locals of approximately 30:1. The Festival is known as 'Fairport Cropredy Convention'.

The crowd at the 2017 Fairport Cropredy Convention (http://www.efestivals.co.uk/festivals/cropredy/2017)

Fairport Convention are a folk rock band who formed in 1967. The 'Fairport Cropredy Convention' music festival had its origins in a private performance by members of Fairport Convention in 1976 at the Cropredy Village Fete and 750 people attended. Several of the band members lived in Cropredy village at the time and it was here that the festival was born. The next year the performance was repeated and fans allowed to attend. In 1978, it was properly organized and moved to a larger site. It became a significant event in the band's history as they played their farewell performance there on 4 August 1979 to

15

around 4,500 fans, who were promised there would be annual reunions. Fairport Convention actually disbanded then, but did return in 1980. The group continued to reappear at the annual summer event and in 1985 reformed and have been continually working as a band ever since. Since 1985, the festival has continued, and grown from a one-day, to a three-day, event.

In 2017 some 20,000 people attended the festival, the audience being limited to 16,000 paying visitors plus children, volunteers, festival crew and support staff. Visitors come mainly from the UK but, also the USA, Canada, Australia, New Zealand and Europe and three generations of the same family are not that uncommon. The majority of attendees camp for the duration of the festival. There are eight separate camping fields adjacent to the arena, one of which is reserved for family parties. The festival is aimed at all ages with an emphasis on families and has developed a reputation as a particularly friendly and safe festival. The main marketing strapline of the festival is 'The Friendliest Festival in England' and it also markets itself using 'A weekend in the country'. Some evidence for the 'friendliest festival' label is that reported thefts from the camping fields are rare, unlike several bigger festivals. As well as a wide range of live music, the event features over 30 stalls selling clothing, books, CDs and food. It also has a large bar, with real ale and the bar is used by festival-goers and performers alike, making Cropredy one of the few major festivals where the public can mingle with the musicians playing there.

The village benefits financially and many residents go out of their way to welcome those attending, with some organisations providing al fresco meals. This includes the village primary school which receives nearly all of its Parent Teacher Association funding via the provision of breakfasts during the Festival. The local church and chapel also gain funding via the sale of food and drink. The two village public houses are the location of 'festival fringe' events. A number of charities also receive support during the festival. A large group of local volunteers, especially young people, assist with the running of the festival in return for free tickets and/or other benefits. An indication of support for the festival from local people is that almost a third of Cropredy village households were involved in making 'scarecrows', using the theme of the festival, during the 2017 event, with festival attenders paying for an entry form and voting for the 'best scarecrow' with all proceeds going to charity. Further confirmation of support for the festival is that when the village church had a new bell installed in 2010, it called it the 'Festival Bell', had the band members' names inscribed on it, and invited members of the band to attend its installation. Additionally, the new village sign includes recognition of the festival, via a depiction of musical instruments.

The festival is not without some negative consequences. Drunkenness is not uncommon, and the noise level, during the festival, in the village is much higher than normal, particularly near the two public houses and some residents actually go away during the festival. There is traffic congestion and traffic is diverted from some village roads and neighbouring roads. The fields where visitors camp can also be (temporarily) damaged following very wet conditions. Despite frequent emptying, the portable toilets on site do not always function appropriately. There is also a greater litter problem, although there are significant attempts at recycling.

However, the festival has been in existence for almost 40 years, so what lessons can be drawn about its continued existence? Key sustainability factors are indicated below:

1  The festival started small and only grew slowly and there is a limit to the number of paying attenders.

2  There is a significant amount of local support, helped by the fact that several band members lived in the village, or locally, when the festival began and some still live nearby and band members take part in local activities.

3  Local people are involved as volunteers.

4  Several local people/businesses/organisations derive economic benefit.

5  The festival raises money for local charities.

6  Locals are kept informed and involved throughout the year.

7  The marketing strapline 'The friendliest festival' is largely supported by the presence of families and a general lack of anti-social behavior.

8  The intended target market of families also encourages new, young supporters.

9  The relatively early finish of events each day in the arena, restricts noise disturbance and also the camping fields are some distance away from the village restricting noise problems.

10 Band members help select each year's performers, based on their own interests as potential audience members, as well as musicians.

11 A number of bands have returned regularly to the festival.

12 The festival is a highly sort after venue for aspiring musicians.

13 Musicians mix with the crowd, as there is no separate back stage bar.

14 The festival attempts to be green, with a significant amount of recycling.

15 Recent additions include a big screen, where attenders can have messages displayed.

16 The Festival produces a range of souvenirs, in particular t-shirts which not only provide revenue, but act as a form of marketing for future festivals.

(Sources: en.wikipedia.org/wiki/Cropredy, accessed January 2017, Oxfordshire Rural Community Council, 2010, Mason, 2017b)

**15**

In an attempt to bring about sustainable development in all fields of human activity, the United Nations (UN) published a number of Sustainable Development Goals (SDGs) in 2015. These SDGs are shown in Table 15.1. Alongside each of the SDGs, related tourism themes have been added to the original UN document. As can be seen one of the goals, SDG 14, focuses on life below water and this is particularly pertinent to the discussion in the case study above concerning the future of the Great Barrier Reef, whilst SDG 11, 'Sustainable Cities and Communities' and SDG 12, 'Responsible Consumption and Production' have relevance to the case study of the Fairport Cropredy Convention.

**Table 15.1:** The 17 SDGs and indicative themes relating to sustainable tourism.

| Sustainable Development Goals (SDGs) | Related Tourism Themes *(Indicative examples only)* |
|---|---|
| **Goal 1. No Poverty** <br> End poverty in all its forms everywhere | Critiques of the green economy <br> Hegemony/gender/oppression/domination/fascism <br> Poverty alleviation through tourism and its critique <br> Pro-poor tourism |
| **Goal 2. Zero Hunger** <br> End hunger, achieve food security and improved nutrition and promote sustainable agriculture | Sustainable food systems <br> Agritourism <br> Permaculture and food movements <br> Food based micro-enterprises <br> Culinary epistemologies for sustainability |
| **Goal 3. Good Health and Wellbeing** <br> Ensure healthy lives and promote well-being for all at all ages | Community development <br> Social capital <br> Tourism and quality of life <br> Tourism as a tool for positive aging |
| **Goal 4. Quality Education** <br> Ensure inclusive and equitable quality education and promote lifelong learning opportunities for all | Critical pedagogy and neoliberalism <br> Collaborative research methods for transformation <br> The role of critical thinking in transforming tourism education <br> International training and education <br> The Global Sustainable Tourism Council (GSTC) <br> Multi-lateral training programmes <br> Educational tourism as a tool for inclusivity |
| **Goal 5. Gender Equality** <br> Achieve gender equality and empower all women and girls | Social complexity, social inequities, structural labours of care and leisure, racialized, gendered, and classed perspectives <br> Multilateral/non-governmental/industry/academic structures of power <br> Ecofeminism and feminist ecology |
| **Goal 6. Clean Water and Sanitation** <br> Ensure availability and sustainable management of water and sanitation for all | Considerations of the quadruple bottom line <br> Water and resource use in tourism <br> Water rights and hegemony in tourism |
| **Goal 7. Affordable and Clean Energy** <br> Ensure access to affordable, reliable, sustainable and modern energy for all | Energy use in tourism <br> Sustainable transport <br> Low carbon energy transitions |
| **Goal 8. Decent Work and Economic Growth** <br> Promote sustained, inclusive and sustainable economic growth, full and productive employment and decent work for all | Considerations of economic growth and de-growth <br> Eco-colonialism and eco-imperialism <br> Indigenous owned and operated tourism business <br> Assumptions of economic growth <br> Leisure and the rights for rest and reflection <br> Workers' Rights <br> Universal basic wage <br> Social Tourism |

| | |
|---|---|
| **Goal 9. Industry, Innovation and Infrastructure**<br>Build resilient infrastructure, promote inclusive and sustainable industrialization and foster innovation | Innovations for sustainability<br>Sustainable energies<br>The use of virtual technologies in Hospitality and Tourism<br>Social entrepreneurship |
| **Goal 10. Reduce Inequalities**<br>Reduce inequality within and among countries | Ethics and bio-cultural conservation: Ecosystems/biodiversity/culture/heritage<br>White/Western privilege<br>Marginalized communities<br>Rights of LBGTQ+ and tourism |
| **Goal 11. Sustainable Cities and Communities**<br>Make cities and human settlements inclusive, safe, resilient and sustainable | Linking urban and rural tourism<br>Tourism systems in the urban context<br>Futurism<br>Humanising cities |
| **Goal 12. Responsible Consumption and Production**<br>Ensure sustainable consumption and production patterns | Critiques of the green economy<br>Considerations of economic growth and degrowth<br>Conscious Consumerism<br>Localisation<br>Slow tourism<br>Participation<br>Certification |
| **Goal 13. Climate Action**<br>Take urgent action to combat climate change and its impacts | Climate actions and activism<br>Paris COP21 Agreement<br>Climate change and structures of power<br>Climate change and aviation<br>Mobility rights and impacts<br>Indigenous activism for positive futures |
| **Goal 14. Life Below Water**<br>Conserve and sustainably use the oceans, seas and marine resources for sustainable development | Tourism and Marine Protected Areas (MPAs)<br>Marine mammals and tourism<br>Tourism and the Blue Economy |
| **Goal 15. Life on Land**<br>Protect, restore and promote sustainable use of terrestrial ecosystems, sustainably manage forests, combat desertification, and halt and reverse land degradation and biodiversity loss | Tourism and Protected Areas (PAs)<br>Linking tourism and conservation<br>The politics of conservation and environmental justice<br>Indigenous cosmologies |
| **Goal 16. Peace, Justice and Strong Institutions**<br>Promote peaceful and inclusive societies for sustainable development, provide access to justice for all and build effective, accountable and inclusive institutions at all levels | Tourism as a conduit for peace<br>Peace building/poverty alleviation/livelihood development/gender equality<br>Cultural interpretations of sustainability<br>Indigenous approaches to interdependence<br>Islamic perspectives on tourism |
| **Goal 17. Partnerships for the Goals**<br>Strengthen the means of implementation and revitalize the Global Partnership for Sustainable Development | Tools that facilitate inclusive and participatory multi-stakeholder dialogue<br>Global Sustainable Tourism Council (GSTC)<br>United Nations World Tourism Organization (UNWO)<br>Greenwashing/Certifications/Accreditations<br>Roles of NGOs as advocates for justice in tourism |

*Source:* Bolak, Caviliere and Higgins-Desboilles, 2017, based on : 'Sustainable Development Goals: 17 Goals to Transform Our World' (2015) with indicative tourism content added.

15

One of the items in SDG 12, 'Responsible Consumption and Production' points to another issue in relation to sustainability. As noted earlier, it is a problem to define sustainable tourism, so that attempting to measure it is fraught with difficulty. This raises the question: 'If it is difficult to define and therefore measure sustainable tourism, how can we tell if it really is sustainable?' SDG 12 provides an indication of how it may be possible to gain information on whether a particular form of tourism activity or product is sustainable, as this SDG makes reference to certification.

Certification is a process in which a product or activity can be assessed using a set of criteria. In more detail, certification is a way to avoid subjectivity in evaluating forms of tourism, and can result in more objective assessments of the activity to help distinguish one type of tourism from another. This will usually involve the use of criteria that can be measured to verify the credentials of companies or organisations that make claims about their tourism products. One particular approach has been through the use of eco-labels. Eco-labels are not confined to tourism and in fact have been used in a variety of settings. A food product that has the word 'organic' or 'bio' on the packaging, is using an eco-label, as this indicates to the consumer how the item was grown, and to be awarded the eco-label the process will have to meet certain criteria.

Eco-labels have been connected with a variety of tourism products and are intended to indicate the 'green' credentials of the product. Eco-labels are predicated on the concept of certification, and this is a formal process in which an independent body certifies to interested parties, such as tourists, marketing bodies and regulators that a provider complies with a specified standard (Buckley, 2002).

Eco-labels have been in existence for over 25 years. Whilst in 1988 there were just three schemes globally, by 2000 there were at least 75 and today there are several hundred in the world. Eco-label awards have been given to destinations, tourism products, tour operators and tourism attractions. Labels can be classified according to whether they cover the whole world, or are regional only and also whether there is one uniform label or they are multi-tiered, which means they have a basic level and advanced level.

The first global tourism eco-label was Green Globe. Although set up by the World Travel and Tourism Council, it remained almost unknown, until it was then taken over in 1999 and became a not-for-profit company, known as Green Globe 21. It has developed three levels of membership 'affiliated', 'benchmarked' and 'certified' (Weaver, 2006). Although the tourism industry, like many other industries, is not always happy about external regulation, eco-labels offer certain advantages to private companies. The award of eco-label certification can lead to positive publicity, which is a form of free marketing. There is then the likelihood of more sales to 'green/discerning' consumers, as well as greater leverage to charge higher prices. A company can also claim there is external recognition of any sustainability claim it makes. Some organisations may also use the external verification of its claim to stave off government attempts to regulate it, by arguing it is not necessary as it already has independent verification of its activities (see Mason and Mowforth, 1996). However, it is vital if eco-labels are to be successful that they are recognised and endorsed by consumer groups, government bodies and NGOs as well as by members of the tourism industry.

The following case study, which is based on an article in a travel industry magazine, provides an indication of the importance of ecolabels particularly from the tourism industry perspective.

## Case study: What do eco-labels bring to tourism?

Sustainability is a trend for holidaymakers and sustainable tourism is growing in popularity. More than 150 international eco-labels have established themselves as a part of the eco-friendly businesses, offering environmentally friendly services even for the travelers. What difference do these eco-labels make?

Tourism is largely a natural experience, but the holidaymakers often damage the environment with their activities. "An awareness of sustainability in tourism has only emerged when more people started travelling and first signs of damage were reported," says the Managing Director of Anders Reisen, an association of sustainable travel companies.

The first ecolabels were created in 1987 – the Blue Flag for coastal zones in Europe. In 1998 the Blue Swallow for environmentally and socially friendly accommodations in Germany was established. In recent years the number has risen sharply. "There are around 150 to 180 labels worldwide for sustainable tourism," reports a lecturer from the 'University of Sustainable Development' (Applied Sciences) in Eberswalde, Germany.

### Criteria for the assessment of eco-labels

It is not always easy to say how to assess the company requiring an eco-label. But there are important criteria: Is there a sustainability strategy? Are visitors counted and the cultural heritage protected? What about environmental factors such as water consumption, recycling, light and noise protection?

There are great differences in the review of these criteria. Some labels are checked from the desk, others send external reviewers to the companies. "The criteria should be presented transparently – that is, publicly," the lecturer from Eberswalde says. 'However, some eco-labels do not publish their evaluation catalogues'.

An important point of orientation for holidaymakers is the question: Was the label recognized by the Global Sustainable Tourism Council (GSTC)? Today, the Council is the largest international interest group for sustainable tourism. It is financially supported by the major tour operator, TUI, among others, but it works independently according to its own statement. The organization checks who is behind a label, what the criteria list requires, how reliable the test procedure is, the sustainability focus of a label and which companies and offers are certified. So far, 26 eco-labels have been recognized by the GSTC.

15

"The question of the best ecolabel cannot be answered on a flat-rate basis. The variety of eco-labels has developed from the diversity of tourism," explains a founding member of the GSTC. There are regional, national and international certificates as well as labels, which distinguish either hotels, camping sites, travel agencies and even car wash systems – or all of this. The labels also differ in the sustainability focal points. Some focus on ecological criteria, such as the Green Key of the Foundation of Environmental Education, which was already awarded to more than 2,500 companies. Other labels cover all three pillars of sustainability, including social and economic components. This includes TourCert, which has been developed for travel agencies and accommodation. They therefore advertise their travel offerings prominently. Green Globe also features hotels, resorts, travel agencies, car rentals and congress centers in a similar fashion. More than 540 events have been held under the ecolabel.

### Attempts for a single certificate failed

In order to create more transparency, six years ago efforts were made to obtain a uniform certificate. The seal of the GSTC should include sustainability criteria for all tourism offerings in the world. The project however failed. A campsite in Austria, for example, has completely different basic requirements than an eco-lodge in the jungle of Borneo.

Are there any black sheep among the eco-labels? A spokesperson for the GSTC who has been working on sustainable tourism since 1987 says: "Greenwashing has not occurred to me during this time." So far, sustainable tourism has been developed on a voluntary basis beyond legal requirements. Greenwashing only occurs when a hotel or region deliberately makes false statements.

The question remains: Does the vacationer look at the labels at all? "For the traveler, this is only decisive in the second or third stage when the destination and price are the same, as the assumption is that sustainable travel is generally more expensive." A member of the GSTC however claims that through sustainable travel, many savings are passed on to the traveler.

The market for eco-labels is likely to develop strongly in the future. The lecturer from Eberswalde refers, for example, to the climate agreement in Paris and the consumer center for responsible and sustainable products. "These developments generate positive dynamics towards sustainable tourism," the researcher believes.

(adapted from *Tourism Review*, 2017)

# Challenges to achieving sustainable tourism

As has been indicated, above one of the main problems in attempts to achieve sustainable tourism is the lack of an accepted definition. The different paradigms in which either economic factors or environmental factors are viewed as dominant is part of the problem. Even definitions that put the economic and environmental aspects on an equal footing have become of little practical value when other themes such as 'community', 'host population' or even the tourists themselves are built into definitions. The 1998 WTO definition presented above may appear detailed and comprehensive as a statement, but trying to put the differing elements together in a real world context will be very difficult.

This vagueness of definition causes problems particularly for the consumers trying to select a sustainable form of tourism. Eco-labels can assist with this choice for consumers, but not all products have eco-labels which means that unscrupulous tour operators can claim (without evidence) that their product is 'more green' or 'more sustainable' in relation to another, and consequently charge more for it. However, the consumer will not be able to discern if this is based on real criteria or is little more than what is termed 'greenwash' – the use of marketing language without supporting evidence (Mason, 2016).

Another significant issue with the application of sustainable tourism is that it usually focuses largely on the destination-end of tourism (in fact, this is what has happened in this chapter). This approach means that the negative effects of vehicle pollution, increased traffic, traffic jams and noise pollution related primarily to transport vehicles used in tourism are largely ignored (Sharpley, 2002). Hence, a tour operator may promote a sustainable holiday experience, using terms such as 'eco-tourism' or 'green tourism' and the actual experience may indeed involve sustainable accommodation, which is aesthetically and architecturally in keeping with the destination, uses local food sources, which are from organic farms controlled by the local community and the residents actually derive significant economic benefits through jobs and income, but if it is in, for example, Costa Rica and the majority of tourists come from Europe, the aircraft that takes them to their holiday will cause air pollution, noise pollution and contribute to global warming!

As long as tourism relies on carbon-based transport and energy sources, it is difficult to argue that it will be sustainable (Holden, 2016). If this reliance continues into the long term future, tourism will continue to contribute to global warming and climate change. Relatively little research, involving modelling and assessment into the long term effects of this reliance on carbon based transport in tourism and how this reliance can be altered to reduce global warming, is currently being conducted (Hall *et al.*, 2013).

As earlier sections of this book have stated, tourism is a highly fragmented industry spanning sectors including accommodation, food and beverages, transport and destinations. At government level where plans are made and regulations created and introduced, tourism does not always fit conveniently into one government department and even if it does, it can have a relatively low status in government, often relegated to a second or third tier (Holden, 2016). This will make planning for tourism sustainability very difficult. Hence, as a result of the fragmentation of tourism as an industry, there is need to integrate it into the planning process and there is a responsibility of governments in democracies to ensure

**15**

the best management of resources, which includes the environmental assets that are used in tourism (Bramwell, 2011). However it is most frequently at the local level that this process occurs (Holden, 2016), as it is at the local level that tourism impacts are often observed. These impacts may be negative, but local authorities can intervene to oppose inappropriate development (Ruhanen, 2013) and local authorities may be best placed to support sustainable forms of tourism as they have local knowledge (Holden, 2016). However, whether sustainable tourism is supported will involve a political decision. The decision makers in democracies are elected representatives of the people, and these elected politicians have different values and usually represent parties that have policies that may, or may not, support sustainable types of tourism. So, it is possible to conclude that political will is very important in the implementation of sustainable tourism.

## Summary

Sustainability is a term that has been an important concept for around 30 years. Notions of sustainable tourism have been derived from concerns with sustainable development. A number of statements on sustainable development appeared in the 1980s, and of particular importance was the Brundtland Report. The first major statements on sustainable tourism appeared in the 1990s. Since then the concept of sustainable tourism has developed and changed, with early ideas usually focused on environmental sustainability. More recent statements have been concerned with socio-cultural and economic factors. The role of local communities has also featured significantly in recent comments on sustainable tourism.

Views on sustainable tourism can be subdivided into groupings such as *techno-centric* or *eco-centric*. It is also possible to discern three traditions, *resource-based*, *activity-based* and *community-based* in the relationship between tourism and sustainability, and to recognize ideal types of sustainable tourism, which range from the *minimalist* to the *comprehensive*. Butler's theory of destination development has been discussed and considered important in relation to the planning and management of destination in attempts to ensure they have long term viability.

However, achieving sustainable tourism has proved to be a very difficult task. Part of the problem is the lack of an accepted definition, which makes assessing and measuring it problematic. Nevertheless, certification has been developed and eco-labels are viewed as one way of providing evidence of the credentials of sustainable forms of tourism, which have advantages for both tourists and the industry. Achieving sustainable tourism is still challenging, but it is very likely that concepts of sustainable tourism will continue to evolve. Perhaps it may be better, as Holden (2008) argues, to think of sustainability not as a desired end point, but rather a process, a guiding philosophy that incorporates certain principles about the way we interact with the environment.

## Student activities

1   What do you understand by the term sustainability?

2   What is sustainable development?

3   What is sustainable tourism?

4   Why could it be difficult to achieve sustainable tourism?

5   How have views on sustainability and sustainable tourism developed since the early 1990s?

6   Study Figure 15.2. Which of the instruments in Figure 15.2 will be particularly effective in bringing about sustainable tourism?

7   How can Butler's TALC theory be used in attempts to achieve sustainable tourism?

8   In relation to the case study of the Great Barrier Reef, why is trying to achieve sustainable tourism here particularly difficult?

9   In small groups, in relation to the case study Fairport Cropredy Convention, discuss:

   a) What you consider to be the major factors contributing to the festival being largely sustainable.

   b) What could lead to the Cropredy festival becoming unsustainable?

10  What are the advantages and disadvantages of ecolabels for:
   a) tourists?
   b) the tourism industry?
   c) governments?

11  What do you think will be the chief components of sustainable tourism in the year 2050?

# References

Bartelmus, P. (1994). *Environment, Growth and Development: The Concepts and Strategies of Sustainability*. London: Routledge.

Benerman, C. and Petit, D. (2007) *Festivals and the Product Life Cycle,: an exploratory study of the Rhone-Alpes region*, Groupe ESC, St Etienne, France.

Bramwell, B. (2011) Governance, the state and sustainable tourism: a political economy approach, *Journal of Sustainable Tourism*, **19**(4-5) 459-447

Bolak, C., Caviliere, L. and Higgins-Desboilles, F. (2017) Trinet message, July 10th, 2017.

Buckley, R. (2002) Minimal impact guidelines for mountain ecotours, *Tourism Recreation Research*, **27**, 35-40.

Butler, R. (1980). The concept of a tourism area cycle of evolution. *Canadian Geographer*, **24**, 5–12.

Butler, R.  (1998). 'Still pedalling along: The resort life cycle two decades on, Paper presented at the CAUTHE Conference, Gold Coast, Australia 1998.

15

Butler, R. and Hall, C. M. (1998). Tourism and recreation in rural areas: myth and reality. In *Rural Tourism Management: Sustainable Options* (D. Hall and J. O'Hanlon, eds.), pp. 97–108. Conference Proceedings, Ayr: Scottish Agricultural College.

Christaller, W. (1963). Some considerations of tourism locations in Europe: the peripheral regions–under-developed countries–recreation areas. *Papers of the Regional Science Association*, **12**, 168–78.

Coccossis, H. and Parpairis, A. (1996). Tourism and carrying capacity in coastal areas: Mykonos Greece. In *Sustainable Tourism? European Experiences* (G. K. Priestley, J. A. Edwards and H. Coccosis, eds), pp. 153–75. Wallingford, UK: CAB International.

Cohen, I. (1972). Towards a sociology of international tourism. *Social Research*, **39**, 164–82.

Doxey. G (1975). A causation theory of resident visitor irritants. In *The Sixth Annual Conference Proceedings of the Travel Research Association*, pp. 195–8.

Doyle, T. and McEachern, D. (1998). *Environment and Politics*. London: Routledge.

ETB (1991). *Tourism and the Environment: Maintaining the Balance.* London: English Tourism Board/Ministry of the Environment.

Hall, C.M., Scott, D. and Gossling, S. (2013) The primacy of climate change for sustainable international tourism, *Sustainable Development*, **21**(1), 112-121.

Holden, A. (2000) *Environment and Tourism*, London: Routledge.

Holden, A. (2008) *Environment and Tourism* (2nd ed.), London: Routledge.

Holden, A. (2016) *Environment and Tourism* (3rd ed.), London: Routledge.

Hunter, C. (1996) Sustainable tourism as an adaptive paradigm, *Annals of Tourism Research*, **24**, 850-67.

Innskeep, E. (1991). *Tourism Planning*. New York: Van Nostrand.

Mason, P. (2013) 'Zoning, land use planning and tourism' in Holden A. and Fennel D. (Eds.) *The Routledge Handbook of Tourism and the Environment*, London Routledge, pp.266-85.

Mason, P. (2016) *Tourism Impacts, Planning and Management* (3rd ed.), London, Routledge

Mason, P. (2017b) Unpublished report: 'Impacts of the 2017 Fairport Cropredy Convention Festival'.

Mason, P. and Mowforth, M. (1996). Codes of conduct in tourism. *Progress in Tourism and Hospitality Research*, **2**, 151–67.

Plog, S (1972) Why destination areas rise and fall in popularity, Cornel Restaurant and Hospitality Administration Quarterly, 12, 13-16.

Ruhanen, L. (2013) Local government: facilitator or inhibitor of sustainable tourism development, Journal of Sustainable Tourism, **21**(1), 80-98.

Saarinen, J. (2006) Traditions in sustainability in tourism studies, *Annals of Tourism Research* **33**(4), 1121-1140.

Sharpley, R. (2002) Tourism and Sustainable Development: exploring the Theoretical Divide, *Journal of Sustainable Tourism*, **8**(1), 1-19.

Tourism Review (2017) What Do Ecolabels Bring To Tourism? June, 13 2017, https://www. hospitalitynet.org/news/4083182.html accessed July 10th.

UNEP/WTO (2005) *Making Tourism More Sustainable: a Guide for Policy Makers*, Paris, United Nations Environment Programme/World Tourism Organisation.

Weaver, D. (2000) A broad context of destination development scenarios, *Tourism Management*, 21(3), 217-34.

Weaver, D. (2006). *Sustainable Tourism*. Oxford: Butterworth- Heinemann.

Wikipedia (2017) Fairport's Cropredy Convention  https//en.wikipedia.org/wiki/ Fairport Convention accessed August 2017.

WTO (1998) *World Tourism 20:20 Vision*, Madrid, World Tourism Organisation.

Zhong, L., Deng, J.  and Xiang, D. (2007) Tourism development and the tourism area life cycle model: a case study of Zhangijajie National Forest Park, *Tourism Management*, **28**(1) 112-127.

**15**

# 16 The Future of Tourism

## Introduction

For the past 50 years or so, tourism as a socio-economic phenomenon has been steadily growing, despite what can be seen today as temporary blips in which growth has slowed or numbers have actually fallen for a short period. Some of these factors leading to a decline or a slowing in growth have been as a result of natural causes and others have occurred following human induced changes. Looking to the future, there are a number of factors that can assist in the further growth and development of tourism and yet other factors that can restrict development and even turn growth into decline. This chapter considers future developments in tourism.

## Key perspectives

Some of the factors that will affect the future of tourism are external to the industry. The most important of these, as noted in Chapter 11, is global climate change. One major result of global warming will be melting of the polar ice caps; the rise in sea level that occurs will cause flooding along low lying coastal areas and in particular will affect a number of islands where tourism is important such as the Maldives and Seychelles. Mountain areas will also be affected by global warming which will disrupt any type of snow-based tourism. Climate change will have dramatic impacts on how, where and when people travel, assuming that they are able to, and will reshape the tourism industry over time (Foundation for the Future, 2009).

As noted in Chapter 12, natural disasters such as earthquakes and tsunamis may have an effect in particular locations; diseases such as SARS may re-occur, new diseases may break out and in either case, be spread around the world by tourists. Terrorism is a relatively recent phenomenon affecting tourism, and in some locations has greatly altered tourist behaviour and motivation to visit, although these changes in tourism do not appear to be permanent.

Other factors that may affect future tourism are internal and will probably include changes in demand for particular types of tourism experience. Changes in demand are likely to occur if prices for holidays and other tourism activities increase in relation to, for example, higher fuel costs. As tourism is in some ways a 'fashion industry' (see Prosser, 1998) new locations and activities will be sought by future tourists, compared with those participated in today.

By the mid-2020s, the UN expects the world population to grow to 8 billion. That's an additional 1.3 billion people, who will place dramatic new demands on the planet as well put pressure on the finite resources for tourism. The growth of the middle classes in countries like China and India has the potential to reshape global tourism flows dramatically. In the current situation, many more tourist visit these countries from the rest of the world than travel in the opposite direction. In the next 30 years or so, movement of tourist from China and India to the rest of the world will greatly increase.

For many commentators conditions are already bad and the following case study indicates for some tourism has already reached a point where drastic action needs to be taken to change tourism.

## Case study: 'Mass Tourism is at a tipping point – but we are all part of the problem'

During August 2017, *The Guardian* newspaper published two very critical commentaries on tourism. Extracts from one of them, written by journalist Martin Kettle, are presented below.

Kettle indicates that about 30 years ago, he was researching to write on global population pressures, and interviewed the zoologist Desmond Morris. During that interview, Morris said something that was hard to forget Kettle indicated. "We have to recognise," he said, "that human beings may be becoming an infestation on the planet".

Those words came back to Kettle as reports were arriving during the 2017 summer about the increasing reaction in several parts of Europe to mass tourism. Kettle noted that very different places, including the Mediterranean coast and the Isle of Skye, were complaining more or less simultaneously about the sheer pressure of tourist numbers in their streets and beauty spots. His reaction was to feel as if the uneasy balance between the visited and the visitors had gone beyond a tipping point.

As he wrote: 'Pictures of a wall in Barcelona saying, "Tourist Go Home", or of protesters in Palma saying, "Tourism Kills Mallorca" should touch an uneasy nerve in anyone whose summer getaway has taken them to places such as San Sebastián, Dubrovnik, Florence, Venice and – further afield – New Orleans and Thailand. For all of these have either taken, or are considering measures to limit the relentless pressure from mass tourism by people like you and me.'

Part of his report focused on Venice, (discussed in Chapter 12). He wrote: "Predictably, Venice is one of the most agonisingly pressured of all. It embodies the increasingly irreconcilable forces of vernacular life, tourism and sustainability in historic parts of Europe.

**16**

But that doesn't stop the millions arriving all the time – 28 million this year, in a city with a population of 55,000, many disembarking from monstrous cruise ships that dwarf the ancient city as they approach the Grand Canal. Each day in summer is a humiliation of most of the things the world treasures about Venice. Not surprisingly, many locals have had enough".

Kettle goes on to argue that far from being unusual, what is happening in Europe during the summer of 2017 is occurring in many parts of not just Europe, but around the world. Kettle suggests that anarchists in Barcelona captured the headlines by holding up tourist buses in protest against the cost of living that they say is inflicted by tourism, especially by short-term-let companies such as Airbnb, which drive up housing costs. He states that the tourism problem is global as human beings across the world make more than a billion foreign trips a year, and this is twice as many as 20 years ago. In Britain, 45 million foreign holidays were taken in 2016, a 68% increase on 1996. He added: "And foreign trips cut both ways. Many of those who were interviewed in the media when the narrow road to Glen Brittle on Skye became jammed with traffic this week were European visitors, attracted not just by the scenery but by the advantageous exchange rate".

Kettle argued that the problem is related to both supply and demand, and claimed that: "There isn't enough room for the many to walk through the centre of Dubrovnik, or enough public loos on Skye for the visitors".  But of particular concern to Kettle is that the number of people wanting to visit such places has been rising for many years, fed by greater global prosperity, cheaper air travel and an increased supply of hotels worldwide. The result Kettle indicated is that: "Tourism is now the largest employer on the planet. One in every 11 people relies on the industry for work".  But he believes this is why the problem is particularly worrying and suggests: "Unsurprisingly, few governments want to put a squeeze on such a source of wealth".

Kettle also believes that governments are not solely to blame, and that consumers have to take some responsibility. As he argues: "We all want to go to places such as Venice. And we are mostly all willing to submit to the indignities and embarrassments that are involved in doing so – whether it's irksome but necessary security checks or overcrowded departure lounges, no-frills flight regulations, car hire price-gouging and all the rest of it…. but few are seriously deterred". So, he contends, all of us are part of this problem, not the solution.

He moves on to consider possible solutions: "Can anything be done to get the visited and visiting into a more sustainable balance? It is tempting to fall back on Morris-like pessimism and to suspect that it can't, that the issues are unmanageable".  He suggests that there are many extremely difficult aspects to the problem, and argues: "The biggest, in a global sense, is the rise of Chinese tourism", but that no-one should be in a position to deny Chinese people the rewards of travel.  Another issue he raises is to do with air travel and indicates: "The tourism industry's carbon footprint is equally problematic. But if people want to take the planes, and the planes are available, who is to say that this should stop?" He refers specifically to the British when discussing the problem of increasing bad behaviour of tourists: "It is beyond question that many British tourists behave badly abroad. The stag-do and hen-do culture is out of hand. But you can't restrict access to Italy to those who know their Giotto from their Duccio".

In his article, Kettle also refers to the other Guardian report that had at that time appeared very recently. He stated: "Writing a few days ago, the writer Elizabeth Becker argued that only governments can handle runaway tourism. Governments can control entry to their countries, can regulate airlines and ships, prevent inappropriate hotel development, and use taxes to shape visitor demand and benefit local people, place limits on rip-off prices that distort markets."   Kettle also adds that Becker admits that most governments prefer things as they are, so the prospect of truly effective coordination by governments remains distant. However he believes: "It would be wonderful if governments could find effective ways to at least mitigate the worst problems … [some] such as those of Thailand and Bhutan, have been bold, even though most restrictions hit hardest at the less well-off and are most easily circumvented by the rich" .

Kettle brings his article to a conclusion by restating that all of us need to be more proactive and take greater individual responsibility. "We have to re-examine the idea that we enjoy an unfettered liberty to travel at will or for pleasure." He believes that we can learn from the American author Henry David Thoreau who suggested that one can travel as much – and develop as much as a human being – in one's own locality as in the far-flung and exotic corners of the globe.

His final thoughts refer to the maxim: 'travel broadens the mind', and argues "But is the person whose air-conditioned tour bus whisks them to a distant glacier in Patagonia or to the Mona Lisa for a quick selfie before depositing them at a characterless international hotel, richer in experience than the one who spends the same amount of time watching the birds or the butterflies in the back garden?" His response, perhaps not surprisingly is: "I doubt it. … Travel can narrow the mind too".

(Source: adapted from Kettle, M., *The Guardian*, August 2017)

The case study makes reference to the work of a writer Elisabeth Becker, and she argues that tourism can only be changed by government involvement. As Becker (2017) claims, it is no longer appropriate to dismiss criticisms of tourism as some form of elitist view of the 'traveller' versus the 'tourist', or a question of who has the right to travel. Becker believes the tourism industry has now grown so large, so quickly that it is a major contributor to the globalisation process and, she argues, it has to be controlled and she suggests it is only governments that can control tourism. As she states:

> *Only governments can handle runaway tourism. Few major industries fall so squarely into their hands – local, regional and national. Governments decide who is eligible for visas: how many cruise ships, airlines and trains can bring in*

**16**

*visitors, how many hotels receive building permits, how many beaches are open to development, how many museums and concert halls are open, even how many farmers receive subsidies to raise food for the restaurants and cafes that tourists frequent* (Becker, 2017:10).

Becker states that currently most governments are unwilling to take action to control tourism, largely because the industry employs such a large number of people and makes very significant financial contributions to many economies. Becker adds however that there is some hope in that a number of countries including France, Bhutan, Costa Rica and Canada have co-ordinated policies of sustainable tourism development, and as she indicates, this has not led to a downturn in tourist numbers. Becker also states that some governments accept that tourism is severely damaging the environment and are turning to alternatives such as ecotourism, and in extreme cases are banning tourists, as was done by the Thai government in relation to Koh Tachai island in an attempt to save it.

In 2009, An organisation made up of tourism industry representatives, academics, government official and non-government organisation staff called 'Forum For the Future' in the UK created a document entitled *Tourism 2023: Four scenarios, a vision and a strategy for UK outbound travel and tourism*. These scenarios, intended to represent possible direction for future tourism, are presented below.

# Four Scenarios from Forum for the Future

## ■ Boom or bust

A booming UK economy and high disposable incomes have fuelled a growth in travel worldwide. People travel further, more frequently, and at faster speeds than ever before. There are many new reasons to go abroad as global political stability and prospering economies have opened up the world to more commerce and visitors. Rapid advances in technology have been crucial, such as the breakthrough in algae-based fuels. Dramatic improvements in efficiencies have allowed the transport sector just about to keep pace with new regulations and their impacts, such as the steadily rising global price of carbon. But expensive trade-offs have been needed and the travel industry has effectively financed the decarbonisation of other sectors of the economy. Margins are tighter than ever and there has been mass industry consolidation. The UK's older population is increasingly mobile, and has time to spare and cash to spend. Hordes go on cheap medical and beauty tourism breaks to Costa Rica and India, which offer substantial savings on operations. More flexible, part-time and semi-retirement working have driven demand for trips, and second home ownership abroad is booming. The UK's legally binding carbon targets are being met – but many are asking how long this can continue. Many destinations are suffering from serious overcrowding. Wilderness is perhaps the scarcest resource as road, rail, sea and air routes have brought mass tourism to the last corners of the planet.

## ■ Divided Disquiet

A toxic combination of devastating climate change impacts, violent wars over scarce resources and social unrest has created an unstable and fearful world. This has made travelling overseas an unattractive proposition. Many destinations were unprepared for the impacts of a changing climate. More extreme weather events, rising sea levels, increased flooding and frequent droughts have battered some places, while food shortages, malnutrition, malaria, and conflict over resources like water and oil have wreaked havoc in others. Tourism is an 'adventure activity' for only the bravest in the worst hit areas: the Sahara to the Middle East and Central Asia, sub-Saharan Africa, South Asian waterways and Small Island States. A lack of cooperation globally has closed down borders and hampered movement. Protectionism is strong and global trade has shrunk. Tight security and additional visa checks make travel cumbersome and time-consuming. Visitors are highly selective in where and when they travel, cramming into a small number of destinations where overcrowding compounds the problems. 'Doomsday tourism' – where visitors rush to see fast-disappearing attractions – is popular in the glacier parks of Patagonia and the bleached corals of Australia's Great Barrier Reef. But many people have begun to think that holidaying abroad just makes the problems worse. A breakthrough in affordable telepresence technology has proved surprisingly popular with businesses that are keen to cut costs. This resulted in drastically reduced numbers of certain air routes, closing them to many holidaymakers.

## ■ Price and Privilege

A dramatically high oil price has made travel punitively expensive. Dwindling supplies and rising demand from the new economies of Asia have pushed energy prices into a series of sharp and unpredictable spikes. The travel industry worldwide has been badly hit and aviation has shrunk dramatically. Fleet replacements have been slower than anticipated and the predicted efficiency gains could not keep pace. There have been mass redundancies across the travel industry and a period of dramatic consolidation across the world. Cost is the primary concern for holidaymakers as everyone asks: how far can I get for my money? Although a small, elite market continues to fly regularly, the vast majority of people simply cannot afford the experience. The days of affordable travel are now just a nostalgic memory. People who want to holiday abroad either save up for years and fly overseas or join the new mass market of overland connections. Pan-European rail, bus and sea networks offer the most cost-effective means of travel for most people. State-of-the-art super-hubs provide seamless connections between different parts of the comfortable and affordable system of overland travel.

## ■ Carbon clampdown

The Government has introduced tradable carbon quotas for all UK households as part its bold plans to tackle climate change. Individual allowances are seen as the fairest way of allocating the 'right to pollute' equally. The public has

16

clamoured for tough action. Environmental impacts are increasingly felt, like the storm-surge disaster in the Thames Estuary in 2012, and people are better educated about climate science. Although there has been no great shift in cultural values, support for regulation is high. The economy is more localised, and disposable incomes are low. The pound's weakness on the international stage means that exchange rates are unfavourable for overseas travel. A crisis over national pensions in 2015 resulted in several large company schemes defaulting on their obligations. This has left many with meagre pensions and costly medical bills in old age. Many British holidaymakers are still keen to travel abroad, but perceptions of the purpose and real costs of travel have changed. Although distance is a key consideration, the reason for the holiday is crucial: what you are doing is more important than where you are. Ethical travel is a new mass market, and the government encourages this with the carbon rebate for volunteering whilst abroad. The UK is experiencing milder winters and hotter, dryer summers. High levels of government investment in local resorts means that many people find their holiday needs can be met closer to home.

## Summary

For the last half century, the number of tourists has steadily increased. At the same time the tourism industry has also grown and in relation to the number of those employed by it, and its contribution to the global economy, it is possibly the biggest global industry. New areas of the world, such as China and India, which were once largely destinations for those from western countries, are generating large numbers of tourists and are likely to continue to do so. The size and scale of tourism have led to some concerned writers to call for governments to step in and control tourism, but in all but a few case this is not yet occurring. A number of possible future scenarios for tourism have been presented in this chapter, but it is far from certain what might actually happen to tourism as an activity and industry in the future.

## Student activities

1   In small groups, discuss whether you agree with the claims made in the case study 'Mass Tourism is at a tipping point – but we are all part of the problem'

2   In relation to the 'Four Scenarios from Forum for the Future', which do you think **is most likely** to occur?

3   In relation to the 'Four Scenarios from Forum for the Future', which one **would you like** to occur?

4   What other possible scenarios do you believe are likely?

5   In the next ten years what do you believe will be: a) the three most important factors that may help tourism to grow, b) the three most important factors that may stop tourism from growing?

# References

Becker, E (2017) Only governments can stem the tide of tourism from sweeping the earth *The Guardian*, August 5th

Foundation for the Future (2009) *Tourism 2023: Four scenarios, a vision and a strategy for UK outbound travel and tourism'*, London, Foundation for the Future

Kettle, M (2017) Mass tourism is at a tipping point – but we are all part of the problem, *The Guardian* August 11th.

Prosser (1998) Tourism. In *Encyclopaedia of Ethics*. Chicago, IL: Houghton Mifflin, Vol. 4, pp. 373-401.

16

# Index